STUDIES IN CHRISTIAN HISTORY AND THOUGHT

Trinitarian Spirituality

John Owen and the Doctrine of God in Western Devotion

STUDIES IN CHRISTIAN HISTORY AND THOUGHT

A full listing of all titles in this series
appears at the close of this book

'The doctrine of the Trinity must stand at the heart of any theology or piety which can claim to be distinctively Christian. It is, of course, a standard criticism of Western theology in general and Protestant theology in particular that this doctrine has been routinely neglected throughout the centuries. Such, however, is not the case as Brian Kay's study of John Owen demonstrates. For Owen, the Trinity was crucial to any understanding of God, of the economy of salvation, and of the believer's response in praise and worship to that salvation; and Dr Kay is to be thanked for bringing the signal contributions of John Owen in this area to the attention of a new generation of Christians.'

Carl R. Trueman, Professor of Historical Theology and Church History, Westminster Theological Seminary, Philadelphia, USA

STUDIES IN CHRISTIAN HISTORY AND THOUGHT

Trinitarian Spirituality

John Owen and the Doctrine of God in Western Devotion

Brian K. Kay

Foreword by J.I. Packer

WIPF & STOCK · Eugene, Oregon

Wipf and Stock Publishers
199 W 8th Ave, Suite 3
Eugene, OR 97401

Trinitarian Spirituality
John Owen and the Doctrine of God in Western Devotion
By Kay, Brian
Copyright©2007 Paternoster
ISBN 13: 978-1-55635-656-8
ISBN 10: 1-55635-656-0
Publication date 1/8/2008

This Edition Published by Wipf and Stock Publishers by arrangement with Paternoster

Paternoster
9 Holdom Avenue
Bletchley
Milton Keyes, MK1 1QR
Great Britain

STUDIES IN CHRISTIAN HISTORY AND THOUGHT

Series Preface

This series complements the specialist series of *Studies in Evangelical History and Thought* and *Studies in Baptist History and Thought* for which Paternoster is becoming increasingly well known by offering works that cover the wider field of Christian history and thought. It encompasses accounts of Christian witness at various periods, studies of individual Christians and movements, and works which concern the relations of church and society through history, and the history of Christian thought.

The series includes monographs, revised dissertations and theses, and collections of papers by individuals and groups. As well as 'free standing' volumes, works on particular running themes are being commissioned; authors will be engaged for these from around the world and from a variety of Christian traditions.

A high academic standard combined with lively writing will commend the volumes in this series both to scholars and to a wider readership.

Series Editors

Alan P.F. Sell, Visiting Professor at Acadia University Divinity College, Nova Scotia, Canada

David Bebbington, Professor of History, University of Stirling, Stirling, Scotland, UK

Clyde Binfield, Professor Associate in History, University of Sheffield, UK

Gerald Bray, Anglican Professor of Divinity, Beeson Divinity School, Samford University, Birmingham, Alabama, USA

Grayson Carter, Associate Professor of Church History, Fuller Theological Seminary SW, Phoenix, Arizona, USA

To Sally

Contents

Foreword
J.I. Packer xiii

Chapter 1
Introduction 1

Chapter 2
The Old Divorce of Spirituality from Theology
and New Reasons for Hope 8
The Historical Roots of the Divorce 11
Integration Projects Old and New 16
   Karl Barth and God's Purpose in Triune Self-Revelation 17
   Re-Asserting the Economy: Strengths and Devotional
   Pitfalls in Karl Rahner 20
Broad Models of Relating the Doctrine of God to Spirituality 23

Chapter 3
In Search of Trinitarian Spirituality:
Definitions, Criteria, and Marginal Successes 29
The Criteria for a Successful Trinitarian Spirituality 30
Explanation of the First Criterion: Orthodoxy in Historical
and Systematic Theology 30
   The Content of the First Criterion: Defining the Doctrine 31
      The Trinity Revealed in the New Testament: Doctrine
      for the Sake of Communion 31
      The Doctrine in Formulation: What Has Been Meant
      by 'Trinity' 33
      God's 'Essential Works' vs. 'Personal Works' 35
Explanation of the Second Criterion: The Trinity of
Redemptive History 36
   Narrative vs. Drama 37
   Non-Dramatic Spirituality and the Critique of Nietzsche 39
   Covenantal Drama and Evangelical Spirituality 42
      Sample Questions 44
Probing Three Devotional Traditions 45
   Early English Quakerism 46
   Popular Puritan Devotion 50

Medieval Devotion 57
   Realist Mysticism on the Continent..59
   Realist Mysticism in Britain: The 'English Mystics' 62
   Owen's Method for Meditating on the Trinity................................68
   Walter Hilton's *Scale of Perfection*: Towards Success....................71
   The *Devotio Moderna*: Realist Mysticism Goes Mainstream............75
      The *Devotio Moderna*'s Tendency Toward Moralism 79
      Counterbalance: The *Devotio Moderna*'s Affective
      Use of Gospel Imagery to Engage the *Historia Salutis* 81
      The Imitation of Christ 84
      Excursis: Owen's Mechanics of Meditating on the Cross............89
   The Two Nominalisms and John Owen..92

Chapter 4
General Features of Trinitarian Spirituality **98**
The Dilemma of God's Incomprehensibility and the Solution
of Salvation History 98
Owen's Dual Affirmation and the Point Where Speculation
Yields to Devotion..103
Owen and the History of One-ness vs. Three-ness............................106
Connecting Theology to Doxology: What is Communion with God?..113
The Enjoyment of Communion Flows from the Fact of Union...........118
Distinct Communion with Each Divine Person..................................120

Chapter 5
Owen's Communion with the Father, Son, and Spirit.......................**124**
Communion with the Father...124
   Responding to the Father's Love: Receiving and Returning.............129
   The Meditative Technique Regarding the Father 132
   The Four Adjectives of Fatherly Love: Free, Distinguishing,
   Unchangeable, Eternal 134
   The Pastoral Context: Confronting Apathy, Instilling Assurance......138
Communion with the Son..145
   Section One: Purchased Grace..147
      Purchased Grace Through Christ's Active Obedience 147
      Purchased Grace Through Christ's Passive Obedience 149
      Three Aspects of the Human Response to Christ's
      Purchased Grace..150
         Aspect One: Responding to Christ through Justification 151
         Aspect Two: Responding to Christ through Sanctification 156
   Section Two: Personal Grace...161

    The *Song of Songs* in Bernard of Clairvaux: The Theology
    of the Kiss 161
    The *Song* According to John Owen 165
Communion with the Holy Spirit 169
    The Spirit's Economic Procession 170
    Indwelling 174
    Union with Christ and the Resulting Prospect of Trinitarian
    Indwelling 177
    The Meaning of the Believer's 'Participation in the Divine
    Nature' 181

Chapter 6
Conclusions, and the Significance of Owenian Devotion 185
The Slipperiness of Evangelical Spirituality 185
The First Test: A One *Substantia*, Three *Persona* Spirituality 187
    Owen and Alignment with the Western Theological/Spiritual
    Tradition 187
    Owen's 'Spirit-Christology' as a Key Ingredient for a
    Trinitarian Spirituality 189
The Second Test: The Devotional Use of Divine Drama 194

Selected Bibliography 200

General Index 211

Foreword

This book, a masterful piece of doctoral research, is important — far-reachingly so, if I am any judge.

A heartening development among Protestant people today is renewed interest, aspiration, and commitment in the field of personal devotion, spiritual formation and direction, and in the practice of prayer and meditation. Since our personal relationship with God is the most important thing in life, this renewal of spirituality and spiritual theology, as it is called, is a welcome and, be it said, long overdue return to the healthful habit of putting first things first. But settling one problem starts another. We who now set ourselves seriously to meditate and pray face a disturbing disconnect between our vision of intimacy with God and our attempts to achieve it, and we act like children on the tennis court who are old enough to admire the professionals but shy off the discipline of being coached so as one day to match them: they choose, rather, to go on having fun knocking balls around haphazardly. Best decision? Hardly.

Worship songs (compositions for congregations, once called hymns) tell the story. Until the twentieth century, these songs took their cue from the Psalms, and were outflows of thought running through praising and petitioning verses, going somewhere, as we would say. Some modern lyrics also do this, but commoner, and certainly more favored, are songs that mark time on a single thought and really go nowhere – static songs, we might call them. But we like them, and have fun singing them, and the quality question – whether they best honor God and mature us – is not raised.

So with other aspects of devotion. The use of argument in petition, and the building of thought in meditation – arts of fellowship with God which the Puritans mastered – are skills unknown to us. We children of God are, by and large, childish in our devotion, and it shows.

Brian Kay alerts us to this by elucidating the devotional reality that John Owen, Puritan colossus and perhaps the best theologian England every produced, lays out in his theologically accomplished, pastorally angled, and profoundly searching treatises on practical religion: most notably, in his landmark book, *Of Communion with the Father, Son, and Holy Ghost, Each Person Distinctly, in Love, Grace and Consolation* (1657). Embodying the developed Reformed theology of his day, with its threefold covenantal structure (of Redemption, of Works, and of Grace), and carrying the almost numinous authority of Bible-based, wide-ranging, tested, contested, and experientially verified insight into the words and ways of the living God, Owen's exposition shows him to be *par excellence* the coach who can take us forward from where we are into full adult devotional maturity. Whether we shall accept Owen's guidance remains to be seen, but I for one am profoundly thankful to God for prompting Dr. Kay to unpack it for us. Should we now start heeding Owen's wisdom on this and some other topics where his thought has been researched recently, it will be for me, I confess, a dream come true, and for the church, in my opinion at least, an immeasurable enrichment. Meantime, I put myself on record as appreciating Dr. Kay's work enormously. May it be widely read and deeply digested. Truly, we have needed it.

J.I. Packer
August 2006

CHAPTER 1

Introduction

The purpose of this work is to answer the question of how the Christian doctrine of God has, and can, make an impact on Christian models of spirituality. Christian spirituality has a long history of describing practical methods of devotion, that is, directives for how a believer may pray, meditate upon, and worship God. The New Testament itself provides the raw material for any such system, and after the apostolic era, from Augustine through the monastic movement, from the Reformation and into the post-Reformation Puritan era, famous models of the spiritual life have risen, flourished, then tapered off in terms of their widespread influence. Because private prayer and worship have such a subjective component, difficulty arises as to how to evaluate a method – is one more right than another, more effective, and on what grounds would one decide? A pre-supposition of this work is that Christian spirituality is practiced before a covenanting God who has rightful claims on his people; consequently, spirituality should be subject to the external controls of divine revelation. Theology, then, the human discipline of drawing conclusions about what God has revealed, has an important voice in the creative work of building models of private devotion – and a role that is more foundational than questions of mere technique. But even if this is true, what exact role should theology play in this process? Without giving an exhaustive answer to such a large question, the narrower focus of this work concerns how the church's classic theological convictions about the Godhead, the Trinity, has played, and might play, a controlling role in shaping Christian spirituality. Current formulations of trinitarian doctrine are not substantially different than what they were fifteen hundred years ago, so devotional practices can be conveniently measured against a doctrine that has remained largely stable over time.[1] My goal is to determine specifically how trinitarian doctrine might shape spirituality, and what benefits accrue when it does so.

---

[1] This is not to deny the existence of current developments in trinitarian theology (some of which will be considered below), but to say that even the most recent contributions are not generally characterized by fundamental novelty, but rather, by a desire to rediscover or newly appropriate an element of ancient formulations, either Greek or Latin.

A special emphasis will be placed on the late-Puritan John Owen (1616-1683) as providing a particularly high watermark for integrating the doctrine of God to Christian practice.[2] Owen will remain a conversation partner throughout this work for more than one reason. On one hand, Owen is an illustrative test case of what kinds of devotional fruit result when trinitarian doctrine is built right into the groundwork of a system of prayer and meditation. Since his eventual ruminations on how the believer can relate to a triune God prove so fruitful, we will routinely compare features of his system with other historical attempts at trinitarian devotion in the west. On the other hand, Owen is an embattled figure of late for at least two reasons, both of which have implications for the possible development of future devotional theology. A considerable body of academic literature has charged that Owen, in fact, helped to ruin Protestant devotion by infusing it with a cold predestinarianism built upon deadening Aristotelian logic.[3] To the contrary, this work will show how certain heights of even emotive response to the Christian God are actually best served by a connection to something like the framework of Covenantal (or Federal) Theology of which Owen was a representative. I intend to argue that Owen illustrates my thesis about the great possibility of doctrine informing and ennobling spiritual practice – and if even the theology of the admittedly dense and scholastic seventeenth-century Calvinists like Owen can be proved so enriching, then hopefully a case will have been made for a way in which theology may serve the Christian at prayer. Some readers will know enough about Owen to be interested in any new argument about his legacy and its much debated place in post-Reformation Protestant scholasticism. However, our focus on Owen is not motivated by the desire to save his reputation, but rather to illustrate the thesis: a robust use of the doctrine of the Trinity is able to shape a quality of spiritual response to God that is not otherwise possible.

The other reason Owen might be considered a problematic figure is his uneasy position within the long tradition in western theology that

---

[2] The most notable biographical sketch is Peter Toon, *God's Statesman: The Life and Work of John Owen* (Exeter: Pater Noster, 1971), which emphasizes Owen's career under Oliver Cromwell. Less critical biographical works include A. Thomson, 'The Life of Dr. Owen,' in *The Works of John Owen*, vol. I, ed. William Goold (Edinburgh: Banner of Truth Trust, 1965); John Asty, 'Memoirs of the Life of John Owen, D.D.' in *A Complete Collection of the Sermons of John Owen, D.D.* (London, 1721); and William Orme, *Memoirs of the Life, Writings, and Religious Connexions, of John Owen, D.D.* (London, 1820); and James Moffat, ed., *The Golden Book of John Owen* (London, 1904) 1-96. The best general introduction to Owen's theology and its pastoral drive is Sinclair Ferguson, *John Owen on the Christian Life* (Edinburgh: Banner of Truth Trust, 1987).

[3] Cf. especially Alan Clifford, *Atonement and Justification: English Evangelical Theology 1640-1790* (Oxford: Oxford University Press, 1990); and R.T. Kendall, *Calvin and English Calvinism to 1649* (Oxford: Oxford University Press, 1981).

emphasizes the absolute unity of action among the divine persons of the Godhead. The kind of trinitarian devotion that Owen produced seems to emphasize nearly the opposite point – that each divine hypostasis contributed certain unique things to redemptive history, and ought to be prayed to distinctively as well. Why does this matter to the present thesis? I contend that a judgment either for or against Owen's adherence to western orthodoxy on this matter is also a judgment about the very possibility of a fully trinitarian mode of devotion within the parameters of western theology. If Owen fundamentally violates this tradition, then my own proposed criteria (stated below) for a successful trinitarian spirituality may also be ruled out as contradictory or impossible, at least within the orthodoxy of the west. If, on the other hand, Owen is within at least the broad parameters of the tradition, then his spiritual model will be a rare and helpful example to many who are looking for further ways to make connections between the classical doctrine of God and spiritual practice.

The next chapter explores the reasons for the unfortunate contemporary phenomena of theology and spirituality operating as disconnected disciplines. Something must account for the somewhat theologically freewheeling nature of Christian spiritual writing, and some historic explanations will be considered. However, utter pessimism about the current state of affairs is also unwarranted because of the recent explosion of efforts to further develop both the doctrine of the Trinity and its implications – and certainly at least *some* of these implications fall in the realm of devotional practice. In different ways, Karl Barth and Karl Rahner can be credited with putting trinitarian theology back on the theological agenda. Barth's placement of the Trinity at the beginning of his *Church Dogmatics* was a statement itself about the foundational role of the doctrine for the whole task of theology, but also, within his language about the trinitarian shape of revelation can be found a helpful connection to the believer's subjective actualizing and experience of the Trinity. More directly bearing on Christian spirituality is Rahner's strong reassertion about *ad extra* works of the Trinity as the prime way for humans to come to knowledge of God's nature and pleasures. However, Rahner's contribution is still a mixed blessing; the ways in which his emphasis on the divine economy ends up undercutting the believer's awe at the Godhead's voluntary acts of love will also be discussed. Jurgen Moltmann, who somewhat follows in Rahner's footsteps, helpfully argues that the event of the crucifixion portrays the trinitarian shape of divine love to the believer like nothing else, yet I will show how, like Rahner, Moltmann's strength is also his weakness when it comes to devotional possibilities. The way in which he over-identifies God with the 'event' of salvation results in a depersonalizing of God, abstracting him in such a way that hinders meaningful response to a God who, scripturally speaking, offers a salvation unto a highly personal communion with himself analogous to the Son's pre-creational glory in personal relation to the Father. The extremely helpful work of James B. Torrance is also considered for its appropriation of some of the best of Barth's later emphases, which flow primarily from Calvin (and I suggest, the Reformed scholastics). Here we find raw material for a trinitarian spirituality that does fuller justice to the personhood of God, as well as emphasizing the mediatory role of Christ as the believer's own vicarious 'communer' with the Father.

With all of these various contributions to the question of how the doctrine of God might impact private devotion, something must be said about what exactly should be the determiners of a truly successfully trinitarian devotional model. The third chapter proposes and defends two criteria for success. First, a good model should draw explicitly (and substantially) from the classic trinitarian doctrine of the ancient formulations. One advantage of this proposal is that the resulting spirituality will be theologically uncontroversial given that the church's doctrine of God has been well established and widely accepted. More importantly, a spirituality based on such a tradition will be theologically rich since the tradition itself has so many nuances about the Godhead's unity, diversity, immanent relations, and *ad extra* functions. The second criterion is that the model make use of the *historia salutis* as the lens through which the believer gazes upon and responds to such a trinitarian God. This emphasis acknowledges what is right about the recent interest in economic trinitarianism and prevents the creedal emphasis of the first criterion from making devotion an overly abstract enterprise. Scripture's own generally narrative mode of revealing the three persons of God and the salvation they accomplish must itself shape devotional response; without this ingredient, theological conclusions about God's nature (even reference to how the external missions of God flow from the immanent processions) deprive the believer of the concrete and dramatic features of God's own method of self-disclosure in history, which are helpful in moving the affections toward adoration. The role of the human affections in responding to God is a sub-theme that recurs throughout this work, and the overarching point is this: affective responses to God most *naturally* result when Christian devotion interacts with trinitarian doctrine according to something like our two criteria. Certainly many of the Christian devotional models we will examine have been exuberant and even properly emotive without being trinitarian in the way that I suggest. However, the two proposed criteria for trinitarian devotion provide a much more obvious, stable, and intricate grounding for a whole range of affective responses to God.

Once these criteria are established, I examine historical models for trinitarian spirituality. Three families of devotion are considered for both positive and negative qualities, as well as their relationship to Owen's thinking which will later be analyzed. Early Quakerism is first discussed, for George Fox's movement was, if anything, an attempt at devotional reform in order to recapture immediacy and vibrancy in relation to God. How did Quaker spirituality relate to its doctrine of God, and in what sense is this God trinitarian? A much longer second section deals with the incredibly long-lived and influential mysticism of the medieval realist tradition. Meister Eckhart stands at one pole of this tradition, while the more theologically orthodox movement of the *devotio moderna* produced classic devotional works still in use in the seventeenth century and beyond. Realist mysticism, especially mediated through the 'English Mystics' (Walter Hilton, Julian of Norwich, Richard Rolle, etc.), has been posited even since the seventeenth century as having a direct influence on some Puritan models of devotion. The Trinity makes regular appearances in such devotion, but in ways that must be evaluated theologically and philosophically, given the neo-platonic tendencies of the whole realist tradition. Thirdly, Owen's own immediate context of Puritan popular devotion will be considered. Contrary to what some have said about Puritanism killing the warm-hearted devotional theology of the Reformers in favor of cold rationalism and introspection, much Puritan writing was experiential and grace-filled.[4] Yet, was it trinitarian according to our criteria? Despite a rich heritage in post-Reformation scholasticism which is explicitly trinitarian in its theological substructure and prolegomena,[5] classic Puritan manuals of devotion failed to appropriate these emphases when it came to prayer and meditation. This tendency is surprising, considering the resplendent trinitarianism of those who the Puritan writers would have eagerly acknowledged as their theological heroes. John Owen stands in contrast to this tendency of his peers, building into the heart of his devotional model a doctrine of the Trinity that reflects characteristics of earlier Reformed scholastics.

---

[4] Alan Clifford and R.T. Kendall certainly make this case, but see also Rolmes Holston III, *John Calvin Versus the Westminster Confession* (Richmond: John Know, 1972); James B. Torrance, 'Strengths and Weaknesses of the Westminster Theology,' in *The Westminster Confession*, ed. Alisdair Heron (Edinburgh: St. Andrews Press, 1982) 4-53; James B. Torrance, 'Covenant or Contract? A Study of the Theological Background of Worship in Seventeenth-Century Scotland,' *Scottish Journal of Theology* 23 (1970): 56-76; James B. Torrance, 'Calvin and Puritanism in England and Scotland - Some Basic Concepts in the Development of "Federal Theology,"' in *Calvinus Reformator* (Potchefstroom: Potchefstroom University for Christian Higher Education, 1982) 264-77.

[5] Cf. Beza's *Tabula Praedestinationis*, Musculus' *Loci Communes*, Vermigli's *Loci Communes*, and the works of John Calvin, Theodore Beza, Zacharius Ursinus, Hieronymous Zanchius, and William Perkins.

Chapters four and five show exactly how Owen wedded the covenantal trinitarianism of Reformed orthodoxy, including its emphasis on the outworking of the divine decree in history, with the experiential heart-emphasis of his own Puritan party. Here we find an emphasis on human affections for the triune God that was later to inform Jonathan Edward's more famous work on topic.[6] Chapter four deals with some of the more general, as well as quite technical, aspects of what it means for a person to be in communion with the members of the Trinity. One of Owen's unique contributions was to stress that believers are to cultivate a distinct relationship with each person of the Godhead, and that these relationships are shaped according to the unique gifts of grace that each divine person bestows on the believer in the economy of salvation. Of course, this kind of language stretched the limits of then current Augustinian assumptions about the unity of the Godhead. This chapter deals with various historically held positions regarding how far the distinctions between the actions of the Father, Son, and Spirit can be pressed while keeping within the limits of orthodoxy. This helps us to consider to what degree Owen satisfies our first criterion of historic trinitarianism. In the end, does it matter to our thesis if Owen fails the test of orthodoxy? If Owen's move to distinguish the saving works of the divine persons is fundamentally wrongheaded, then doubt arises as to whether or not western orthodoxy itself is equipped to produce the kind of trinitarian spirituality that this thesis is advocating. A judgment about Owen, one way or another, becomes a judgment about the possibility of distinctively trinitarian devotion in a tradition generally marked by an emphasis on divine unity.

Chapter five is an extended case study of how both our criteria, when taken together, produce certain positive results for devotion. If, in the final analysis, Owen largely satisfies both the criteria of fidelity to ancient creedal formulas as well as reliance on redemptive history,[7] it will be worth looking over his shoulder to observe how such commitments might affect prayer and meditation. In probing Owen's own devotional program here, we are simply using him to validate the original criteria from a more pragmatic angle: here are features of a rich devotional life that are not fully attainable apart from something like the two criteria we have been arguing for. Another fact that this chapter demonstrates is that seventeenth-century Federal Theology, often chided as dry and philosophical, actually provides very helpful footholds for the worshipping Christian. The greatest reason for this may be its interest in historical and intra-trinitarian covenants that have so much to say about distinct actions of the divine *hypostaseis* in loving the believer. While

---

[6] Edwards refers to Owen at least six times in the twenty-two Yale volumes of his *opera omnia* published to date (New Haven: Yale University Press, 1957-), including once in *Religious Affections* (original Yale manuscript) 143.

[7] More of the evidence for this determination will be offered in the final chapter.

Federal Theology abounds in excruciating distinctions and legal language, it also draws great attention to the multi-faceted significance of God's past and present work to minister salvation to the believer. These facets of God's saving work have rich possibilities for the meditating Christian, and, in the end, do more to provoke affectionate responses to God than they do to bog her down with theological minutiae (as the common charge goes). The idea that Federal Theology might actually provide unparalleled resources for Christian devotion will certainly be a controversial claim today, so much so that the benefits may need to be seen to be believed. Owen will help demonstrate the way in which the commitment of Federal Theology to the *historia salutis* evokes especially rich human responses to a triune God.

The final chapter offers concluding analysis about Owen's system in respect to the two criteria for trinitarian spirituality that were originally proposed, as well as suggestions about how our criteria might address weaknesses in the Evangelical/Reformed tradition of spirituality through to the present. A somewhat qualified 'yes' is answered as to whether Owen keeps within the tradition, for while he stretches the usual Western conceptions of divine unity, he does so by exploiting underdeveloped and latent allowances in the tradition itself. The significance of Owen's Spirit-centered christology is also evaluated for its ways of connecting the experience of the believer with the person of Christ and then to the work of the whole Trinity. A christology so conceived injects a trinitarian influence into spirituality, as the believer's union with Christ turns out to be therefore an explicitly trinitarian affair itself. The second criteria, which looks for a devotional use of the Trinity through the *historia salutis*, shows Owen making the covenantal structure of Federal Theology central to devotional practice in way that his theological allies often left undeveloped for spiritual practice. Here Owen succeeds where the realist mystical tradition, for all its willingness to name God as a Trinity, remained weak. Failing to dwell on the particularity of salvation on the plane of public history neglects an important aid to the imagination of the believer as she seeks to kindle her affections with impressions of God and his publicly demonstrated love. The significance of such a focus on redemptive history is also curative to some tendencies within Reformed/Evangelical spirituality following Owen. When theology itself is sensitive to the *historia salutis*, devotional application is an easy jump to make, and a trinitarian flavor emerges organically and without overwrought technique.

CHAPTER 2

The Old Divorce of Spirituality from Theology and New Reasons for Hope

One of the most celebrated features of later twentieth-century theology has been its rediscovery of the doctrine of the Trinity. While the classic formulations of the doctrine had rarely been denied by most theologians, nor did the Apostle's or Nicene Creed completely drop out of liturgical use,[1] the church seems until recently to have forgotten why this defining Christian doctrine really mattered. Karl Rahner could make the observation as late as 1967 that 'should the doctrine of the Trinity have to be dropped as false, the major part of religious literature could well remain virtually unchanged.'[2] In post-Enlightenment Western culture, ideas — especially theological ones — in which no one finds an immediate practical value to shape or improve the self or the world are soon shirked as being an unfortunate vestige of a less rational or efficient age. The doctrine of the Trinity itself, as perhaps Christianity's most nuanced and irresolvably mysterious belief, has all the makings of a doctrine that should have been destined for permanent streamlining. And yet, not only has Liberal rationalism and even Evangelical pragmatism failed to entirely extinguish the old doctrine, trinitarian studies seems now to be enjoying a renaissance across the theological spectrum – Roman Catholic, Protestant, and Eastern Orthodox theologians have all made notable contributions to the present revival.

What has begun in the last half of the twentieth-century is not merely a repristination of the old creedal formulas. Without denying those formulas, indeed, often using them as a platform, the new emphasis is on how the doctrine makes a difference to the life of the church in its daily mission and even to the individual Christian. The writings that will soon be mentioned deal, therefore, with the implications of the doctrine of God: most of the time, even when they are working through a more abstract topic like the *ad intra* relations of the divine Persons, they do so in order to show how those relations go on to order the divine missions,

---

[1] However, many branches of Evangelicalism have dropped the saying of historical creeds in corporate worship.

[2] Karl Rahner, *The Trinity* (New York: Crossroad Publishing Company, 2002 rept.) 11.

and beyond that, how they effect human beings in one way or another. Only a cynic would say that the secular age which demanded relevance and practicality was the primary motivation for the church to produce such new writing. Rather, the consensus among the modern authors, if anything, is that the scriptures themselves are the reason for a restored confidence that the doctrine matters. The New Testament is concerned to announce a Trinity that is *pro nobis*, that is, a substantial union of divine Persons who reveal their relations in order to make us understand how it is that we have been saved and are being saved, and on that basis how such a Trinity compels some kind of response to such three-fold grace. This is the Trinity of Paul and the Gospels, not any speculative tri-unity that is purely mysterious to us without any significance to human sinners beyond merely being an article of belief.

An important question for the church near the beginning of the twenty-first century is to what degree this renewal has penetrated all the arenas of Christian life and thought that it might. The initial theological work, especially of Karl Barth and Karl Rahner, has been seized on and creatively expanded by later writers such as Jurgen Moltmann, Robert Jensen, John Zizioulas, Colin Gunton, Alan Torrance, James Torrance, David Cunningham, and Catherine Mowry LaCugna, to name a few. To be sure, the breadth of applications of the economic Trinity that many of these later writers are finding is impressive and helpful. One of the recurring themes is the social model of the Trinity as an impetus for Christian community life (the divine Persons are diverse though unified and interpenetrating, and so must we be), political involvement,[3] gender relations,[4] corporate worship,[5] and even the practice of science.[6]

As fruitful as these directions are, we would expect that if the nature of the Trinity is best understood through its own economy of salvation, there would be also, and perhaps even more fundamentally, an impact on the way a human person who has been an object of such saving trinitarian love relates directly back to such a God in prayer and worship. In other words, our doctrine of God should have some kind of impact on our spirituality when the God in question is one who reveals himself most clearly through saving acts which happen to bear a particularly triune imprint. Rahner's accusation can be applied to practical works of

---

[3] Cf. Jurgen Moltmann, *The Trinity and The Kingdom* (Minneapolis: The Fortress Press, 1993 rept.); and *The Crucified God* (Minneapolis: The Fortress Press, 1993 rept.) 291-340.

[4] Catherine Mowry LaCugna, *God For Us: The Trinity and the Christian Life* (San Francisco: HarperSan Francisco, 1993).

[5] J.B. Torrance, *Worship, Community, and the Triune God of Grace* (Downer's Grove, Ill.: InterVarsity, 1996).

[6] Colin Gunton, *The Promise of Trinitarian Theology* (Edinburgh: T. & T. Clark, 1997(.

Christian spirituality as well, I suggest, for upon examination most contemporary models of the spiritual life would be unharmed if the doctrine of the Trinity proved untrue. That is to say, we need help to get from what are functionally unitarian models of spirituality to something more robustly trinitarian, especially now that the Trinity is being rediscovered not just as a hard-to-relate-to ontology, but as a grace-giving economy. If the biblically revealed God is explicitly both a Trinity in essence and a Trinity who acts *pro nobis* in salvation, and if salvation involves the freeing of human persons from the shackles of sin, death, and the power of the devil in order that they may worship *this* particular God for all eternity, then it would seem that present spirituality should have a distinctively trinitarian character which reflects both the source of salvation (from the Father, through the Son, in the Spirit) as well as specify, in kind, the appropriate mode of the church's worshipful response (glory to the Father, through the Son, in the Spirit) .[7]

'Spirituality' is a notoriously slippery word, of course, so anyone who uses it probably needs to make his own meaning as clear as possible in order get the traction needed for clear communication. In this work, 'spirituality' is used narrowly to speak of the personal response to God of someone who is indwelled by the Holy Spirit and thus is united to Christ and on that basis restored to the Father. All to say, I am limiting the word to describe specifically the New Testament kind of spirituality, the kind that describes responses to God from humans who possess the Spirit of Jesus Christ because of the gracious determination of the Father. Also, by 'response' I am further narrowing the definition to only refer to actions such as prayer, private worship (which is certainly incomplete without corporate worship), and meditation about God and his gospel for its further impact on the believer's own sanctification. In these terms, even the classic spiritual practices of mortification and vivification, for example, fit well within the bounds of spirituality. Sometimes, in recent writing, broader Christian engagement with the world is also grouped under the heading of spirituality, for instance, feeding the poor as a response to God's feeding his people in Christ. Such connections are legitimate and necessary, but too broad for inclusion here. The value of the previously mentioned writers is exactly that they do make those connections to the broader mission of the church, but the narrower concern of this work is to ask how a God who is revealed as a Trinity-who-saves makes impact on the believer's life when lived self-consciously

---

[7] The American Lutheran writer Robert Jensen suggests that in light of the gospel events, the Christian God must now be named as 'whoever raised Jesus from the dead,' and that, more fully, Christians should address their God with the proper name 'Father, Son, and Spirit.' Christian worship after the resurrection thus requires a trinitarian naming of its object. Cf. Robert Jensen, 'The Triune God,' in C.E. Braaten and R.W. Jensen (eds.), *Christian Dogmatics* vol.1 (Philadelphia: Fortress Press, 1984) 87-92.

coram deo, in a one-on-one (or one-on-three) relation. A basic contention of this work is that those interested to develop a trinitarian spirituality owe much to certain predecessors, both in the twentieth-century and before, and yet the Protestant Scholastics, in particular John Owen, provide especially helpful suggestions for constructing a biblically faithful model of the Christian spiritual life that does full justice to God's revelation of his triunity.

The Historical Roots of the Divorce

The vacuum of trinitarian spiritualities suggests the larger problem of a tendency of both theology and spirituality to operate as overly distinct disciplines that can be pursued without reference to one another. In other words, spirituality as a discipline has often been guilty of doing its work as if theology barely mattered. Sandra Schneiders has actually argued in favor of this separation, suggesting that while the two disciplines properly inform one another, they are essentially autonomous.[8] On the grounds she provides, spirituality should therefore not be considered an outworking of the practical application of doctrine, but is properly cut free from it. In fact, because of the a-doctrinal basis of spirituality, non-Christian and Christian religious scholars can work together toward the advancement of the discipline. But, contrary to Schneiders, if the revealed Trinity turns out to have a properly foundational role in shaping Christian experience in the way that this work will suggest, then the model of two autonomous disciplines is challenged, and neither will non-Christian spiritualities find much neutral territory in the triune spirituality that biblical history gives rise to. On the other hand, some of the blame for the divorce of spirituality from theology falls on theologians themselves when they are not interested enough to show how their discoveries might go on to effect Christian devotion. Philip Sheldrake has noted hopefully that recent changes in theological method toward inductive and experiential modes may be giving spirituality a new voice in the study of theology – yet, of course, this observation simply raises the question of why it was until recently absent in the first place.[9]

---

[8] Sandra Schneiders, 'Theology and Spirituality: Strangers, Rivals or Partners?' *Horizons*, 13 (1986), 253-74; 'Spirituality in the Academy,' *Theological Studies* 50 (1989), 676-97; 'Spirituality as an Academic Discipline: Reflections from Experience,' *Christian Spirituality Bulletin* 1/2 (Fall 1993), 10-15; and 'A Hermeneutical Approach to the Study of Christian Spirituality,' *Christian Spirituality Bulletin* 2/1 (Spring 1994), 9-14.

[9] Philip Sheldrake, *Spirituality and Theology: Christian Living and the Doctrine of God* (Maryknoll, New York: Orbis Books, 1998). Sheldrake's analysis of the historical development of such a rift has greatly influenced the following section.

When did the post-apostolic church arrive at a place where spirituality came to do its business without reference to doctrine, especially to a doctrine of God?[10] To begin at the beginning, the work of patristic authors show that the problem was not always with us, for they often held theological reflection and spiritual response closely together. Augustine's *De Trinitate* is thus a famous theological and spiritual treatise simultaneously. In books XII-XIV he states that God is not known by *scientia* but by *sapientia*, that is, not by logical demonstration resting on self-evident first principles — which is a legitimate but lower functioning of the mind — but rather God is known by a kind of contemplative knowledge that is characterized by its love, desire, and worship of its divine object, the Trinity itself.[11] For Augustine, to have knowledge of God essentially meant to worship the Trinity. Put another way, to be wise in one's spiritual life (that is, a life of *sapientia*) can only mean to have a life characterized by worship-knowledge of the triune God. We might say that a theologian is a worshipper in the thinking mode as she considers the nature of the one whom she adores. Someone who excels at practical wisdom is someone who first worships the triune persons. This kind of patristic 'mysticism' should thus not be confused with later developments toward a subjective neo-platonic other-worldliness, but instead, mysticism in this earlier sense was the life of every baptized Christian who sought to experience 'the mystery,' the revelation of God in Jesus Christ through the illumination of the Spirit. Such mysticism was experiential, but grounded in the objectivity of the actions of the triune God outside and above the worshipper who has, as it were, come down to humanity through the Christ of history, and into the worshipper through the ongoing mediation of Christ by the Holy Spirit. This is a devotion marked by its actualization of doctrine and can still function as a model of how both disciplines properly depend on one another.

The unity between the objective knowledge about God and the devotional contemplation of God perhaps found its highest early expression in the Golden Age of monastic theology, from Gregory the Great in the sixth century to Bernard of Clairvaux in the twelfth. During this time two developments may serve to illustrate the marriage of doctrinal reflection and piety. The *Quadriga*, primarily a medieval model of biblical exegesis and interpretation, was also highly devotional and mystical (perhaps to a fault). Of the 'four senses' of Scripture, the first

---

[10] This is to suggest that other doctrines are not as poorly represented in spiritual writing as is the doctrine of the Trinity. Theological anthropology, for example, may be a more regular feature; however, without a doctrine of God along side it, anthropology becomes human-centered and itself misleads any model of Christian living. Cf. the popular acknowledgment of this in Will Metzger's *Tell the Truth* (Downer's Grove, Illinois: InterVarsity Press, 1983).

[11] Augustine, *On the Trinity* (New York: New City Press, 1991) 334.

alone was the 'literal,' while what followed were the three 'spiritual senses': the allegorical, the tropological (or moral), and the anagogical (mystical or eschatological meaning). The spiritual senses, especially the allegorical, could unfortunately become a license to unhinge the text altogether from authorial intent. Yet, while exegetes from the Reformation to the present rightly criticize this feature of the *Quadriga*, the method itself certainly suggests that this earlier age believed that, in a sense, the spiritual application of scripture was three-fourths of a right understanding of it. Exegesis and spiritual application here are very closely interwoven: for example, the reader of an Old Testament text that might routinely mention the city of Jerusalem, but who fails to hear God calling him through that text to live a life worthy of the *spiritual* Jerusalem ruled by Christ, has actually failed to understand the Old Testament text in the fullest purpose for which God inspired it. There was no right understanding of the text without a right submitting oneself to it. Another telling illustration of doctrine's former marriage to devotion is the medieval expansion of the *lectio divina*. Drawing on a more rudimentary ancient practice, the Carthusian Guido II in his *Ladder of Monks* turned the ancient *lectio divina* into a four-stage method designed to guide the whole life by a meditative reading of scripture.[12] The first stage was simply *lectio*, reading for basic meaning, followed by *meditatio*, *oratio*, and finally, a rare experience for the mature believer, *contemplatio*. While the stages of meditation, prayer, and contemplation represented successive advancements in expertise that surely encouraged spiritual elitism, evident also is the assumption that the spiritual life was ultimately rooted in the biblical text and the doctrine it taught. Even the very mystical (and yes, perhaps neo-platonic) *contemplatio* remains somehow a contemplation of the text itself. Whatever their excesses, these two medieval methods of unfolding the doctrinal content of Scripture are simultaneously also methods of prayer and devotion.

A change to a more scientific approach to theology begins to show itself after the time of Peter Abelard (1079-1142). Aristotelian categories and methods of study began accumulating during this period, and while that alone is no necessary predictor of changing theologies, such modes of doing theology eventually gave a greater allowance for intellectual speculation. A new tension appears between the new 'theology of the schools' and the continuing monastic theology.[13] The centers of learning during this time, of course, were moving from the monasteries to the new 'cathedral schools' that would eventually become the universities. While

---

[12] Guido II, *The Ladder of Monks* (Cistercian Studies 48, Kalamazoo, Michigan: Cistercian Publications, 1981) ch. 2.

[13] Cf. Jean Leclercq, 'The Renewal of Theology,' in Robert Benson, Giles Constable and Carol Lanham (eds.), *Renaissance and the Renewal in the Twelfth Century* (Toronto, 1991 edition) 68-87.

it would be wrong to make too much of this shift in merely the physical location where study was pursued, certainly the fact that the theological enterprise was no longer situated in the community of religious life would have its effect on the discipline itself. It is telling that when the Reformers and Protestant Scholastics who will be emphasized later would draw from medieval sources, they usually looked to the monastic tradition rather than the school theology. Protestant writers who desired to somehow unite doctrine to spirituality were furnished with a host of allies in what might seem be an unlikely place, the cell of the thoroughly medieval monk. Wolfhart Pannenberg suggests that, after all, the Reformation was a response to a spiritual crisis, not merely an intellectual one: the best of medieval spirituality was concerned to pursue communion with God, though sometimes seeking to do so through various humanly invented forms of mediation that were believed to bridge the God-human gap.[14] The Reformation principle *sola fide* responded negatively to this multiplying of mediators, but certainly without denying something of the original monastic goal. If this is true, then *sola fide* and *solus Christus* are principles that while being essentially theological, are at the same time seeking to reform a spirituality from idolatrous fixation on objects and persons (and persons' works) who are in the end inadequate at the job of mediating God's presence to the believer.

Thomas Aquinas represents a somewhat transitional figure in the growing separation of spirituality and theology. While he tried to unite theological reflection and contemplation, he still placed spiritual concerns in the second part of the *Summa*, as a sub-category of moral theology, apparently distinct from dogma. Karl Rahner has further criticized Thomism for separating the doctrine of God into two treatises, 'On the One God' and 'On the Triune God.'[15] While the distinction itself may be legitimate for purposes of study, the tendency of the church following Aquinas, and especially that of the Roman Catholic 'neo-scholastics' who drew from Aquinas and whom Rahner was seeking to rebut, was to describe the One God as he whose essence and attributes can be known almost thoroughly by reason and without any reference to the divine *hypostaseis*. By the time the Trinity is eventually treated, there is very little left to say about God. The triune character of God's essence is only a mysterious fact of revelation about which little can be said except to simply assert it as a doctrine to be assented to. Says Rahner, had the school theologians recognized what the Greeks knew about the New Testament, they would have realized that *theos* does not refer to God as an undifferentiated divine essence, but particularly to the Father. And the

---

[14] Wolfhart Pannenberg, *Christian Spirituality and Sacramental Community* (London: Darton, Longman and Todd, 1983) 13-17, in Sheldrake, *Spirituality and Theology*, 213.

[15] Even Peter Lombard had dealt with the unity of God as a subjection of the treatment of his Trinity, notes Rahner. Cf. Rahner, *The Trinity*, 15-21.

Father, as Father, cannot himself be ontologically understood without reference to a Son or his economic sending of the Son and the Spirit. If Rahner is right, *theos* is only understood when his relation to all the events of salvation history which flow from those divine processions and missions are in view. The damaging effect of the medieval scholastic way of doing theology was to isolate who God is from what he does, diminishing both theology and devotion.

The result, I contend, of making theology proper more about God's immanent, unified attributes than God's trinitarian action is to greatly handicap Christian devotion from the start. The worshipper may be able, in some general sense, to be awed by God's abstract attributes, to feel some moral force of the divine law, and to seek to appreciate God's mercy, but he will always have difficulty in deeper levels of these responses. This is because, by comparison, a God who is first thought about as trinitarian, and particularly so by virtue of his self-revelation in the *historia salutis,* much more naturally provokes deep human response: the otherwise abstract divine attributes are now given historical reference points, concreteness, specificity, and, with respect to the event of the Incarnation, quite literally given flesh and bones. Worship and thankfulness are not then dependant on merely experiencing God in the present moment of encounter nor through intellectual abstractions about his attributes.

To cite one example, the devotional goal of feeling the weight of divine law on one's life is best realized not when a person merely thinks the thought 'God is holy and so ought I be,' but when the incarnate Son of such a holy God is remembered as hanging on a tree because of one's own transgressions, or, positively, when the Son is observed in the Gospels as perfectly loving God and neighbor, thereby fulfilling the law in his own obedience. The weight of the law is thereby demonstrated, not just asserted. Differently, the otherwise abstract proposition 'God is gracious' now turns out, in light of Jesus' high priestly promises, to mean the following specific thing to the believer: citizenship in a new Jerusalem, a kind of perichoretic relationship with Father and divine Son, and enjoyment of the divine Son's own sonship rights by those who have themselves only merited the Father's abandonment. God as 'omnipresent' now more wondrously includes the indwelling presence of the Holy Spirit who first came at Pentecost and now mediates Christ's presence even to one's inward parts. Models of spirituality that are not trinitarian in these ways fail to be specific or concrete enough to inspire sustained interest and tend toward, at best, boredom,[16] whereas the trinitarian history of salvation is compelling drama, a true story that while

---

[16] And at worst, narcissism, since without a compelling picture of God, the gaze turns inward.

executed in history, has the believer's transformation as part of its goal and can thus sustain the believer with rich content for prayer and meditation. More of these themes will be explored, but some of the present harvest of abstract and therefore bland, even speculative spiritualities[17] seem to owe something to a time when, inconceivable to the patristics let alone the apostles, Christians began to write volumes about God and only appendices about the Trinity. Hans Urs von Balthasar writes that only after the epoch of Albert the Great, Thomas Aquinas, and Bonaventure, towards the end of the thirteenth-century, can we see the 'disappearance of the "complete" theologian... the theologian who is also a saint,' and I suggest that an equally troubling disappearance is any substantial reference to the Trinity-in-redemptive action in many prescriptions for the life of prayer.[18]

Integration Projects Old and New

In direct contrast to the scholastic separation of spirituality and the doctrine of God was the High Middle Ages renewal of interest in Dionysius and affective, mystical methods of seeking God. While this emphasis often tended in the neo-platonic direction, the Victorine monastery in Paris actually combined some of the Dionysian mysticism with the doctrinal precision of the school theology in such a way that was more palatable for the theologically orthodox. The Victorines in turn influenced works such as the *Cloud of Unknowing* as well as the *devotio moderna* movement, which will both be evaluated in more detail in the next chapter as to their degree of success in re-engaging spirituality with trinitarian theology. However, it must be said that both of these movements tended (with notable exceptions) toward the realist emphasis on the unity of divine persons, with little to say about a trinitarian economy of salvation or its devotional relevance. By the end of the Middle Ages, two of the very few significant figures in this period whom Philip Sheldrake categorizes as 'mystic theologians' were Jean Gerson and Nicholas of Cusa, the former, however, was a theological nominalist and therefore virtually Pelagian in his doctrine of sin, and the latter a theological realist in the fairly unorthodox tradition of Meister Eckhart.[19] Evidence such as this suggests that while integration projects were attempted, many were not in the end satisfactory to those who remained within the theological mainstream of the church. Sheldrake is more optimistic than perhaps is warranted about such early signs of reintegration of a doctrine of God and spirituality since even where they

---

[17] Some of these will be discussed by name in the final chapter.

[18] Hans Urs von Balthasar, 'Theology and Sanctity,' in his *Word and Redemption: Essays in Theology* (New York: 1965) 57, in Sheldrake, *Spirituality and Theology*, 40.

[19] Sheldrake, *Spirituality and Theology*, 41-43.

are not theologically problematic, they deal very sparingly with the economically revealed Trinity of the New Testament.

Karl Barth and God's Purpose in Triune Self-Revelation

The modern era has seen many more credible attempts to draw out some of the implications of a doctrine of God. For purposes of rough categorizing, these contributions tend to run either in the 'social' direction, that is, drawing lines from the relationality within the Godhead to human social relations in politics, ethics, gender, and church community, or in finding such implications of God's inner-relationality in improved understandings of the ontology of the divine *hypostaseis* and sometimes, by extension, clues as to the nature of human personhood. Both social and ontological directions owe much to the pioneer work of Karl Barth. Opposite to the ordering of *loci* demonstrated by his early hero Schleiermacher, Barth located the Trinity at the beginning of his *Church Dogmatics* because he believed that all revelation of God to sinful humanity, and thus all dogmatic reflection about such revelation, depends on the actions of God as Father, Son, and Spirit in self-disclosure. Given the sinful resistance of humanity to God, the very fact that humans might succeed in receiving such revelation requires an explanation. Humanity will necessarily be passive in any reception of revelation because of its sinful incapacity to hear, so the process of revelation itself is subject to the sovereign autonomy of God. This is true in three senses: God is simultaneously the subject of revelation (the 'revealer'), the act of revelation (God the Word is 'revelation' itself), and the revelation's object ('revealedness').[20] More succinctly put, '*God* reveals himself. He reveals himself *through himself.* He reveals *himself.*'[21] In trinitarian language, the Father reveals himself through the Son, while the Spirit provides the capacity to hear to the human recipient (*Offenbarsein*).

Stated in a slightly different way, the testimony of scripture about divine revelation poses three questions to its hearer: Who reveals himself? What does God do to reveal himself? And, most provocatively for our present purposes, 'What is the result? What does this event do to the man to whom it happens?'[22] Fascinatingly, the third of only three questions that Barth thinks reveal the nature of God ends up being about revelation's impact on the human recipient. The Revealer himself is actually known by looking at his effect on his elect, 'with a reference to what the Revealer wills and does with them, to what His revelation achieves

---

[20] Barth, *Church Dogmatics*, ed. Geoffrey W. Bromil and T. F. Torrance, 13 vols. (Edinburgh, T. & T. Clark, 1969) .I/1, 295.

[21] Barth, *Church Dogmatics*, I/1, 296.

[22] Barth, *Church Dogmatics*, I/1, 296, emphasis mine.

in them.'[23] The trinitarian self-revealer is also fundamentally the trinitarian transformer of humans who receive the revelation. While the list of modern economic trinitarian theologians usually begins later with Rahner, here in the very heart of Barth's articulation of the trinitarian character of revelation is a claim that the Trinity itself is better understood when the question of how revelation impacts the human receiver is answered. Part of the answer to this third question is that such a 'man is now "in Christ," a future has been won, and along with it a present between the times.'[24] While the *Church Dogmatics* is not a devotional treatise, built into its very trinitarian foundation is the sense that God reveals his trinitarian nature as he answers for us the question of revelation's purpose, which in the end is to unite a sinner to Christ and usher him into the *eschaton*. Further, the implication here is that trinitarian doctrine cannot be understood apart from consideration of the believer's subjective realization of the saving benefits of the Godhead, an assertion that would seem to provide a trinitarian theological grounding and framework for devotional response to God.

Hans Urs von Balthasar, who was until at least recently one of the most credible interpreters of Barth,[25] makes more explicit such Barthian themes. Balthasar was opposed to liberal rationalism in theology as well as suspicious of the turn to experience in spirituality (unlike Rahner, who eagerly embraced it). Instead, all human forms of spirituality were to be rooted in the self-revelation of the triune God, supremely achieved visibly in Jesus Christ who was a window to God's inner-trinitarian reality.[26] Here is a check against subjective spirituality, replaced with an objective ground established by Christ, the revealer of the Trinity, which for Balthasar helped to ground spirituality in the incarnation and preserve its objectivity by anchoring it to celebration of the sacraments. Again, while none of this makes specific any spiritual method to be used by a believer, it is significant to see such a necessary connection drawn between the doctrine of the Trinity and human subjective realization of God's revealed triunity. The work of Barth and Balthasar on those points begs to be fleshed out in the direction of practical spirituality.

---

[23] Barth, *Church Dogmatics*, I/1, 298.

[24] Barth, *Church Dogmatics*, I/1, 298

[25] Cf. Hans Urs von Balthasar, *The Theology of Karl Barth: Exposition and Interpretation*, trans. by Edward T. Oakes, S.J. (Ignatius, 1992). Balthasar's analysis of Barth's theological development has been challenged and perhaps corrected by George Hunsinger, *How to Read Karl Barth: The Shape of His Theology* (Oxford: Oxford University Press, 1991); and Bruce L. McCormack, *Karl Barth's Critically Realistic Dialectical Theology: Its Genesis and Development 1909-1936* (Oxford: Oxford University Press, 1995).

[26] Hans Urs von Balthasar, *Word and Redemption: Essays in Theology* (New York: Herder and Herder, 1965); and *The Glory of the Lord* (Edinburgh: T. & T. Clark, 1982-92).

Some of the most helpful work done in the Barthian tradition for the purpose of uniting the spiritual life and the Trinity is being done by James B. Torrance. While Torrance's greatest concerns are corporate worship and community life, his base-line definition of worship is fruitful for our purposes here: 'worship is the gift of participating through the Spirit in the incarnate Son's communion with the Father.'[27] As our great high-priest, Christ is therefore the 'real agent in all true worship.' We might add to this by saying that the believer should relate to Christ as her substitutionary or vicarious communer with the Father, rather than simply seeing him as giving the believer mere access or enablement to approach the Father. If this is true, Torrance's observation leads to helpful ways to explain why scriptural accounts of Old Testament worship deal so heavily with the duties of the priests but comparatively little about the worship roles for private believers. The trajectory of salvation history has always been in the direction of God accomplishing things for his people, including, it appears, even accomplishing for them the very task of communing with himself. Might the scripture de-emphasize private worship in the Old Testament in order to prepare its audience to understand vicarious communion (through the Levites), and finally, the vicarious communion with the Father by Christ that ultimately defines an individual's own relationship to God on account of one's Spirit-given union with Christ? Whether or not the believer employs such reliance on Christ alone in effect determines whether worship is really trinitarian or sub-Christian and unitarian: unitarian worship is primarily something humans do; God's grace helps them to do it, and Jesus is believed to teach them how to do it and to perhaps set the example. In other words, humans are virtually their own priests in such a unitarian model. In trinitarian worship, by contrast, Christ is the one priest because of his unique privileges that allow him an approach to his Father that no fallen human could ever possess in himself. Just as the Reformers stressed the sole priesthood of Christ versus the necessary mediation of the *ecclesia* or *magisterium*, the idea of Christ as vicarious communer-with-the-Father reforms private devotion by showing that even prayer to the Father is, in a sense, first a work of the Son on our behalf. Christ communes perfectly with the Father because his divine nature is held in common with the Father's, but as a human, as mediator, he can commune in the place of the humans he represents. Torrance's observations in this regard will help us to evaluate various practical models of trinitarian spirituality that we will soon encounter.

---

[27] James B. Torrance, *Worship*, 20.

Re-Asserting the Economy:
Strengths and Devotional Pitfalls in Karl Rahner

In a different way than the Barthian tradition, Karl Rahner's work also moves theology and (trinitarian) spirituality back into each other's orbits. Rahner was critical of a two-fold disjunction which he identified in Roman Catholic 'neo-scholastic' theology: a separation of God as one from God as Trinity, as well as a rift between the economic and the immanent Trinity. As we have seen, Rahner seems to blame the first disjunction on Aquinas, or at least the later Western tradition of overly dividing Aquinas' 'One God' and 'Triune God' treatises. This later tradition explains God in terms of attributes of the divine nature in general, so that God as Trinity is primarily, and merely, 'mysterious,' but even this only in the sense of being 'puzzling.' Rahner laments that a primarily 'mysterious' Trinity has no power to explain the classic hope of heaven which has always been framed as the Christian's beatific vision of a specifically triune God: 'we must inquire how this could be true, if between man and each one of the three divine persons there is no real ontological relation, something more than mere appropriation. How can the contemplation of any reality, even the loftiest reality, beatify us if intrinsically it is absolutely *unrelated* to us in any way?'[28] The value of this observation is to show that unless each of the divine persons can be explained as relating to us in some real, differentiated sense, we will slip into a devotional unitarianism, even if not fully doctrinally so. Owen will be later shown to have a similar reticence about over-wrought uses of the Western doctrine of appropriations, a doctrine which has the effect of eclipsing the distinct contributions of each divine person to the believer's salvation as well as undercutting an appropriately triune form of devotion.

The other disjunction that Rahner was worried about, a severing of the economic Trinity from the immanent Trinity, he countered by his famous slogan, 'the economic Trinity is the immanent Trinity and the immanent Trinity is the economic Trinity.'[29] The expression might be taken in two ways.[30] Less controversially, Rahner may simply have meant that the God who in the work of salvation appears as triune is triune in himself. Father, Son, and Holy Spirit are not roles which God assumes for purposes of salvation, but their roles in salvation reveal their essential being in relation to each other. However, it seems likely that Rahner meant more than this, and he seems to have perhaps overly equated the triune missions in the

---

[28] Rahner, *The Trinity*, 15.

[29] Rahner, *The Trinity*, 22.

[30] J.A. Di Noia, 'Karl Rahner,' in *The Modern Theologians: An Introduction to Christian Theology in the Twentieth-Century*, ed. David F. Ford (Malden, MA: Blackwell Publishing, 1997) 127-29.

world with the *ad intra* triune processions. For Rahner, the processions and missions are explicated in terms of God's self-expression and self-possession. To say this, however, creates a problematic implication that the Trinity is not fully itself apart from the orders of creation and redemption. Rahner's philosophical substructure to this understanding seems to rely heavily on his 'ontology of the symbol' (which also factors in his christology, ecclesiology, sacramental theology, and exegesis). A 'real symbol' not only expresses something, it does something. An entity becomes itself (does something) in expressing itself (saying something). The Father expresses himself in the Son in order to possess himself in the Spirit, and the processions of the Son and Spirit are also thus processions of self-expression and self-possession. Indeed, in more traditional theology the external missions of the Trinity are extensions of the processions; however, these missions were understood as freely chosen actions, described in terms of efficient causality of the respective divine person. Rahner's model appears to make the free actions of creation, incarnation, and other saving events into necessary acts of each of the given *hypostaseis* apart from which they would fail to express, possess, or really be themselves. All of this seems reminiscent of the Hegelian assertion that world history is the process of God realizing himself: here 'history' might be substituted with 'salvation history,' but the general effect is the same – the work of God in the world is fundamentally about God growing up into his mature identity.

Even given this critique however, the positive aspect of Rahner's general direction is to turn the attention of the believer toward the economy of salvation in order to discover whom she is actually worshipping. So, more than worshipping God in an abstract and undifferentiated sense as the Supreme Being, or even a supremely loving, compassionate, merciful, just, and holy God, broadly conceived, she worships the God who can be trusted to have all these attributes for the primary reason that he has demonstrated such traits as he has revealed himself as the God of Abraham, Isaac, and Jacob, the God of the theophanies, the God of the Exodus deliverance, the God who promises to restore the exiles from Babylon, the God who saves through his Suffering Servant. Even without a fully manifest trinitarian devotion resulting from such probing of the Old Covenant story-line (though the theophanies and Isaiah prophecies, for example, are extremely suggestive of a second divine person active in salvation, and the Spirit also as somehow distinct), if this pattern is continued into the New Testament saving events, the explicit trinitarianism of these latter scenes of the redemptive story result in a cure to the devotional unitarianism to which Rahner's critique alerts us.

Negatively though, Rahner's necessitarian tendencies have the effect of undercutting the believer's awe at being loved by such a God. At its worst, the trinitarian work of salvation so conceived becomes a story more about God expressing and possessing his own nature than his free love to sinners. Of course there is a sense in which 'necessary' actions which are organic expressions of a person's own character are not the same as actions that are made necessary by an external force or coercion, and this perhaps mediates some of the negative effects of Rahner's necessitarianism. Yet, the freeness of God's saving activity outside himself as distinct from his necessary attributes has been a feature that some have rightfully as seen especially needful to preserve. The Protestant scholastics, drawing on medieval sources, recognized a difference between the *voluntas necessaria sive naturalis*, the necessary or natural will of God, which he must have and must manifest according to his own nature and by which God necessarily wills to be himself in his own attributes of goodness, love and justice, etc., and, on the other hand, the *voluntas libera*, the utterly free will according to which God executes his decrees of creation, providence, and the plan of salvation. The *voluntas libera* deals with the *ad extra* works of God and will have an important devotional value for a believer who realizes that the Father's determination to save in league with the Son and Spirit is, however mysterious, an external, free, act of the triune God, however in line with God's immanent attributes. Sinners are loved not because God needs to love them, but because he chooses to.

Rahner, of course, is not going as far as to say that God is being forced to save by an external power, and a critique of his necessitarianism that does not make this distinction would be unfair. Still, even the degree to which Rahner articulates his version of the Trinity's need to save as expressed in its processions and missions perhaps, in a different way, becomes too human-centered. Bluntly, does God need sinners to save in order to actualize himself? Is not the triune God delighted in himself apart from and prior to his acts of creation and redemption? If he is, then for the believer to be taken up by Christ into communion with such self-fulfilled, intrinsically glorious, and personally complete triune members is a deliverance into a perichoretic participation that is wondrous, utterly beyond her and independent of her own usefulness to God. Devotionally, the believer is surprised by the invitation into the inner-life of divine persons who would not have been thought to need her company, yet somehow freely sought it. Beyond this, the high-priestly prayer of Jesus suggests that a believer will in fact, through Christ, enter into the glory that the Son shared with the Father *before* the creation of the world, and thus before God's historical works of redemption. Of course, it is the result of trinitarian saving missions that such a salvation is accomplished for the believer – the external activities in history of the Father sending the Son into the world incarnate as Jesus Christ, mediated to believers through the Spirit – but this salvation is *unto* something beyond the historical acts themselves. Downplaying this fact over-identifies the trinitarian saving acts as part of the Trinity's essence. Perhaps we should say instead that the economic Trinity saves the believer into communion with the immanent Trinity. These are the same Trinities, but the external acts and being of the Trinity can still be thus distinguished. For all Rahner's admirable desire to draw attention back to the economy of salvation as a basic rubric for understanding the Trinity, he loses something crucial in the process. By equating the Trinity's essence with its work, God *in se* with God *pro nobis*, to so great a degree, the divine essence to which such external work points, illustrates, and induces worship becomes insubstantial beyond the events themselves. The believer would be tempted to worship God as the saving event more than the God who saves through the event, and whom the event saves them *unto*. Again, the devotional harm is in the arena of awe: if the ontology of God is to be understood as incomprehensible as it properly is in classic theology, there is a price to pay for over-identifying God's visible work with his essence, his revelation of himself with who he is in himself. The inherent incomprehensibility of God and a Godhead who exists above his works (however rightly he is revealed by those works) is a feature of a doctrine of God that preserves awe. As we will see, such theological assertions can be maintained (with their payoff for spirituality) even while taking seriously Rahner's rightful demand that the *historia salutis* is the only place to learn about the triune character of the God who saves.

Broad Models of Relating the Doctrine of God to Spirituality

In order to gather up so many loose ends and set them in context, it might be said that the modern history of spirituality suggests three overall models regarding ways to appropriate the doctrine of God.[31] The first model is that of Liberal Protestantism, defined by the likes of Adolf Harnack[32] and John Hick, where spirituality deals with the soul's immediate access to God. The role of Jesus, since he is not more than a perfect man, is to model his own communion with the Father and point the way for others to merely imitate him. The main block to communion with God is the believer, and the believer, with (perhaps) divine assistance, provides her own path to return. Such a view, says Torrance, 'made deep inroads and accounts in measure for the moralistic view of Christianity . . . free grace disappears, replaced by ethics.'[33] A second model characterized by the existential, present-day experience of God represents the early Barth, Bultmann, and perhaps surprisingly, major strains of

---

[31] Identified by James B. Torrance, *Worship*, 25ff.
[32] Adolf Harnack, *What is Christianity?* (New York: Harper, 1957).
[33] Torrance, *Worship*, 25-26.

contemporary Evangelicalism. Here, God gives himself to a person in a present moment of encounter and the response of the believer is variously to exercise faith, repentance, make a decision, etc., but, unlike the former Liberal model, such a response is only made possible by the work of Christ on the cross. In general, the event of preaching (*kerygma*) is what gives rise to the hearer's response. The more radical Bultmannian side of this model would suggest that while the *kerygma* certainly has a content and should make reference to the cross (for example), no direct belief in the atonement, the Trinity, or the incarnation is required as part of the proper response of faith. Evangelical versions of this model would counter that an explicit response of the believer to Jesus as God and the value of his atoning sacrifice for sin is in fact necessary. However, what unites these two otherwise very different theological visions is the central weight placed on the believer's existential response to the prior movement of God. While Evangelicalism with its Protestant roots will seek to do justice to *sola gratia* and *sola fide*, the weight placed on human response subtly undercuts both such principles: though this kind of Evangelicalism is clear about God's initiative and movement toward human sinners through Christ's work alone, the response to that initiative is all the sinner's. In practice, the quality, intensity, and genuineness of that human response determines the quality of a person's spirituality or relationship to God. This kind of theology of experience results in a two-dimensional worship between God and the sinner, implying that God, while offering salvation through Christ, then simply awaits a response. While the Evangelical-existential model advocates the need to believe in the Trinity, the doctrine of God itself does not inform the two-dimensional worship exchange. In other words, while the believer intellectually acknowledges that God is triune, the form of dialogue with that God is not particularly shaped by such a conviction. Missing is a recognition that God himself has already provided the response that alone is acceptable to him, for in fact 'whatever else our faith is, it is a response to a response already made for us and continually being made for us in Christ, the pioneer of our faith.'[34] In trinitarian terms, while the existential model applies the Son's sacrifice for sin to the believer, it under-realizes the believer's participation in Christ's own response of faith and obedience to his Father, as well as the ongoing intercession of the Spirit on behalf of believers who themselves really do not know how to pray.[35] Likewise, the incarnation of the Son may have value as a condition by which God makes Christ's death an appropriate substitute for human sinners, but little additional value is seen in Christ's perfect human

---

[34] Torrance, *Worship*, 29-30.
[35] Rom. 8:26-27

response to the Father for other humans who will never themselves respond as purely.

A third model, which Torrance advocates, thus seeks to do full justice to the incarnation and the Trinity, defining worship as the gift of participating through the Spirit in the incarnate Son's communion with the Father. For, at the center of the New Testament stands not the believer's spiritual experience of God, but Jesus' relationship with the Father. His response, always perfectly obedient, prayerful, decisive, faithful, is mediated to sinful believers who are then given an analogous knowledge and access to the Father, for 'no one knows the Father except the Son and those to whom the Son chooses to reveal him.'[36] While Torrance does not say so, there is a kind of Federalism to this brand of spirituality; the 'spiritual' response of Christ to the Father is credited to the believer before there is any talk of the believer responding with her own faith, adoration, etc. Human spirituality is not first a 'practice' but a gift to be received from one who brings us into his own communion with the Father. The cross is central to the revelation of this intra-trinitarian relationship: between the Father and Son is a 'unique relationship of mutual love, mutual self-giving, mutual testifying, mutual glorifying... indeed there is a one-ness of mind between the Father and Son revealed supremely in the cross "to bring many sons to glory" (Heb.2:10), "that we might receive the adoption of sons" (Gal.4:5ff.).'[37] Crucial also is the Holy Spirit's role, for Jesus is conceived by the Spirit, baptized in him, driven by him into the wilderness, raised from the dead by him, and Jesus receives the Spirit from the Father in his own humanity, and then with the Father sends this Spirit into believers.

Jurgen Moltmann operates somewhat from within this model when he speaks about the crucifixion as the clearest revelation of the Trinity, since at the cross we see God relating to God, God the Son to God the Father, and, in fact, the abandonment of the Father amounting to the punitive removal of God the Spirit from Christ (for without such a Spirit-centric formulation of Christ's abandonment it is impossible to conceive of how, generically, God could abandon the God-man without the problematic assertion that he was emptying the crucified Jesus of his divinity – instead Christ was deprived of only the anointing of the Spirit).[38] How does this realization effect prayer, for example? The triune God revealed at the cross should not be approached as merely a 'personal God,' but in reference to the three persons who were revealed there: 'one does not simply pray to God as a heavenly Thou but prays...through the Son to the Father in the Spirit . . . the New Testament made a very neat

---

[36] Mt.11:27; see also Jn.1:18; 17:25-26.
[37] Torrance, *Worship*, 31.
[38] Jurgen Moltmann, 'The "Crucified God": God and the Trinity Today,' in *New Questions on God*, ed. J. B. Metz (New York: Herder & Herder, 1972) 31-5.

distinction in Christian prayer between the Son and the Father. We ought to take that up, and ought not to speak of 'God' in such an undifferentiated way, thus opening up the way to atheism.'[39] But the cross does not just show the Christian the trinitarian God whom she is to respond to, for the love of this God toward her that is both provided and evidenced at the cross (1) motivates her own love by the very sight of it, and (2) acts simultaneously as God's fulfillment of his own mandate to humans. In light of the cross, to say 'God is love' is not an abstract assertion of a static attribute he possesses, but 'an *event* [emphasis mine] in a loveless, legalistic world: the event of an unconditioned and boundless love which comes to meet man, which takes hold of those who are unloved and forsaken, unrighteous or outside the law, and gives them a new identity, liberates them from the norms of social identifications and from the guardians of social norms and idolatrous images. What Jesus commanded in the Sermon on the Mount as love of one's enemy has taken place on the cross through Jesus' dying and the grief of the Father in the power of the Spirit, for the godless and loveless.'[40]

In other words, what God commands of his people he also gives to them at the cross, and what he gives he gives there as a unified though differentiated work of the Father, Son, and Spirit. This crucifixion is on behalf of beloved sinners through which the Trinity both loves them and fulfills the requirement that they are to themselves love (which begins to mesh with Torrance's interest that the believer view Christ's work as the fulfillment of the spiritual life properly lived). Like Rahner though, Moltmann is open to some criticism for the extent to which he identifies God with his actions, in this case his actions in the crucifixion. Surely he is over-extending the principle to say as he does, '"God" is not another nature or a heavenly person or moral authority, but in fact an "event".'[41] As important as what the event accomplishes and reveals by and about God, why not allow for God to exist before and outside it? And while the crucifixion ought to be seen as the center of gravity for spirituality, the value of the crucifixion is made more complete when the resurrection is linked with it, tandem events of what together are the pinnacle of salvation history and trinitarian self-revelation. Adding reference to the resurrection would complete for the believer the reality of the joy, victory, and glory shared between Father and Son and therefore could act as grounds for the believer's similar response of joy before God as she contemplates her own resurrection in Christ.

If this modification to Moltmann is observed (to add reference to the resurrection and to not reduce God to an event), then the

---

[39] Moltmann, *The Crucified God*, 247.
[40] Moltmann, *The Crucified God*, 248.
[41] Moltmann, *The Crucified God*, 247.

crucifixion/resurrection event can become two things for a trinitarian spirituality. On one hand the event itself, in the way that it reveals the triune God in action on behalf of sinners, becomes the prime impetus of the believer's own responses to God – the sinner who realizes she has been saved by such a loving conspiracy between the Father, Son, and Spirit has now ultimate grounds for humility, thankfulness, joy, etc. In other words, no believer knows more fully how costly her sins, how much she has been willingly forgiven of, how glorious her destiny, than when she is looking at what happened to Christ on Good Friday and Easter. On the other hand, because the event centers around Christ's vicarious display of the ultimate human response to God, imputed to the believer, the cross (especially) spells the end of Christian spirituality's sometimes pretentiousness. That is, the very spiritual response to God that the crucifixion/resurrection induces in a believer when she considers it, is already perfectly acted out by Christ for her – Christ prayed fervently, he humbly submitted to the Father's will, he bore up under present suffering 'for the joy set before him,' he finally ascended to commune with the Father face-to-face. If Christ has really done all these things as her priest, her stand-in, then by virtue of her union with Christ she has already, in a sense, reached the pinnacle of human response to God. The value of this fact for a believer who seeks a vital daily relationship with God is, among other things, to immediately prevent the overwrought sense of the value of her own spiritual response. Not only has her eternal salvation been accomplished by Christ, but so has her present spiritual life. Has she not been thankful enough? Christ has been thankful to the Father, in her place. Are her prayers weak? Christ's were strong, and his prayers cover hers (and the Spirit of Christ's prayers somehow even transform her bumbling prayers after she utters them, cf. Rom. 8:26-27). In this sense, Christ's own spirituality is the end of Christian spirituality: it completes it while, in another sense, it undercuts its pretensions. Because Christ's own spiritual life is itself *pro nobis*, the believer who understands it as such is not discouraged as if Christ set an imposing standard to live up to; rather, her own life of prayer, moral exertion, etc., is freed more than ever to become a simple, uncalculated response to grace received rather than a program of spiritual achievements.

Whatever degree of fuzziness there might seem to be in the connections made above between trinitarian actions and human response, or more particularly, between the actions of the three divine persons in and around the crucifixion/resurrection event and the believer's response to such actions, it is accounted for because we have not yet developed a theology of each divine person's unique contribution to the saving plan (Owen will help us). In other words, if there exists at all an explicitly trinitarian spirituality, it would seem to require explicit statements about how each divine person has uniquely brought about salvation, and how the believer would respond to knowing these distinct contributions. Much more can be said about the saving work of each divine *hypostaseis*. The Protestant Scholastics are good conversation partners in this regard, partly because of their sometimes elaborate Covenant Theology. The scholastic Covenant of Redemption is particularly fruitful because it identifies the divine persons themselves (especially the Father and the Son) as parties of a covenant by which they differently bring about human salvation. John Owen did not write any of the foundational works of Covenant Theology; however, his elaboration on its themes, especially on the unique roles of each divine member, provided for him the theological backbone of a model for spirituality that is full of clues for anyone seeking to make a more robust appropriation of the doctrine of God in private worship. The next chapter will analyze in further depth examples of devotional movements in church history where trinitarian thought (or lack of it) positively (or negatively) impacted the way in which the believer was understood to commune with God. John Owen will eventually emerge as a particularly helpful writer for his strong linking of spirituality and a doctrine of God.

CHAPTER 3

In Search of Trinitarian Spirituality: Definitions, Criteria, and Marginal Successes

Some of the contemporary individuals and models that were introduced in the previous chapter suggest the broad strokes of a trinitarian spirituality, though most of what has been mentioned is more theological and conceptual than directly suggestive of a practical model for believers in their devotion. To summarize the best of what we have discovered in contemporary theologians: Barth tells us that the Trinity's self-revelation is completed only when we observe such revelation's transformative impact on the human recipient; Rahner tells the believer to look for the nature of God in his three-fold saving work for us; Moltmann says that the event of the crucifixion alone compels the highest thoughts of God's nature and love; and Torrance says that worship is the gift of participating through the Spirit in the incarnate Son's communion with the Father. But can any of these observations cohere in a practical way for the Christian who sits down to pray, repent, worship, meditate? This chapter is concerned to analyze moments in the history of Christian devotion where something of a doctrine of God was put into action in such a way that orthodox trinitarianism can be said to have programmed a whole spirituality—or tellingly failed to do so. To do this, we will first posit two overarching criteria for a successful trinitarian spirituality. In the remaining bulk of the chapter we will evaluate three families of historical devotion for their relative successes and failures to appropriate those criteria: 1) the Marginal Trinitarian Orthodoxy of Quakerism, 2) the Trinity within (Popular) Protestant scholasticism, and 3) the God of Realist Mysticism.

As the three traditions are examined, we will increasingly introduce the ideas of John Owen by way of comparison, especially in the last section on medieval realism. Why? The conclusion of this work is that Owen comes closer than most other figures in western spirituality to integrating a doctrinally rich trinitarianism into the heart of a spiritual method. So, in order to evaluate the three strains of spirituality, we will sometimes look through the lenses of Owen, especially in places where, I believe, he succeeds in meeting the specific criteria for trinitarian spirituality that are established below. On the other hand, Owen did not derive his system *de novo*, but stands at the end of a long history of spiritual writers who were interested to integrate properly the Christian doctrine of God. While he stands in contrast to some of that tradition, certain partial allies will appear, sometimes in the unlikeliest of places. Therefore, the other reason to compare Owen to some of the medieval spiritual schools is to understand his own system better, and to see where he is developing emphases that already existed in the western tradition.

The Criteria for a Successful Trinitarian Spirituality

For the sake of clarity, our two criteria will first be stated, then explained:

Criterion #1
   Given the 'Great Tradition' of the relatively stable doctrine of the Trinity, Christian spiritualities can be evaluated by how well they comport with this doctrinal tradition, or even better, to what extent they explicitly draw from it.

Criterion #2
   The commendable recent emphasis that the Trinity is revealed most clearly through the divine acts in salvation history suggests that a thoroughly trinitarian spirituality will anchor itself in obvious ways on the *historia salutis*.

Explanation of the First Criterion: Orthodoxy in Historical and Systematic Theology

The term 'Great Tradition' is borrowed from Thomas Oden and others who have recently argued for a renewed weight on doctrine that has been believed 'everywhere, always, and by all.'[1] While the Great Tradition model can be justly criticized for sometimes ignoring significant differences between the patristics, or for undervaluing the principle of *sola scriptura* as the only 'norming norm' for church dogmatics, few would argue today against the foundational value of especially the patristic tradition when it comes to making sense of the biblical content regarding the Trinity. So, if the doctrine of God has been so stable across Christian communions and over time, we would expect such formulations

---

[1] Thomas Oden, *The Rebirth of Orthodoxy: Signs of New Life in Christianity* (San Francisco: HarperSanFrancisco, 2003); Thomas Oden, ed., *Ancient Christian Commentary on Scripture* (Downer's Grove, Illinois: InterVarsity, ongoing); James S. Cutsinger, ed., *Reclaiming the Great Tradition: Evangelicals, Catholics, and Orthodox in Dialogue* (Downer's Grove, Illinois: InterVarsity, 1997). Interestingly, Oden cites John Owen as one of the noteworthy Protestant Scholastics who operated with vast knowledge on the ancient writers, cf. unpublished interview by Daniel Reed, Senior Editor, InterVarsity Press.

to be uncontroversial as a basic ingredient in any recipe for how a believer should relate to this particular God of Christians. As we might expect, many Christian spiritual models do in fact endorse traditional trinitarian orthodoxy, but the criterion proposed here also asks that such models would actually feature such doctrine in some central way for spiritual practice. Put more strongly, *a spirituality that meets this criterion should come completely undone if the doctrine of the Trinity were proved untrue.*

The Content of the First Criterion: Defining the Doctrine

To say that a given model of spirituality is especially reliant on a given doctrine suggests that the depth and nuances of that doctrine are somehow visible in that model's practices. The Trinity, among all doctrines, has a notably complex vocabulary that has developed over centuries, so identifying the elements of a deeply trinitarian spirituality requires at least a short foray into the details of the historical terminology. Without its making some reference to such formulations, spirituality that is supposedly trinitarian can become either shallow or overly subjective. Positively put, the greater the degree that legitimate nuances of the doctrine are in mind, the more content there is to draw from for devotional application. Great amounts of historical rehashing here are unnecessary, though a few points are worth making in reference to the scriptural sources of the doctrine, as well as early Greek and Latin formulations. We would expect that any claimed trinitarian spirituality would deal to some degree with both the Trinity as it has been revealed in scripture as well as the carefully constructed formulas of the early ecumenical tradition.

THE TRINITY REVEALED IN THE NEW TESTAMENT: DOCTRINE FOR THE SAKE OF COMMUNION

The classic creedal formulations were of course trying to make sense of biblical content – but the context of those biblical texts already tells us something about the way the doctrine of God was originally intended to be *used*. So before dealing with later patristic formulas, the first thing to be said about the New Testament references is that they reveal an original context that is more about enriching the believer's life in fellowship with God than building a doctrine as an end in itself. B.B. Warfield's observation that trinitarian doctrine in the New Testament is more 'overheard' than directly spoken[2] raises the question of what the topic of the overheard conversation was first about – and the answer usually has

---

[2] Benjamin B. Warfield, "The Biblical Doctrine of the Trinity," in *Biblical and Theological Studies* (Phillipsburg: Presbyterian and Reformed, 1968) 32.

something to do with furthering the Christian's conscious experience of God's saving activity. That is, the Trinity is revealed in biblical texts that deal with establishing the believer's assurance of God's favor or that draw attention to other present benefits of the gospel. Thus Paul *encourages* the believers with the pastoral reminder that 'through [Christ] we both have access to the Father by one Spirit,' (Eph.2:18), and John *comforts* by saying that 'truly our fellowship is with the Father and with his Son Jesus Christ,' (1 Jn.1:13). And, if pastoral encouragement about fellowship with and access to God are at the center of the New Testament's trinitarian conversation, so also are trinitarian reminders about the manner in which God give gifts to his people, for 'there are different kinds of gifts, but the same Spirit. There are different kinds of service, but the same Lord. There are different kinds of working, but the same God works all of them in all men,' (1 Cor. 12:4-6). And without added theological commentary Paul is able to *bless* the Corinthians with the almost off-handedly trinitarian formula, 'May the grace of the Lord Jesus Christ, the love of the Father, and the fellowship of the Holy Spirit be with you all,' (2 Cor.1:14). These are the classic texts used to prove and explain trinitarian doctrine, yet the actual original context, without fail, is apostolic encouragement that believers variously experience the God of their salvation. The conclusion is that the triunity of God has been articulated since the beginning in order to answer the practical questions about how and to whom the believer is to respond (in worship and service) as she comes to realize the triune author of her redemption. All of this is to stress the importance and legitimacy that the doctrine be applied, not just believed merely in the old sense of *noticia*.[3] It also licenses (even urges) Christians to find models of the spiritual life that are distinctively Trinitarian, if this original New Testament context is to remain a normative guide.

Yet, admittedly, perhaps the very New Testament 'over-heardness' of the doctrine itself suggests a certain restraint about the way to apply the conclusions of our present project. Warfield notes that when Paul's clauses refer to each divine person, they often do so without further comment merely because 'God, the Lord, and the Spirit lie in the back of his mind constantly suggesting a threefold causality behind every manifestation of grace.'[4] If this is true, then a trinitarian spirituality need not always be flying its colors in elaborate distinctions between the persons of the Godhead. Theological richness in a spiritual model need not always spell longish prayers where each divine person is dwelt upon in depth for his distinct processions and missions. A full trinitarian

---

[3] Protestant scholasticism defined saving faith as a combination of knowledge (*noticia*), assent to that knowledge (*assensus*), and trust (*fiducia*).

[4] Warfield, "The Biblical Doctrine,"48.

spirituality may sometimes be only partly in evidence since the threefold causality of grace must be, in some cases, only at the 'back of the mind.' Simply put, the most properly elaborate models of trinitarian devotion that we may discover in our historical inquiry need not demand that every prayer be so elaborate. If anything, the New Testament model is that trinitarian theology inform the believer's worship and prayer, but without regimenting any particular form of prayer or meditative structure – the trinitarian character of Christian devotion should be so deeply rooted as to manifest itself spontaneously in different degrees of complexity. We are of course in this study seeking out explicitly trinitarian models of the spiritual life, yet since the New Testament often weaves in trinitarian doctrine without fanfare and in ways that are hardly formulaic, we must view even the most doctrinally rich spiritualities from church history as helpful guides but not inspired techniques.

THE DOCTRINE IN FORMULATION: WHAT HAS BEEN MEANT BY 'TRINITY'

All of the above being said, the question still remains as to what theological propositions about the Godhead might be appropriated for a spirituality to be considered highly trinitarian. Here some reference to theological formula becomes important. We would expect that a trinitarian spirituality would be dependant on some amount of these relatively settled doctrinal distinctions. Tertullian (c.220) established the beginning of a doctrinal vocabulary when he rebutted the modalistic monarchian heresy of Sabellius by asserting that God is one in *substantia* and three in *persona*. Strangely, Sabellius himself first coined the term *homoousios* to describe the Son's relationship with the Father, though not in the sense of the later orthodox meaning of the term. For Sabellius, the Son emanates from the Father and thereby shares his essence, but so do other lesser created things such as angels, rocks, and trees. For the Son is exalted because he is closer to God on the chain of divine emanation than other created things, but is he is still lower than God himself. Tertullian opposed this idea by saying that each divine *persona* shares equally in one divine *substantia* — the person of the Son is not essentially lower on the ontological ladder of God-ness, as Sabellius had said, but has equal God-ness with the Father. By the time of the Council of Nicea in 325, a new form of monarchianism, now 'dynamic monarchianism,' was being derived from the writings of Paul of Samosata, Lucian of Antioch, and more famously, Arius. The Arians were eager to guard the one-ness of God and did so by seeing Jesus as the most exalted of God's creations, adopted by God on account of his perfect obedience which demonstrated his 'one-ness' with God – a one-ness only, however, of purpose and mission. The Council responded that the Son was 'begotten' not in reference to his beginning in time as the Arians said, but in the filial sense, calling attention to the Son's eternal son-like relationship with the

Father. In an ironic choice of words, Athanasius and the Council of Nicea affirmed that the Son was *homoousios* with the Father, deciding that it was worth the risk of reviving the old heretical usage of the word by the Sabellian gnostics[5] for the sake of defending the full deity of the Son. In fact, the nagging aroma of modalistic monarchianism that the *homoousios* terminology might have suggested at this later date was only finally avoided by the achievements of the Cappadocian Fathers: Basil of Caesarea, Gregory of Nyssa, and Gregory of Nazianzus. The Cappadocians argued for one *ousia* but three *hypostaseis*, with the *hypostaseis* seen as particular instances of the *ousia* much in the same sense that Peter, James, and John are particular individuals of the essence which is humanity. The opposite error of tritheism is almost implied in this formulation, of course, so the Cappadocians went on to specify that the entire divine *ousia* is indivisibly present in the three *hypostaseis*, or more technically, that the *hypostaseis* are eternally subsistent relations in the one *ousia*.

The West largely accepted these distinctions, but struggled somewhat in relating Greek concepts to Latin terminology. Eventually, the Greek *ousia* was accepted as the equivalent of Tertullian's already familiar Latin *substantia*, and the Greek *hypostasis* was rendered as *persona*. So, one *ousia* in three *hypostaseis* could be termed one *substantia* in three *personae*. To make things clearer though, Latin-speaking scholastics eventually added *subsistentia*, a more transparent word than *persona* to mean a particular instance of a *substantia*, as well as using the phrase *modus subsistendi* in order to express the idea that each *hypostasis* is a relation within the Trinity. For the West this *modus subsistendi* also guarded the coequality of the persons, since ideas like 'order' and 'relation' do not imply subordination but instead comport with full equality.[6] For the West, the Father and Son both proceed the Spirit, who is the bond of love between Father and Son, and is the reciprocal relation between them. Both Greek and Latin theories, though, described the common possession of the entire divine essence by each person as a coinherence of each person in one another and in the essence of divine nature: this *perichoresis* in Greek was the *circumincessio* in Latin. Such divine mutual indwelling, or 'inter-penetration,' is a universally recognized aspect of trinitarian identity that will have impact, perhaps both properly and improperly, on devotional movements that we will consider.

---

[5] Again, that the Son is of one substance with the Father in the sense that he is on the same chain of being with him, though, like the rest of creation, still a lower emanation of the Father's essence.

[6] Richard A. Muller, *Dictionary of Greek and Latin Theological Terms* (Grand Rapids: Baker, 1985), 308.

GOD'S 'ESSENTIAL WORKS' VS. 'PERSONAL WORKS'

Another scholastic distinction worth noting in reference to devotional possibilities, is that between the *opera Dei essentiala* and the *opera Dei personalia*. First, the 'essential works of God' are those performed by God in reference to his one-ness, such that each divine person is equally involved. These works include both the *opus Dei essentialis* **ad intra**, meaning the eternal decree, as well as the *opus Dei essentialis* **ad extra** which flow from the decree, i.e. the works of creation and providence, including the economy of salvation. The more famous formula associated with the latter idea is *opera trinitatis ad extra sunt indivisa*, 'the external works of the Trinity are undivided.' An immediate objection which arises to this formula is that some external works do seem to be more properly attributed to one person than another, especially in the works of redemption, where the Son alone takes human nature, the Spirit alone is said to conceive the Christ-child, etc. The scholastic solution was to concede that each divine person has his own *modus agendi*, manner of working, where the Father acts through the Son and in the Spirit, or more elaborately, the Father is the *fons actionis* ('fount of activity'), the Son is the *medium actionis* ('means of activity'), and the Spirit is the *terminus actionis* ('limit of activity'). It seems that such refining of the doctrine of the *Dei essentiala* guards it against undue smoothing over of divine distinctions, yet the emphasis remains on the one-ness, with the three-ness more of a concession to events in salvation history that would be hard to explain otherwise. It will take bolder practical writers like John Owen to press the distinctions between the work of each divine person into service for the believer's fullest response to God, taking these distinctions further than some scholastics would have emphasized. A scholastic theology of the Trinity applied to devotion, in the end, would need to somehow make use of the different senses in which God's saving work is both one and three. However, our interest is in the direction of appropriating the distinctions in hypostatic activity, and the tradition certainly in the East and even here to a degree in the West seems to allow us, hesitatingly, to do so. Owen in particular will articulate a way to pray that depends heavily on the distinct saving work of each *hypostasis*, and I suggest this is technically licensed, though perhaps not enthusiastically, by such Western formulas, which are more concerned to highlight the non-distinctiveness of each divine person's work.

Perhaps a greater foundational recognition of divine distinctions is seen in the doctrine of the *opera Dei personala*, which refers to the *ad intra* operations of the individual members of the Trinity to and amongst themselves. Here now are actions that everyone agrees are fully distinct, and the potential hedging of the above formulas seems to fall away: such 'personal works of God' are the activity of the Father begetting the Son, the Father and the Son (in the West) spirating the Spirit, the Spirit passively being spirated, and the Son passively being begotten.[7] These are interior works/relations in which the differences between the persons are acknowledged as irreducibly distinct (and are not to be confused with the *ad intra* works of the *opera Dei essentiala*, which is a reference to only the eternal decree as a unified work of the Godhead). Owen's fairly elaborate and certainly heavy reliance on divine distinctions in the saving economy probably, again, should not be interpreted as an obvious outflow of such elements of the Western tradition's acknowledgment of immanent-three-ness, for only loosely does Owen connect his observation of distinctions in the economy with the distinctions in God's personal emanations. Certainly for Owen, the objects of the Christian's meditation were to be each of the divine persons' saving acts in history, and such acts would easily fall under the category of the Godhead's 'external work' – the very work that the Latin formula warns must not be thought of as divided amongst the persons. There definitely exists some tension between Owen and this aspect of Western tradition. However, on the above grounds of the scholastic admission of at least *some* appropriate distinctions, we should not see Owen as altogether alien to the Western formulas either (the doctrine of appropriations and the 'personal works of God' are both justly footholds for him). To press against the Western emphasis on unity and indivisibility, even to press against the limits of the doctrine of appropriations, is possible in ways to which tradition itself seems to give some credence. Chapter six will deal with a more sustained critique of the doctrinal appropriateness of Owen's method in particular. However, stated in the most cautious way, the ancient and scholastic formulas of the Trinity recognized some kind of one-ness and three-ness about God's essence as well as his saving work, but so often the three-ness, however described and with whatever qualifications, has made little impact on devotional theology. If it had, as a quick example, a prayer of thanksgiving to the Son would involve reference to his distinct as well as shared role in providing certain saving benefits, and an act of praise might exult in his unique actions while he was incarnate in Palestine as well as for his divine nature which he shares with the Father and Spirit. We move on though to briefly consider the second criterion that would identify success in such an effort to appropriate the classical three-ness of God within Christian spirituality.

Explanation of the Second Criterion: The Trinity of Redemptive History

Again, this criterion states: The commendable recent emphasis that the Trinity is revealed most clearly through its acts in salvation history

---

[7] These are also known as the four 'personal relations,' *relatio personalis*.

suggests that a thoroughly trinitarian spirituality will anchor itself in obvious ways on the *historia salutis*. If the nature of God himself is humanly perceived from the plot-line of redemption rather than by any other means, we would expect that dealings with such a God would not be divorced from that story but would dwell on it in significant ways. How well do prayer models, exercises for meditation, motives for mortification of sin and vivifying of the new self, etc., refer to the plot-line of redemption and the divine persons who differently act it out on the stage of the biblical world? The previous chapter introduced the concern for an emphasis on redemptive history, but the nature of this criterion requires more explanation and defense.

Narrative vs. Drama

So far we have used 'narrative' and 'drama' almost interchangeably, but some of the features of contemporary 'narrative theology' require us to distinguish more carefully what we are claiming that is different from that school. Narrative theology, as a movement, tends to see as irreducible certain polarities such as reader vs. text and intratextual reality vs. extratextual reference. The result is that certain events in the biblical story, such as Jesus' resurrection, are seen as essential because of their helpful function in the Christian community, not first because they occurred in time and space. For narrative theologians to advocate taking the biblical story-line seriously is a move in the right direction from the demythologizing tendency of Liberalism, but to make the 'community value' of the narrative the reason for this move is still to undervalue what this story is about. 'While modernity enshrined the sacred self, postliberalism enshrined the sacred community,' says Horton.[8] But if the scriptural narratives are reporting 'true truth,' that is, actual historical events of God's own public acts, then the reason to take such narratives seriously is because they report events that really happened and, by God's purposes, really accomplished something even apart from whether the self or community recognizes it. The value of an historical-dramatic model for understanding scripture is that it transcends the dichotomies of textual event vs. historical event by putting the Author and the reader in the same play. Since God has acted on the stage of history, 'and not merely within the narrative text, we are able to provide legitimate space for both the individual and the community,'[9] but only as both are written and directed by the God of the drama. The value of the narrative events come not from how the individual, nor the community, may use them, but

---

[8] Michael Horton, *Covenant and Eschatology: The Divine Drama* (Louisville, Kentucky: Westminster/John Knox Press, 2002) 96.

[9] Horton, *Covenant*, 96.

by virtue of their objectively taking place in the historical plane that we as individuals and as a Christian community share with God. So while we may rightly say that the covenantal 'narrative' is what shapes a fully trinitarian devotion, it may be more clear, given the different use of this term in the lexicon of Yale postliberalism (perhaps narrative theology's heartland), to talk instead about the covenantal *drama*. To speak of the drama of redemption makes more clear that these are not mythic tales but events that have taken place in space and time, on the stage of observable history. A devotion based on a drama that has been historically enacted will be less given to the kind of subjectivity that is inherent in reader-centered or even community-centered criticism, criticism that is less grounded on events that really took place during fixed dates on the stage that was ancient Palestine, Egypt, and Mesopotamia.

But despite the advantages for our project, is it really legitimate to liken this covenantal mode of scripture to such a stage-play, and if so, how would doing so inform particularly trinitarian devotion? It has been said that the hallmark of the 'redemptive-historical' (or 'eschatological') method of God's self-disclosure is that the divine plan unfolds in scripture through a 'word—act—word' pattern, or more fully described, 'announcement—accomplishment—interpretation.'[10] If so, to really learn about God requires reflecting on God's performative action in the world, including the prophecies that first predict the action, the action itself, the scriptural interpretation of that action, and, by natural extension, even our own participation in the action, since God has announced that he is drawing us into his own saving acts as both recipients and respondents. To call this 'drama' is especially appropriate since we quickly notice that we are dealing with all the elements of a play: a playwright (the triune God), a script (the Scriptures), a stage (the created world), actors (Father, Son, and Spirit as the main characters, and every human playing a role as well), and an audience (humanity and the angels). So, while the Scriptures record the past acts of the play, the present moment is also part of the play as God continues to move the redemptive story along through his own acts and our responses (which themselves are part of the his script, assuming theological double-agency of divine and human will). Since the script is written and published, we know the ending already – that the kingdom will be consummated, the conflict of sin and death resolved, and the Lamb will be enthroned.

Why is this dramatic mode so important for models of spirituality to reckon with? One reason is that drama affects a person holistically – the intellect is involved, yes, but so are the emotions, as we have noted, and

---

[10] Horton, *Covenant*, 5.

even the senses are played upon.¹¹ The Father's offering up the Son humbles us, the Son's willingness to endure Calvary strikes us as terrible and yet wondrous, the prophetically foretold images of the *parousia* give us hope that the Spirit's work will one day be completed in us and in the world. Good drama is enveloping; the audience surrenders to it and is changed as a result. To deal with God through the drama of his own acts of creation and redemption is to invite a kind of enthrallment of the whole person. And, since the drama in question is the particular one played out in the biblical covenants, this will not be a primarily subjective enthrallment akin to some forms of mysticism, but a content-rich encounter based on the historical facts describing how a Father, Son, and Spirit have sought us out. As it turns out, this particular biblical play does not star a purely monotheistic deity, but a three-in-one-God who is busy redeeming a people for himself according to his own processions and missions. Dorothy Sayers said that 'the dogma is the drama,'¹² meaning that out of the story-line, and nowhere else, comes our access to doctrinal truths about this particular God, and, I would add, the story remains the center-of-gravity for our devotion to God as well. If we are really watching this drama, and not one of our own making, we see that the starring role is played by one who increasingly portrays himself as a three-in-one hero. If covenantal narrative really controls devotion, then devotion will be trinitarian in shape. Conversely, devotional models that are not grounded on redemptive history will have a hard time keeping anything but an ontological Trinity in view – the economic Trinity will be elusive since the drama is the only place where this truth about God comes clearly into view.

Non-Dramatic Spirituality and the Critique of Nietzsche

Outside criticism of Christian spirituality also teaches a lesson in this regard. One of Nietzsche's problems with Christianity was that its God was a 'bad fiction.'¹³ Not only was the Christian God untrue, but belief in him was as harmful to the believer and to society as a bad book is to someone who gets wrapped up in it. Nietzsche should therefore be understood as much a critic of Christian spirituality as of theology, for he believed that the Christian fiction acted as a kind of destructive 'Platonism for the masses,' a drug which made believers detached and

---

¹¹ The Lord's Supper, for example, is a sort of reenactment of the Christ's death scene, which communicates to us not through the ear, but through the other senses of seeing, tasting, and smelling.

¹² Dorothy Sayers, *Creed or Chaos* (Manchester, New Hampshire: Sophia Institute Press, 1974) 5.

¹³ Brian Ingraffia, *Postmodern Theory and Biblical Theology* (Cambridge: Cambridge University Press, 1995) 7, in Horton, *Covenant*, 22.

complacent in the present world, yearning for heaven, the Christianized world-of-the-forms. Yet Nietzsche makes a valid criticism of platonic spiritualities that pay little attention to the New Testament eschatology, and, as a result, languish in abstract spiritual values and communion with a static deity. If redemptive history sets the tone, on the other hand, the expression of spiritual strength in the Christian's life is neither modeled after the image of Apollo (a resignation to defeat – what Nietzsche criticized in Christianity) nor of Dionysius (the will to power which he advocated), but the image of a Lamb who was slain for us and is now alive for us.[14] While the Christian life involves much self-denial, humility, and perseverance under suffering, these are not timeless values *per se*, but eschatologically appropriate values for this point in the story. As such, the ideal of 'weakness,' for example, takes on a very different meaning inside an eschatological spirituality of the biblical drama than in the timeless brand of spirituality that Nietzsche was rightly bothered by. The Son who in humility subjected himself to his enemies is certainly a model whom his followers seek to emulate – however, the same Son will, in the play's last act, return to the stage in glory (not humility) to judge his enemies (not to turn his cheek again) and will gather up his people to join him in having joyful dominion over a new creation (not to keep groaning in the old fallen one). Because the *eschaton* reminds the believer that his destiny is to be in perfect union with the triumphant Lamb while in a body and mind that has been entirely transformed by the Spirit, even Christian 'weakness' now is simply a different kind of strength.[15] The believer's present weakness (physically, economically, morally, whatever) drives him to find a new power, not in pretended Nietzschean autonomy, but in dwelling on the efficacious active and passive work of Christ for him, which affords him a new identity as a loved child of God, a temple for the Spirit, and a future citizen of the glorious *civitatis dei*. With this narrative controlling his mind and affections, he is not made apathetic, but empowered to work and serve the triune God's present kingdom purposes in this world. The 'already' of Christ's victory mediates some of the pain of the 'not yet' aspects in his present experience, with the promise that the last scene of the play will resolve the dialectic in favor of victory and unbroken communion with Father, Son, and Spirit. So, not only does the redemptive-historical 'theology of the cross' keep in check any self-indulgent, ill-timed 'theology of glory,' as Luther urged, but it also contradicts misuse of otherwise admirable spiritual or moral ideals

---

[14] Horton, *Covenant*, 22

[15] Miroslav Volf says, 'theology as reflection on the word of the cross must be embodied in the community of the cross whose particular kind of weakness is a new kind of power inserted into the network of the powers of the world,' in *The Future of Theology: Essays in Honor of Jurgen Moltmann*, ed. Volf, Carmen Krieg, and Thomas Kucharz (Grand Rapids: Eerdmans, 1996) 109, in Horton, *Covenant*, 43.

that, without emplotment, are not really distinctively Christian and truly are insipid. Christian spirituality, when derived from the covenantal storyline, will not make the believer flee 'this glorious theater' of Calvin's description; neither will he become self-indulgent. The believer is 'not on a pilgrimage from this world to another, but from this world under the reign of unrighteousness to the newness that has already dawned in Jesus Christ...,' for they know that in a decisive future moment all people will 'behold that tragicomic incongruity of a lamb who was slain seated triumphantly on a throne.'[16] A theology of God that is not also eschatological, plot-driven, redemptive-historical (to gather up some terms) has none of these resources that are so necessary to make devotional anchor-points for the believer.

I suspect that one of the reasons Christian history offers so few models of adequate trinitarian devotion is that the doctrine of the Trinity was originally articulated in formulaic theological language (as was necessary), without as much regard to the covenantal emplotment through which the trinitarian God discloses himself.[17] Formula does not grip the soul the way a story does (never mind give it a vision of history's whole meaning), so it should not surprise us that God happens to have chosen story for the form of his own self-disclosure.[18] This is not to fault early dogmatic statements about the Godhead, since systematic-theological formulas are valuable and necessary, especially in stating doctrine succinctly and in the face of controversy. But as we will see in some of the examples of medieval spirituality, the Trinity sometimes appears with more of the static look of mere systematic theology, as if the believer were dealing merely with the three *hypostaseis* in their naked divine attributes. Certainly the Augustinian emphasis on what unites the divine persons rather than what distinguishes them has had an effect – we would expect that this emphasis, like any theological assertion, would carry through to devotional practice with the same inherent strengths and weaknesses. An over-emphasis on divine unity, among other things, is a drama killer, for three divine actors are reduced to one, and the moving interplay between them in their enacted conspiracy to redeem their people is lost. Yet if, as Owen will be shown to say, (1) the true God is made up of three persons who are really capable of some kind of distinct (though unified) action, and, (2) that these divine persons have in fact

---

[16] Horton, *Covenant*, 45.

[17] The notable exception, of course, is the mini-narrative about the Father and the Son in the Apostle's Creed.

[18] Certainly the Bible contains interpretation of the redemptive story as well (the epistles, for example), but this is not the same as formula. Romans 1-8, for example, is considered one of the more doctrinally complex parts of the Bible, yet even here Paul is weaving in and out of the redemptive story from Abraham to Moses, and through to Christ's activity as completion of the earlier covenants.

acted on the stage of history in ways respecting their immanent processions, then redemptive-historical modes of devotion will be better suited to commune with this particular God than devotion which grows from systematic-theological soil alone. Even doctrinal formulas that get right the biblical distinctions in action between the divine persons, i.e. formulas that capture the simultaneous unity and distinction in the Godhead, even these are not structurally sufficient to communicate action nor to affect the worshipper the way the drama can. The content of the best systematic-theological formulas must be portrayed to the devotionalist through covenantal drama if growth in the love of God, and not simply improved knowledge about him, is the goal. When the drama of God's own writing/performing is central in the worshipper's gaze, *fiducia* is stoked, and, since the drama naturally gives rise to systematic-theological reflection (for even the Bible's own didactic genres interpret the narrative events), the components of *noticia* and *assensus* are not compromised either.

Covenantal Drama and Evangelical Spirituality

How might the emphasis on covenantal drama inform contemporary Evangelical spirituality? One might think that in the family tree of Christian spiritualities, those flowing from Reformation and post-Reformation Covenant Theology might contain rich dramatic elements because of that tradition's fascination with divine and human parties acting out various covenant obligations to one another. Ironically, inheritors of Reformed scholasticism themselves have not always maintained an interest in the dramatic mode of theology, nor devotional models that might flow from it. One of the classic institutions that has shaped Reformed theology in America (and broader Evangelicalism as well) was the 'Old Princeton,' a popular designation of the seminary from the year of its founding in 1812 to its dramatic shift in 1932 toward higher-criticism and theological Liberalism. Charles Hodge and B.B. Warfield were among the celebrated theologians of the Old Princeton, and both sought to defend Calvinist orthodoxy in the face of modern challenges in science and theology.[19] Hodge's method of doing theology, though, was in many ways shaped more by the post-Enlightenment milieu of intellectual discourse than it was by the redemptive-historical method of his Reformed predecessors in the sixteenth and seventeenth centuries. Hodge famously says, 'The Bible is to the theologian what nature is to the man of science. It is his store-house of facts; and his method of

---

[19] See *Reformed Theology in America: A History of Its Modern Development*, ed. David F. Wells (Grand Rapids: Eerdmans, 1985), and *The Princeton Theology, 1812-1949: Scripture, Science, and Theological Method from Archibald Alexander to Benjamin Warfield*, ed. Mark A. Noll (Grand Rapids: Baker Book House, 1983).

ascertaining what the Bible teaches is the same as that which the natural philosopher adopts to ascertain what nature teaches.'[20] For Hodge, the mode of doing theology was like scientific induction – bits of data on a given subject are drawn together from wherever they occur in the texts and then assembled to determine the Bible's view on the matter. As we might expect, Hodge's still widely used *Systematic Theology* has plenty to say on the traditional heads of doctrine, with Calvinist conclusions abounding, but it features almost no reference to the categories of unfolding historical covenants that so controlled the theological method used by Owen and the early Reformed scholastics. By contrast, for the likes of Owen, redemptive-history (not scientific induction) provided the very methodology by which one could prove that Reformed distinctives of systematic theology were biblically defensible. For example, while Owen defended the systematic-theological claim of 'limited atonement,' he did so not by proof-texting verses about God's attributes but mostly by reference to the inviolable promise of the Father to the Son (in the Covenant of Redemption) to not punish any for whom Christ died.

The limitations of Hodge's very different general method is contrasted by that of a far lesser known Old Princeton luminary, Geerhardus Vos. While Vos remained appreciative of systematic theology, he was first concerned by what various biblical texts reveal about the redemptive work of God in history. The Bible, said Vos, 'is not a dogmatic handbook but a historical book full of dramatic interest.'[21] Vos was first struck by the 'epochs' which appear in the Bible, epochs which not only tell the story of God's dealing with his people but which unfold the nature of God and how he is to be approached by human sinners within the epoch in which they live.[22] The contribution of Vos is to show that the methodological questions about how to do theology are not something to be settled neutrally, before exegesis begins, but by sensitivity to the Bible's own dramatic epochs as God's chosen mode of self-disclosure. Vos's school of 'Biblical Theology' will certainly inform systematic-theological conclusions, but without the danger of importing a pre-exegetical prolegomena into theology that would certainly color the final conclusions. Hodge and Warfield (who had similar scientific methods) are still the more famous names in American Reformed theology, while few of the broader Evangelicals who still pay respects to Old Princeton will today know the name of Vos at all. It is beyond dispute that

---

[20] Charles Hodge, *Systematic Theology*, vol. 1 (Grand Rapids: Eerdmans, 1946 rept.) 10.

[21] Geerhardus Vos, *Biblical Theology* (Grand Rapids: Eerdmans, 1948) 17.

[22] It should be noted that Vos was no friend to dispensational theology and its more radical disjunction between these epochs. Vos, following the Reformed scholastics, saw a primary unity between the epochs, though with some important developments that tended to be underplayed by those less sensitive to redemptive history.

contemporary Evangelical theology has Hodgean traits, but for that reasons it also suffers from the thought-modes of Enlightenment rationalism that have become stowaways in otherwise biblical Evangelical theological methodology. A remedy to these problems may be found in Vos, Owen, and a reappraisal of redemptive-history as a guide to theological prolegomena rather than an uncritical use of scientific induction to derive doctrine.

What does this have to do with devotion? One goal of this work is to show that devotion must stay connected to doctrine to remain robust as well as fully Christian (in any historical sense). Many current spiritualities suffer because they have more to do with Hodge than Vos, with realist mysticism than narrative trinitarianism. When Vos argues for the primacy of biblical drama as the building block for a healthy prolegomena to theology, we may extend his urgency equally to devotional practices. To put it another way, the danger to theology of ignoring 'a historical book of dramatic interest' must be at least as great a danger to spirituality, since spirituality of any stripe admits from the start that it is concerned with what might improve our subjective 'interest' in God. What a loss if the triune God has said, 'Let me tell you a dramatic story about what I've done for you that will move you to love me in return' and we have responded by saying, 'Better yet, we have other techniques that we think will affect our hearts more deeply.' Devotional models, as much as theological methods, can be undermined by pre-critical decisions about method. To argue for a redemptive-historical foundation for spirituality is only to say that the scriptures of God should be the first place to look for the way to relate to that God, and when we begin with that expectation, we at once find the scriptures are about God telling the grand story of his three-personed plan to reclaim his fallen world. Without, for a moment, adding further nuanced directives about how to relate to that God through his story (like Owen does in his elaborate *Communion with God*), we would expect, if nothing else, that covenant drama would somehow make a discernable mark on our devotional model if the scriptures are given any role at all in determining the *method* of spirituality, and not just its content.

SAMPLE QUESTIONS

In terms of our two criteria, candidates for a trinitarian spirituality may be said to face two tests: the test of historical systematic theology and the test of redemptive history. Given both of these criteria as a basis, the following flurry of questions serve as sample guidelines to evaluate the trinitarian content of any spiritual model. Does the particular model tell the believer to dwell on the priority of the Father's electing love and the Son's saving work rather than her own effort to love God? Is God described in an adequately personal way rather than as aloof (as in deism) or as a impersonal Divine Being (as in pantheism)? Are Father and Son relations understood as between real persons, or are they reduced to pure metaphor (which would be a speculative, anti-historical act of theologizing by trying to see behind the God-of-the-story-line, behind the supposed metaphor, to arrive at some eternal essential meaning of the *hypostaseis*)? Is the Spirit supposedly accessed by the believer in a way that is excessively individualistic rather than through a Spirit-indwelt community? Do dealings with the Spirit adequately center on the Spirit's central role which is to glorify the Son? Is God overly transcendent and mysterious (to deny that revelation has occurred) or overly immanent and accessible (to deny that it needed to occur)? Is there a practical modalism that, for example, would have difficulty understanding that salvation involves a human experiencing the glory that the Son had with the Father before the creation of the world? Is there a balanced eschatology between the already and not-yet of the believer's knowledge and access to God? Is the Father seen as both holy and compassionate, just and forgiving, with the cross borne by the Son as the ultimate place to see these attributes resolved? Is the unity of divine action emphasized so that the believer sees the love of the Father during the crucifixion (not just the Son's) so that the Father is not interpreted as grudgingly being bought off by the Son's self-sacrifice? Does the intercession of Christ before the Father make any difference to Christian practice now? Do believers relate to each divine person uniquely for his role in the economy of salvation?

These questions assume certain things about how the divine *hypostaseis* relate to each other, as well as to events in the earthly history that they have determined. In terms of our criteria, questions like these assume and extend the doctrine of the historic trinitarian formulations (which tend to deal with God's ontology) as well as the story-line especially of the Gospels (which explicitly reveals God's trinitarian external workings).

Probing Three Devotional Traditions

Does the history of Christian devotion show any signs of the doctrine of the Trinity shaping a model of spirituality? The three traditions to be explored are early Quakerism, the mysticism of late-middle ages realism, and sixteenth- and seventeenth-century popularized Protestant scholasticism. Why these three? On one hand, each is illustrative of very different approaches to spirituality that vividly illustrate consequences, positively and negatively, of using or dismissing our two criteria. Also, since this work contends that John Owen's spirituality represents a particularly high watermark in making practical the classic doctrine as well as redemptive drama, these are three schools that in some sense help us to understand Owen better. Quakerism was one of Owen's most recurring concerns in his polemics, while pre-Reformation devotion was the soil from which many of his devotional ideas grew (or as often, rebelled), and Protestant scholasticism and the popular Puritan spirituality which drew from it represents Owen's own nuclear family of both theology and practice. In regards to popular Puritan devotion, however, it will be shown that Owen carries through trinitarian concerns into practical spirituality more consistently than some of his Puritan brethren, who, mysteriously, often under-utilized the strikingly trinitarian emphases of their Protestant Scholastic forbearers. By far the longest section is that of the late medieval realist mysticism, for here we see an explosion of devotional writing that attempted to deal with the Trinity at the level of prayer and meditation. Medieval successes are carried forward by Owen to some degree, while that era's failures also illustrate what happens when a somewhat neo-platonic philosophical substructure of Platonism eclipses the emphasis on the Trinity revealed in the *historia salutis*.

Early English Quakerism

The most obvious theological distinction about Quakerism which makes an impact on devotional practice is the doctrine of the 'inner light.' George Fox exegeted passages such as John 1:9 ('the true light which lighteth every man that cometh into the world') to mean that every individual was born with the light of Christ within. Though the light (which is often identified as the Holy Spirit) is darkened by sin, it can be rekindled through quietness and spiritual listening.[23] Christ, therefore, shines anew on the heart apart from the normal means of grace such as preaching and reading the Scriptures. Owen, for one, was actually willing to grant that some 'edification ... is attainable in the silent meetings of the Quakers'; however, the Quaker doctrine of the inner light was a misunderstanding of both the person and the work of the Holy Spirit.[24] The constant emphasis on the Spirit within-the-soul was a subtle form of an exaltation of the Spirit by the Spirit, especially since the Spirit rarely was understood by Quakers to point the believer back to the objective work of Christ's sacrifice. For Owen, the purpose of the sending of the Spirit was instead to glorify the Son, as per the words of John 16:14: '[the Spirit] shall glorify me; for he shall receive of mine and shall show it to

---

[23] Michael R. Watts, *The Dissenters* (Oxford: Clarendon Press, 1978) I, 203; T.L. Underwood, *Primitivism, Radicalism, and the Lamb's War: The Baptist-Quaker Conflict in Seventeenth-Century England* (New York: Oxford University Press, 1997) 105-111, in Michael Haykin, 'John Owen and the Challenge of the Quakers,' in *John Owen: The Man and His Theology*, ed. Robert W. Oliver (Philipsburg, New Jersey: Evangelical Press and P&R Publishing, 2002) 137.

[24] John Owen, *Works*, 23 vols., ed. W. H. Goold (London: Johnstone and Hunter, 1854 rept.) IV.331; all additional references to Owen's *Works* will be cited by volume an page numbers.

In Search of Trinitarian Spirituality 47

you.' The message of the Quakers was thus an inversion of 'the order of the divine dispensations,' for the Spirit's mission is to make the Son 'glorious, honourable, and of high esteem in the hearts of believers' and to 'shed abroad the love of God in our hearts.' The Spirit's mission is therefore parallel to the Son's being sent by the Father 'to suffer at Jerusalem ... for us' and to bring glory to the Father who sent him.[25] At its heart, the failure of Quaker worship was that it got the Trinity's work of redemption wrong. Owen summarized the failure of Quaker spirituality as first a failure of trinity:rian theology, 'Convince any of them of the doctrine of the Trinity, and all the rest of their imaginations vanish into smoke.'[26]

But were the Quakers really un-trinitarian? Rarely, if ever, did George Fox criticize the classic form of the doctrine. His *Journal* never mentions the Trinity. In 1671, though, Fox wrote a letter to the governor of Barbados defending the practice of Quakers against rumors that they denied 'God and Jesus Christ and the Scriptures of truth.' His response to the criticism was not exactly that of a resounding trinitarian, but his positive affirmations would have seemed quite reassuring: 'We believe in God, the only wise, omnipotent and everlasting God' and that Jesus Christ is 'his beloved and only begotten Son...who was conceived by the Holy Ghost...who is the express image of the Invisible God...who tasted death for every man, shed his blood for all men, and is the propitiation for our sins...he is our Mediator that makes peace and reconciliation between God offended and us offending.'[27] When under pressure of criticism, at least, Fox admitted to fairly orthodox beliefs about God and his work. It would seem, though, that Fox's confession did not capture the real direction of the movement when it was speaking without the threat of harassment. One is amazed to find his younger associate William Penn (1644-1718) making a direct and stinging attack on the doctrine of the Trinity:

> Before I conclude this head, it is requisite that I should inform thee, reader, concerning the origin of the trinitarian doctrine: Thou mayest assure thyself, it is not from the Scriptures, nor reason, since so expressly repugnant; although all broachers of their own inventions strongly endeavor to reconcile them with the holy record. Know then, my friend, it was born about three hundred years after the

---

[25] II.257-58; and Haykin, 'John Owen,' 142.

[26] III.66

[27] George Fox, 'Letter to the Governor of Barbados, 1671,' in Eighth and Bicentenary edition of the *Journal of George Fox* (London: Friend's Tract Association, 1891).

ancient gospel was declared; it was conceived in ignorance, brought forth and maintained by cruelty.[28]

So, to the extent that at least William Penn can be credited with articulating Quakerism's theological foundations, one would conclude that early on the movement had become decidedly anti-trinitarian. John Punshon's history of the Quakers admits as much, saying that the movement never formally adopted the doctrine of the Trinity, but instead, the functioning theology proper is closer to pantheism.[29] Quakerism excels at drawing lines between such a doctrine of God and a corresponding spirituality: since the Spirit of God fills the universe and all men, silent and unstructured worship is the most fitting human response. The universality of the divine light is best recognized when no particular thought content is prescribed, or story-line adhered to. A nebulous doctrine of God leads naturally to a nebulous, unstructured form of worship. This view of God, in fact, makes the scriptures redundant, since, as Fox and others stressed, the cotemporary believer has the same or clearer experience of God as the biblical prophets. Our two guiding criteria for trinitarian spirituality are both dismissed, actually, since not only are the classic *hypostaseis* unacknowledged in both their *ad intra* an *ad extra* workings, but the Bible is not recognized as an historical narrative of the personal accomplishments of the divine persons. Rather, the scripture is more like a record of ancient men who had their own 'showings' of the divine light, experiences recorded in order to prompt us to do the same. The Bible is a guidebook only in this way, but not as a record of how God has constituted the believer's present salvation by past historical acts. A later Quaker puts it this way: 'Quakerism is better off emphasizing pantheistic and universalist perspectives. Our mode of worship is especially well-suited to this theology. Other denominations probably better serve people who are looking for strict adherence to doctrine (i.e. Roman Catholicism) or for Christ crucified as a personal Savior (evangelical Protestantism).'[30]

Since the focus of this work is on ways that doctrine pushes through into devotion, a look at Quaker devotional writing will help demonstrate the practical consequences of such an amorphous doctrine of God. Stephen Crisp's *A Short History of a Long Travel from Babylon to Bethel* is something of a Quaker devotional polemic.[31] Specifically, it is a rebuttal and parody of John Bunyan's *The Pilgrim's Progress*, and, as

---

[28] In Hugh H. Stanus, *A History of the Doctrine of the Trinity in the Early Church* (London: Christian Life Publishing, 1882 rept..) 7.

[29] John Punshon, *Portrait in Grey: A Short History of the Quakers* (London: Quaker Home Service, 1984) 158-167.

[30] Ted Goertzel, Rutgers University, unpublished article.

[31] Published by the Tract Association of Friends, Philadelphia (1691).

such, acts as a vivid example of what Puritan values the Quakers hoped to correct. In the Quaker allegory, Pilgrim sets off to find 'the Father's house.' He first follows a self-assured guide who claims to know the way, but always has his head buried in his 'guide-book' and ends up making both of them further lost. Eventually, the guide falls asleep and Pilgrim rejects the approach of such 'booklearning.' A second guide leads him within sight of a large house, and tells him the house is full of rules since God is a God of order. Upon entering, he finds the house full of cobwebs, spiders, and shallow people, two of whom are arguing about money with heated words. Pilgrim is shocked at their conduct and confronts his guide, who admits to the failings of the place. Pilgrim responds, 'What! Dost thou talk of human frailties in the house of God?' He is incensed that sin exists in these supposed people of God and concludes that it is not the house he is looking for. Journeying on, he falls asleep under a great tree and then awakes in the dark to find a small light near him. The light begins to move, he begins to follow it – up a mountain, through a field of dangerous serpents, across valley full of mire and puddles, and eventually, to another great house on a mountain top. The house has one tower, but no paintings or artistry. A voice beckons, 'take off your old garments so you may enter.' He does so, and is given a new garment of pure white linen. As he walks through the house he finds it clean; the people are kind and make pleasant conversation, never quarrelling.

Obvious in this allegory are critiques of people who depend on the Bible as a rule, traditional (and even non-conformist) ecclesiology, and the presence of sin in those who claim to know God. More telling though is the view of salvation that is proposed. Salvation is, primarily, acceptance into a visibly holy human community. The story has no functioning doctrine of God at all, except perhaps an allusion to the Spirit as the tiny light. The final destination, the goal of divine guidance, is not so much toward God, but toward other godly people in a kind of utopia. The garment of sin is first removed, but without the need of a mediator, or really any divine forgiveness at all. While we should not require Crisp's allegory to be a doctrinal manual, it must be remembered that it is itself a critique of Bunyan's allegory which describes a Celestial City where God dwells with quite obvious references to his trinitarian saving actions in behalf of the protagonist, Christian. In other words, for Crisp to attack Bunyan while himself allegorizing no doctrine of God beyond his role as a guide is a significant silence. Perhaps by so emphasizing the role of the Spirit as a guide to the exclusion of any other aspects of God or his work in the world, early Quaker devotion has difficulty defining the Christian life as much more than the best way toward moral progress and harmonious community living. The devotional works of seventeenth-century Quaker poet Thomas Elwood shows a similar vagueness about God, even in poems entitled 'Hymn to God' and 'Song of Praise.'[32]

In the end, Quakerism did not originally go out of its way to deny trinitarian doctrine (though William Penn was a significant exception), but tended to describe the spiritual life as if the Trinity did not exist or matter. Even though Fox himself, under pressure, might have expressed something quite close to an orthodox theology of God which incorporated the role of the Son as an historical mediator, none of these admissions filtered down into actual spiritual practice. The emphasis on the 'Spirit of Christ' seems to therefore have no connection to the Jesus who lived in Palestine, and the 'inner light' does not particularly illuminate the saving purposes of either Father or Son. Seventeenth-century Quakerism, therefore, prayed, or listened, in a way that would be largely unaffected if the Trinity were proved untrue.

Popular Puritan Devotion

English Puritanism can be viewed as either a scholastic or a popular enterprise, and one of the strengths of the movement was that those who were writing the defining theological treatises were also usually preachers to the laity. The same people who wrote theology using the sophisticated philosophical categories of either Aristotle, or, more likely, Peter Ramus, were also writing sermons, tracts, and preaching to the unlearned about how to know God in deeper ways. In light of this fact, A.C. McGiffert's charge that Protestant scholasticism was characterized by a 'rigid sterile rationalism lacking either religious warmth or intellectual originality' is wrong on both counts.[33] Certainly the vast numbers who packed into the non-conformist churches to hear the preaching of these Puritan intellectuals, often risking their own reputation to do so, were finding something life-giving about what they heard.

A brief look at the development of Reformed scholasticism, in fact shows a largely organic relationship between theology and devotion. The post-Reformation era naturally divides into three stages, the first two of which concern us: Early orthodoxy runs from the publication of the Heidelberg Catechism (1563) to the waning of the careers of the commissioners at the Synod of Dort (1630-40), and the second stage runs from the beginning of the Puritan parliament in 1640 through the end of

---

[32] Cf. *History and Life of Thomas Elwood, Written by Himself* (Lanham, Maryland: Rowman and Littlefield, 2004) 158, 203.

[33] A.C. McGiffert, *Protestant Thought Before Kant* (New York: Harper Torchbooks, 1961) 105.

the seventeenth century.³⁴ The first of these two periods is characterized by the consolidation of the Reformation's original theological outbursts into more organized systems that could be taught at the university level, could be explained by the use of older theological and philosophical language, and were precise enough to be defensible in the face of increasingly exacting critiques from Roman Catholics, rationalists, and even from friendlier rebuttals across the Luther-Reformed divide.³⁵ This consolidation does not prove that the original fire of the Reformers was being systematically extinguished, as some think, though certainly a refining of the original convictions was taking place. Significant to our study is what these newly coined systems were proclaiming as central themes. The caricature of this period is that it was obsessed with the doctrine of predestination and made most other doctrines dependant upon it, with the ultimate dismal effect of making God appear cold and arbitrary even to those who believed they were of the elect.³⁶ Richard Muller has shown, however, that predestination was not an organizing principle for the Reformed scholastics, because these scholars almost always viewed predestination through the primary lens of christology.³⁷ Beyond this, predestination and christology interrelate for this movement at two levels: 'the level of the eternal intra-trinitarian relationships of Father, Son, and Spirit, and the level of the temporal effecting of God's will.'³⁸ To put this in terms already familiar to us: the immanent Trinity, and the Trinity's external saving work in history, are the ground for understanding all other doctrine. The mysterious workings of God's eternal decree, for example, can only begin to be grasped by the human mind when in reference to the scriptural testimony to the inner relationship between the members of the Trinity in their joint project of redemption, and to the public outworking of that trinitarian project in history. Admittedly, when the doctrine of predestination is considered without the context of the Trinity, and the Trinity-in-history, it becomes something other than what it really should be. Muller avoids the old pitfall of identifying any one central *loci* in Calvin or the Reformed

---

³⁴ These divisions follow the framework of Otto Weber, *Foundations of Dogmatics*, 2 vols. (Grand Rapids: Eerdmans, 1981-1982), 1:120-27. Otto's third period begins in 1700 and catalogues the decline of Reformed scholasticism's vitality.

³⁵ For a defining work on post-Reformation Lutheranism, for example, see Robert D. Preus, *The Theology of Post-Reformation Lutheranism*, 2 vols. (St. Louis: Concordia, 1970).

³⁶ This is the thesis of R.T. Kendall, Alan Clifford, et. al., following Basil Hall's 'Calvin Against the Calvinists,' in *John Calvin*, ed. Gervase Duffield (Grand Rapids: Eerdmans, 1966) 19-37.

³⁷ Richard Muller, *Christ and the Decree: Christology and Predestination in Reformed Theology from Calvin to Perkins* (Durham, North Carolina: Labyrinth, 1986).

³⁸ Muller, *Christ and the Decree*, 10.

scholastics, though, he says, 'we can speak of one ground of doctrine ... because all aspects of the system relate to and derive from the saving intention, eternally conceived, by the three persons of the one God in the unity of their will and wisdom.'[39] For the Reformed scholastics, then, the Trinity is at the absolute center, especially in the plan and execution of salvation. If this is true, then the natural direction of spirituality based on this Reformed scholastic theology is not cold speculation or morbid personal introspection. Rather, because the trinitarian saving intention has been executed on the temporal plane in various redemptive acts that finally led to Christ's resurrection and ascension, a believer's contemplation (even of such a predestinating God) naturally begins with meditation on God's objective self-revealing in his saving love-acts in Scripture, culminating in the events of Passion Week. The point of noting this is to support the argument that the two aspects of approaching the Trinity that we have held up as a kind of ultimate ground for spirituality – classic trinitarian doctrine and regard to the economic outworkings of a saving drama – were in fact present, perhaps more than anywhere before, in the theological systems of those such as Bullinger, Vermigli, Zanchius, and Beza.[40] If the reader can get past the oftentimes dense philosophical language of these writers, he will see the Trinity-in-action behind every bush and will see the superstructure of covenant promises and historical fulfillments of those promises upon which he can base his prayers of adoration and thanksgiving.

So, the Protestant scholastics (who so greatly informed the Puritans) had both a strong trinitarian theology and a dramatic-historical mode of *doing* theology. Further elaboration on the basic plot-line of that narrative, as they saw it, will be helpful as we assess its potential value to trinitarian Christian devotion. The Covenant Theology (or Federal Theology) that the Protestant scholastics produced was concerned to deal seriously with the fact that the turning points of the scriptural story seem to hinge on various historical covenants that God initiates with his people (or that were formed between God's own *hypostaseis*). For the Federal theologians, the story goes something like this: The world was created by the initiative of the Father, who through his Son, the divine Word, formed the universe through the active agency of their Spirit. Human beings were uniquely formed in the image of this triune God, and, through a Covenant of Works, Adam was told that if he obeyed God during a probationary test in the Garden, his active righteousness would be imputed to all following generations as well as the reward for such obedience – personal and bodily glorification and unbroken communion

---

[39] Muller, *Christ and the Decree*, 181.
[40] Cf. Musculus' *Loci Communes*, Vermigli's *Loci Communes*, Beza's *Tabula Praedestinationis*, Ursinus' *Doctrinae Christianae Compendium*, Zanchius' *De Tribus Elohim*, Perkin's *A Golden Chaine*, and Turretin's *Institutes of Elenctic Theology*.

with God forever. But, if he disobeyed, his guilt and pollution would be imputed instead. The human race fell with Adam, but immediately the Father initiated a Covenant of Grace whereby he revealed, at first only in glimpses, that the curse would be eventually reversed by a human seed of Eve who would conquer death and the devil, though at the cost of his own blood. So, while Adam was the first federal head of the human race, Christ as the second Adam is the head of redeemed humanity. This promise to humanity is really the public broadcasting of the pre-existing Covenant of Redemption between the eternal Father and Son, in which the Father promised to give to the Son as his treasured subjects all those whom he would atone for in his future mission to the world as the self-sacrificing God-man. As history progressed towards the eventual incarnation of the Son, the Covenant of Grace was carried forward by various sub-covenants (and the exact division and nature of these is not fully agreed upon by the Federalists): the Covenant of Abraham made the original redemptive promise more clear, that those who received its benefits would do so not by virtue of their own merit but by simply trusting God's graciousness; the Covenant at Sinai showed that sin can only be removed by the shedding of blood, and that God is willing to accept the blood of a substitute; the Covenant with David pointed to the fact that God's salvation is unto a kingdom, ruled by a beneficent king. When the time had fully come, the Son fulfilled his obligation to the Father within the Covenant of Redemption and released his grasp on the full benefits of his divine nature, uniting himself with human nature through the creative agency of the Spirit. Jesus Christ, the God-man, then unveiled the New Covenant, the climactic manifestation of the ancient Covenant of Grace, revealing himself as the ultimate king, the final sacrificial substitute, the greatest 'blessing' once promised to Abraham. As the second Adam, Jesus' moral righteousness is imputed to his people, reversing the ill-effects of the first Adam's unrighteousness. In his death and resurrection, Jesus conquered the dominion of evil, reversed the curse of death itself, and inaugurated the final kingdom of God. Since that time, as history progresses, the Spirit has been active in advancing this kingdom by bringing human sinners into union with the exalted Jesus Christ, imparting to them the judicial rewards of his obedience and death, as well as the first-fruits of resurrected life as he re-creates them in the image of the triune God.

One might expect that the devotional implications of such a drama, both in its starring role for the Trinity as well as its whole narrative arc, would have showed themselves in popular writings of the day that supposedly drew from the theological offerings of Reformed scholasticism. Did they? Yes, and no. In keeping with our timeline, the second period of post-Reformation development was 1640-1700, which happens to be fairly closely aligned with John Owen's career. This period at large is marked by further refining of the scholastic systems, and, I would argue, an unparalleled explosion of devotional writings that are self-consciously Reformed. The Puritans were incredibly prolific, both in the pulpit and with the pen, and with Puritan power consolidated in England, people were freer than ever to print and buy books. I believe Owen represents the closest pastoral appropriation of the theological trinitarianism of the Reformed scholastics of the prior stage, but Owen's emphases are somewhat unique when compared with other famous devotional writings of the period.

Consider the features of a few of the bestsellers among Puritan devotional manuals. In about 1599, Arthur Dent wrote *The Plain Man's Pathway to Heaven*, which became wildly successfully by the mid-1600's, eventually reaching a fortieth edition by 1704 with more than one-hundred thousand copies sold.[41] The book's allegorical model is said to have inspired John Bunyan to write *The Pilgrim's Progress*. The form of Dent's book is, actually, more of a dialogue among the following fictional conversation partners: Theologus (a divine), Philagathus (and honest man), Asunetas (an ignorant man), and Antilegon (a caviler and atheist). The pathway to heaven that Theologus explains is descriptive of a strategy similar to the Heidelberg Catechism's – it begins with the fact and reasons for human misery, then shows how personal regeneration through the gospel brings spiritual relief. However, the section of the book that deals with these ideas takes up only twenty-six of the book's three-hundred thirty-two pages, and the treatment of regeneration is almost solely restricted to the subjective experience of the soul, with scant reference to the actual work of Christ that effects regeneration. In a sense, the pathway to heaven is framed as an *ordo salutis* without a *historia salutis* in sight. The following chapters (the bulk of the book) are detailed explications of various sins – 'On Pride,' 'On Whoredom and Adultery,' 'On Covetousness,' 'On Swearing,' etc., and ways to 'remedy' such sins. The remedy is almost always described as a list of moral steps that, frankly, could be as easily taken by the Antilegon character without contradicting his own non-existent doctrine of God. Arthur Dent himself was not theologically naïve, and his book is filled with references to famous classical and theological works.[42] Why such an underdeveloped presentation of the gospel itself? One answer might be that the writers in Puritan England could be confident that their readers had already heard and understood the gospel. Many writers would have re-emphasized the moral requirements of Christian living to challenge casual professors of

---

[41] Arthur Dent, *The Plain Man's Pathway to Heaven* (Pennsylvania: Soli Deo Gloria, 1994 rept.). The books fiftieth edition came long after the Puritan era, actually, in 1860.

[42] Dent was famous for standing up to Bishop Aylmer for Puritan theological distinctives, and was reputed to be quite learned, cf. editorial remarks in Soli Deo Gloria edition.

the Protestant gospel who by now were falsely assured of their salvation and were guilty of anti-nomianism. However, in a manual that actually took on the task of describing the spiritual path to heaven from start to finish, we are surprised to see so little of a doctrine of God, and so underdeveloped a mention of Christ's person and work. Even if one knows the gospel by heart, is the Christian life well-served by such scant reference to the foundation for one's salvation in the saving work of God in the gospel? Dent's case suggests that even those who presumably possess a rich doctrine of God will not always carry that doctrine through to its implications for the devotional life.

Another famous manual of this period was Lewis Bayly's *Practice of Piety*, probably first published in 1611.[43] By 1643 it reached its thirty-fourth English edition (to say nothing of Dutch, German, French, and Polish versions). Bayly earned a doctorate in divinity at Oxford in 1613, became chaplain to the king three years later, and was eventually consecrated as bishop of Bangor where he died in 1631. The bishop's book was so popular among non-conformists, however, that some argued it impossible for such a work to be written by someone within the English church, and sought to deprive him the credit as the author.[44] Interestingly, as an explicitly practical manual of devotional exercises, the book begins with a twenty-five page treatment on the doctrine of God and why knowledge of God's nature should matter for the pious Christian. In the first of these pages, the doctrine of the Trinity is carefully developed in many of its historically formulated nuances, followed by a longer section treating the scriptural names of God and various divine attributes. Bayly seems especially zealous about God's triune nature, even arguing that in Genesis 1:1 the Hebrew word *bara* ('to create') has an embedded trinitarian code; the consonant *beth* points to the Son (*ben*), *resch* connects with the Spirit (*rouach*) and the *aleph* signifies the Father (*ab*). The real value of this section is that Bayly connects the attributes of the Godhead to meditative applications that could ennoble the believer's communion with God:

> From a true and lively sense of God's attributes, there is bred in a man's heart a love, awe, and confidence in God...if therefore, thou doest believe that God is almighty, why dost thou fear devils and enemies and not confidently trust in God?...if thou believest that God is the sovereign good, why is not thy heart more settled upon him than on all worldly good...if thou doest truly believe that God is most wise, why doest not thou refer the events of crosses and disgraces to him who knoweth how to turn all things to the best unto them that love him?...and if thou believest that God is beauty and perfection itself, why dost not thou make him

---

[43] Lewis Bayly, *Practice of Piety* (Pennsylvania: Soli Deo Gloria, 1997 rept.).

[44] *Dictionary of National Biography* 1:1369, in Joel Beeke's introduction to Soli Deo Gloria edition.

alone the chief end of all thine affections and desires? For if thou lovest beauty, he is most fair; if thou desirest riches, his is most wealthy; if thou seekest wisdom, he is most wise...and when in heaven we shall have an immediate communion with God, we shall have them all immediately communicated to us...by the light of his own word, we have seen the back parts of JEHOVAH Elohim, the Eternal Trinity; whom to believe is saving faith and verity...[45]

Is this the trinitarian devotion we are looking for? Almost. Bayly carefully draws devotional applications from the doctrine of God which are profound and heart-searching. He knows that the only God that Christians deal with is triune, and he is sure that this God is the one that believers meet with when they pray. However, while his doctrinal section is even interested to show the distinguishing marks between the divine persons, he has nothing to say about the impact of such distinctions or divine missions on mediation or prayer. That is, Bayly believes in a highly sophisticated doctrine of the Trinity, but the only aspects of the doctrine of God that actually get devotional treatment are the simple attributes shared by all the *hypostaseis*. None of this is to say that Bayly is sub-trinitarian overall: in later portions of the book he makes recommendations that people meditate on the work of Christ, on the love of the Father, and on the Spirit's regenerative and cleansing power. In some cases his language sounds almost like the *Book of Common Prayer*, which is not shy about featuring trinitarian language. However, it is somehow telling that in the very section of his book in which Bayly admirably delves into the devotional implication of trinitarian doctrine, he says nothing about the saving action of the Trinity or the very theater of redemption where God makes his triune nature most clear. Again we have high trinitarian doctrine that unfortunately only gets developed as far as a unitarian devotional practice.

The example of Bayly and Dent do not prove that Puritan devotion is somehow anti-trinitarian, nor is Owen the only Puritan who sought to appropriate the doctrine of the Trinity for its devotional uses.[46] The case, however, is that the substantial trinitarian emphases of the Reformed scholastics – who were the very theologians that the likes of Bayly were reading while at Oxford – often were inadequately translated in any sustained way to the otherwise elaborate Puritan devotional models. The doctrine of God was failing to connect to spirituality, at least the well-developed Reformed doctrine of a grace-filled Trinity who historically revealed himself in various ways surrounding the incarnation, life, death, resurrection, and heavenly session of Jesus Christ. From this perspective, the real weakness of some Puritan devotion is not that it was too doctrinal,

---

[45] Bayly, *Practice of Piety*, 26-27.

[46] Owen's friend, Thomas Goodwin, for example, will also be examined for his trinitarian emphases.

but that is was not doctrinal enough, especially by the standards of the Reformers and Reformed scholastics from which they could have so naturally drawn. Owen's contribution to Puritan writings should not then be seen as exacerbating any spiritually arid tendencies in the movement, but quite the opposite: so often he appraised the most affectively-pregnant aspects of Covenant Theology for more regular application to a family of practical devotion that sometimes overlooked its own rich inheritance.

Medieval Devotion

There are at least three reasons to look deeper into the history of English devotion as a valid interpretive context for Owen's own program of spirituality. The first is nowadays considered to be common sense historiography: no man is an intellectual island, not even a man like Owen who speaks as a leader of a 'non-conformist' or 'reformational' school of thought. Therefore, the highly cultured Owen could not have avoided the impact of the tremendously influential devotional thinkers that preceded him, even if their influence was merely to give him a goad to kick against (as certainly was the case, some of the time). Secondly, it is impossible now in the wake of Heiko Oberman's body of work to even consider that the Reformation itself was without a considerable organic relationship to other strains of medieval piety and theology.[47] If Owen represents the crème of the Puritan movement, and if Puritanism was even somewhat faithful to the theology of Calvin and his second-generation Continental scholastics, and if, as Oberman says, such Reformers were knowingly dependent on medieval and patristic teachers to whom they appealed in order to prove that their own emphases were not entirely novel, then we should expect that Owen's devotional theology will also have some pre-Reformation sources (whether or not he acknowledges them). Lastly, the vast citations of others' works within Owen's corpus proves the degree to which he knew he was at times influenced by his own heroes, or foes. For example, the list of writers which Owen quotes *more frequently* than his perhaps expected favorites, Luther and Calvin, include Aquinas, Chrysostom, Horace, Aristotle, Arminius, Grotius, Ambrose, Jerome, Justin Martyr, Origen, Socinus, Tertullian, and Virgil. Based on the number of citations, Augustine is by far his greatest influence, whom he quotes (positively) more than twice as frequently as anyone else (206 references; compare with Calvin at 27). While in one place he declares that Bucer, Calvin, Martyr, and Beza are the 'principal' authors,[48] he often

---

[47] Cf. Heiko Oberman, *The Harvest of Medieval Theology* (Grand Rapids: Baker Book House, 2000); *The Reformation: Roots and Ramifications* (Edinburgh: T. & T. Clark, 1994); and *Forerunners of the Reformation* (Philadelphia: Fortress Press, 1966).

[48] IV.229

shows great appreciation for Thomas Aquinas as 'the best and most sober of all your [Roman Catholic] school doctors,' and is not beyond occasionally praising the Jesuit and Dominican scholars whom he saw as helpful torch-bearers of contemporary Thomism.[49] In 1684 the contents of Owen's personal book collection were auctioned, and for the first time there was pubic evidence of exactly what he was referring to when he once made passing reference to 'my own small library.'[50] In fact, he owned almost three-thousand volumes which included the major patristic, medieval, and contemporary theologians, and large number of Greek and Roman philosophical and historical classics. He owned the *opera omnia* of Calvin, Vermigli, Davenant, Junius, Gomarus, Cameron, and, showing his interest in Reformed scholasticism, the significant works of Maccovius, Downame, Usher, and Ursinus.[51] But his library proves him to be a man of many and diverse influences, and his pattern of citations suggests that he was equally interested in demonstrating when possible that his doctrinal teachings were in fact non-innovative, but rooted in a time before the Reformation.

The goal of examining this period is to discern how the Trinity made an appearance in medieval devotional writing, and when it did so, to what degree it was (1) the Trinity of historical orthodoxy, and (2) a Trinity that is somehow known through its self-disclosure in redemptive deeds. Subsidiary themes that touch upon both of these questions will also arise, especially in regards to religious epistemology (which for our purposes answers how a human being can come to know such an invisible triune God). Also, I will highlight places where the literature variously asserts that the prime arena of human response to God is either in the affections, or the will, or the naked intellect. The conclusion toward which we are moving is that trinitarian theology that is developed in a redemptive-historical mode seems to have certain advantages when it comes to eliciting the believer's affectionate response to a triune God. Our interaction with Owen will also now increase, since his methods for devotion often bear certain resemblances to medieval traditions, even while the content of his theology remains post-Reformation Protestant. At times, he will seem to offer a version of certain medieval trinitarian emphases that is more sensitive to particular trinitarian actions in history.

---

[49] Quotations of Diego Alvarez in X.52, 73, 86, 107; XI.21-22, 71, 72; Rodrigo de Arriaga in XII.140; Juan Azor in 14:235, 416, 439; Cajetan in XII.71, XVI.285; Fransesco Suarez in X.614; XI.73; XII.71; XIV.201, among others Jesuit and Dominican authors are pointed out by Sebastian Rehnman in his 'John Owen: A Reformed Scholastic at Oxford,' in *Reformation and Scholasticism*, ed. Willem J. van Asselt and Eef Dekker (Grand Rapids: Baker Books, 2002) 193.

[50] X.471

[51] Edward Millington, ed., *Bibliotheca Oweniana, sive Catalogus librorum ... Rev. Doct. Vir. D. Joan. Oweni...* (London, 1684), in Rehnman, 'John Owen,' 184.

The dialogue between Owen and especially the complex *devotio moderna* will help to illuminate both traditions.

A helpful first step in understanding the nature of medieval devotion is to take note of two opposing philosophical schools which dominated high medieval scholasticism. It is common to identify 'realism' as the dominant philosophy of the early high scholastic period (c.1200-1350), which was then overtaken by 'nominalism' in the latter half of high scholasticism (c.1350-1500).[52] Realism emphasized the existence of universals which exist above and beyond any real world particulars; in other words, it was a Platonic system which had been somewhat Christianized. The most influential theological schools which made use of realism were Thomism and Scotism. Normally, these two schools are discussed in terms of their particular epistemology and ontology; however, their ideas helped define an approach to God that may be broadly categorized as mysticism. Even so, it is probably more accurate to consider that the kind of mysticism that flows from philosophical realism is really only one of mysticism's multiple varieties. Nominalism, in fact, produced its own kind of mysticism. Nominalism, the second philosophical school of high medievalism that we will consider, produced two very different theological movements: the *via moderna* and the *schola Augustiniana moderna*. Despite their different conclusions, both the *via moderna* and the *schola Augustiniana* explained how nominalistic philosophy can have implications for the devotional life. Thus, perhaps surprisingly, philosophical nominalism went on to inspire two very different kinds of devotional theology. So, with some danger of oversimplifying, we may say that the philosophical theology of the Middle Ages produced three strains of Christian devotional practice – realist mysticism, devotion of the nominalist *via moderna,* and devotion the differently nominalist *schola Augustiniana moderna*. These schools are not always water-tight in terms of their practical methodologies, and individuals such as Owen can be seen to borrow the philosophy of one school while rejecting its theological/devotional assertions in favor of another's, – but overall, these distinctions illuminate three brands of piety which survived into Puritan times.

REALIST MYSTICISM ON THE CONTINENT

Thomas Aquinas was more a philosopher/theologian than a mystic, yet his realist Christian philosophy had many practical consequences for contemplation that he was not reluctant to draw out. However, Aquinas is not an easy figure to categorize as founder of any single devotional school, for his mature thought in the *Summa* clearly proves him to be a

---

[52] Alister McGrath, *Reformation Theology* (Grand Rapids: Baker Book House, 1995) 71.

theological friend of the Augustinians, who were very dissimilar in mystical practice from other devotionalists who thought themselves to be drawing from the same Thomistic realist heritage. For example, Aquinas' description of the beatific vision as the perfection of theology, while in line with typical antecedents going back to the major church fathers, was taken in a very different direction by the famous mystical follower of Aquinas, Meister Eckhart of Hochheim (d. 1327). For Eckhart, who in this regard perhaps owes as much to platonism as to Aquinas, God is the Absolute One who is not only beyond the creation but beyond the Trinity. How can creatures commune with such a distant God? The problem of separation from God for this kind of Eckhartian realism is not ethical but ontological – human sin in the face of a holy God is not a barrier to communion as much as the fact that God is wholly other than anything in the created world of particulars. For Eckhart, the human soul occupies the only middle ground between humanity and God.[53] Why? The soul includes within itself a divine nucleus, which is identical with the Absolute One; therefore, the nucleus of the soul is where God can be born into a human life. The value of Christ is that he is an example of how perfect the union between God and a man can be – thus, the Incarnation was at the center of Eckhart's theology rather than the Crucifixion or Resurrection. A person is saved by entering into himself, in a sense, in order to unite to the divine, to invoke a kind of new Incarnation within himself. This is done following the classical three stages of mysticism: purification, illumination, and union. We should quickly remind ourselves here that after his death, key points of Eckhart's system were officially labeled as heresy – the exact words of Pope John XXII sound almost like a rebuttal of realism's whole project, a condemnation of dabbling in the theological equivalent of the world of the forms. Pope John simply put it, 'we are indeed sad to report that in these days someone by the name of Eckhart from Germany...wished to know more than he should.'[54] However, though officially heretical, Eckhart's definition of each of these three stages of mysticism sound remarkably similar to other much more widely accepted devotional texts,

---

[53] Essential primary texts of Eckhart can be found in *Meister Eckhart*, ed. Edmond Colledge and Bernard McGinn (New York: Paulist Press, 1981). See also McGinn's *The Presence of God: A History of Western Christian Mysticism*, Vol. 2, *The Development of Mysticism* (New York: Crossroad, 2002); and Bengt Hägglund, *History of Theology* (Saint Louis: Concordia, 1968) 203-207.

[54] From the bull 'In agro dominico' (March 27, 1329), in *Meister Eckhart* ed. Edmond Colledge and Bernard McGinn, 77. As Oberman points out, it is not surprising that the pope's charge is the exact opposite of the one that is commonly leveled against nominalists, which is that they were skeptics who had given up on the usefulness of reason in matters of religion, cf. *Harvest*, 326.

the *Cloud of Unknowing* and *The Imitation of Christ*, which we will soon consider.

First, though, it is worth considering in more detail the three mystical stages as Eckhart defines them. For, while his system is an unorthodox amplification of less controversial realism-based mystical principles, I believe it remains organically related to them in often striking ways. The first stage, *purification*, consists of repentance and the active mortification of sinful urges, as well as a fight against sensual indulgence. Nothing at this stage might seem to suggest a unique commitment to platonized Christianity, necessarily. However, the reason why fleshly appetites are to be avoided is that they inhibit the believer from transcending the veil of creation and attaining the intellectual perception of transcendent reality. That is to say, purification is not the believer's response to an ethical problem between himself and God, nor the repair of a breach of covenant, nor the cleansing of a sullied personal relationship with God; rather, it is a technique to transcend the dirtiness of creaturely embodiment. The second stage, *illumination*, consists of the believer's imitation of Christ's suffering and obedience to the Father. The tools toward this end are contemplation of Christ's sufferings as an example to be followed, and surrendering one's own will in order to be absorbed in the will of God. The emphasis in this stage is on the value of suffering in the believer's own life, for, as Eckhart says, 'the quickest way to reach perfection is suffering.'[55] This theme of suffering as agent of personal perfecting will turn up again with vigor in *The Imitation of Christ*. The last stage, *union* of the soul with God, is the result of the believer's freedom from both created things and, as a subset of all created things, freedom from his own individuality. The human soul loses its individuality as it merges with God, the ultimate One, the only reality. Whatever else might be said of Eckhart's version of the three stage mystical ladder, it certainly bears a family resemblance to the neo-platonic systems of Plotinus and Dionysius more than anything particularly Pauline or Augustinian (whereas the latter would say that the created world and embodied humanity are fallen things that need to be redeemed, but not jettisoned). Eckhart's views should count as negative evidence against the occasional claim that the real value of any mysticism is that it rescues Christian devotion from the cold grip of philosophical theology and returns it to its more relational, scriptural moorings. The dominant modern critique of Owen and Reformed scholasticism is along such lines: Owen's use of Aristotelian categories and various scholastic theological *loci* is believed to make him *de facto* a weak guide into vibrant devotional living and thus an enemy of the real scriptural call to heartfelt worship and experience of God. Yet, here in Eckhart one finds a

---

[55] Cited in Bengt Hägglund, *History of Theology*, 204.

vibrant mystical system that, of all things, is clearly more the servant of a realist philosophy than it is of scripture or any other authority. Eckhart's devotional method bears more resemblance to an undiluted neo-platonism than any rigorously exegetical meditation on what the human soul might be experiencing when it is united to God through Christ. On the other hand, Eckhart's model proves that the presence of philosophy within a devotional system does not necessarily stymie the devotional warmth and vibrancy – which Eckhart did have, in his own way; but neither does such immediacy by itself prove that the model is derived from scripture rather than philosophy. Put another way, devotional immediacy is not necessarily defeated by the presence of disciplined philosophical categories and analysis, but neither does it guarantee doctrinal orthodoxy. Eckhart also provides an extreme example of how abandoning the world of particulars also involves an abandonment of the *historia salutis* and any valuing of what the triune God has accomplished in time and space. Even the Incarnation, the one enacted event that Eckhart features, is not a saving event as much as an example of a timeless spiritual ideal to be imitated by anyone at any time. It is, of course, easy to critique Eckhart since his brand of mysticism is an outlier on anyone's spectrum of Christian practice. However, less pantheistic versions of Eckhart's devotional realism show up in some of the definitive works of English mysticism which we will consider next, as well as a major school of devotion which deeply penetrated pre-Reformation England, which we will examine after that.

REALIST MYSTICISM IN BRITAIN: THE 'ENGLISH MYSTICS'

Sometime in the late fourteenth century an unknown English author penned *The Cloud of Unknowing* in Middle English, perhaps the earliest mystical devotional manual in the language, as well as a related work known as *The Book of Privy Counseling*. Both owe much to the evolving apophatic tradition begun by Gregory of Nyssa and Dionysius the Areopagite,[56] who both suggest that God is best known by negation. For Dionysius, there are two ways to know God – through reason (which involves positive statements about God and, even better, negative ones) and through the way that is even more pure: mystical contemplation. Such contemplation requires the believer to 'leave behind the sense and the operations of the intellect...and strain upwards in unknowing, as far as may be, towards the union with Him Who is above all things and knowledge.'[57] For the author of *The Cloud*, all religious thoughts and

---

[56] For the medievals, Dionysius was the apostle Paul's convert, though now he is agreed to be a Syrian monk of the early sixth century.

[57] Dionysius the Areopagite, *Mystical Theology*, I,1. in William Johnston, ed., *The Cloud of Unknowing and the Book of Privy Counseling* (New York: Doubleday, 1973) 26.

images must therefore be intentionally buried by the worshipper beneath a 'cloud of forgetting' while her naked love (divested of thought) will rise toward union with God in a 'cloud of unknowing.' The author's contribution to the apophatic tradition is his particular emphasis on loving God as an element of this mystical contemplation. Showing a Thomistic strain (for Aquinas was also influenced by this tradition), he believes that love by nature is ecstatic because it takes a person out of himself and into the thing that he loves.

There is a trinitarian shape to this kind of devotion, however, given the role that Christ plays. Christ is not so much concrete or bodily existent since his resurrection, but more a cosmic-Christ so that 'the contemplative puts on the mind of the cosmic Christ and offers himself to the Father for the salvation of the human race.'[58] This is a surprising twist in the idea of communion with the Trinity, for it gives the believer himself some kind of Christ-like role in the redemption of other people. The author clearly promises that in the work of contemplation, if one forgets every earthly thing, 'your fellow men are marvelously enriched by this work of yours, even if you may not fully understand how.'[59] As the mystic gives himself up to the cloud of unknowing, leaving his own particularity behind, he somehow conveys to others the merit of Christ, who also gave himself up. Of course, while Owen uses strong language to describe trinitarian communion, the believer is Christ-like in the sense that he is given communion with the Father based on the privileges of sonship transferred to him by the only begotten Son, not that he shares in the Son's saving capacity in the way *The Cloud* describes.

But a further comparison between Owen and *The Cloud of Unknowing* is the description of the contemplative prayer that brings one into fuller communion with God. In what follows, Owen will be shown to advocate a kind of prayer and meditation that is particularly centered on the comforting proofs of trinitarian love toward the believer as it is demonstrated in the person and public deeds of Christ. In other words, his kind of meditation is not on God in an abstract sense, but on particulars – the definitive acts of a trinitarian God whose glory and love transforms the believer as she contemplates the Jesus of the Gospel story, and especially the meaning of his death and resurrection in history. It is a kind of meditation full of thinking, interpreting, and applying truths to oneself. *The Cloud*, on the other hand, turns the apophatic and realist tradition into a method that results in almost a directly opposite way of approaching God. That is, while it never seems to redefine the very nature of God or humanity in the novel and problematic way of Eckhart, it

---

[58] *The Cloud of Unknowing*, 19.
[59] *The Cloud of Unknowing*, 48

makes full use of realist principles in describing the means of prayer as a way to leave behind anything in the world of particulars:

> Say to your thoughts, 'You are powerless to grasp him, be still.'... Don't be surprised if your thoughts seem holy and valuable for prayer. Probably you will find yourself thinking about the wonderful qualities of Jesus, his sweetness, his love, his graciousness, his mercy. But if you pay attention to these ideas they will have gained what they wanted of you, and will go on chattering until they divert you even more to the thought of his passion....Soon you will be thinking about your sinful life and perhaps in this connection you will recall some place where you have lived in the past, until suddenly, before you know it, your mind is completely scattered.[60]

And later, as if to admit that at least some minimal thoughts of God are necessary for prayer to be meaningful, there is the following hesitating qualification:

> Think only of God, the God who created you, redeemed you, and guided you to this work. Allow no other ideas about God to enter your mind. Yet even this is too much. A naked intent toward God, the desire for him alone, is enough...likewise it is wrong for a person who ought to be busy with the contemplative work in the darkness of the *cloud of unknowing* to let ideas about God, his wonderful gifts, his kindness, or his works distract him from attentiveness to God himself.[61]

There is a broad conflict between this method and the general Reformed assumption that God cannot actually be known as 'God himself' apart from his self-disclosure in redemptive history – that is, no knowledge of God is possible apart from his acts of self-disclosure in the world of particulars.[62] Yet, as to the question of method, one might say that everything *The Cloud* says not to do is exactly what the Reformed, and especially Owen, command. For Owen, as will be shown, the only way to achieve the desire for God and rest in him is to contemplate his sweetness, love, graciousness, mercy, and especially, the work of Christ's mediation. Thoughts that *The Cloud* sees as leading to unfortunate mental 'scattering' (for example, the Passion) are the very thoughts that for Owen are one's best mental anchors for meaningful communion with God.

One long-held legend is that *The Cloud* was written by a Carthusian, and by the Puritan era the work was considered to be a vestige of Roman Catholic spirituality and therefore officially proscribed. However, the book and those of its ilk certainly had helped to shape English devotion by then and were by no means extinct in England. For example, the

---

[60] *The Cloud of Unknowing*, 55
[61] *The Cloud of Unknowing*, 56, 59.
[62] Calvin, *Institutes*, ed. Ford Lewis Battles, trans. John T. McNeill, (Philadelphia: Westminster Press, 1960) II.9ff, 61ff.

recusant Catholic leader and Benedictine Augustine Baker (1575-1641) lists Walter Hilton's *Scale of Perfection* and the similar *Cloud of Unknowing* at the top of his list of books most helpful for the contemplative soul.[63] Even still, could such banned Catholic books have found any widespread readership in England into the seventeenth century? Yes, in more ways than one. Black-market and smuggled works from overseas were not hard to find, albeit at prices double or triple that of legal books. Perhaps more interestingly, contraband books of piety were sometimes acquired by English Protestants traveling abroad who sent the works home to their equally Protestant loved ones, as is shown by this letter from Isaac Basire (a well-known Anglican divine during the reign of Charles I) to his fiancée. In sending her a present of books he writes:

> These two I send you myself are, 1. An Introduction to a Devout Life, etc. 2. The marrow of the Oracles of God: two books which next to God's owne, my soul hath been much taken with. The first was made by a French Bishop, yet is the booke free from Popery, (for which I have read it aforehand for your soule's saecke): only where you see a crosse at the margent, there it maybe mistaken by some; else, all is safe.[64]

The first book that Basire is referring to is by St. Francis de Sales (1567-1622), a Roman Catholic bishop who spent part of his career preaching in Geneva in order to help undo the work of Calvinists. And if Anglicans were reading Roman Catholic devotion, so were the Presbyterians. Richard Baxter, in fact, was converted by such a Catholic book, albeit in a somewhat edited form. While it is widely known that Baxter in his *Reliquiae Baxterianae* describes his own awakening to be the result of his reading 'Bunny's Resolution,' it is less known that Baxter admits that Edmund Bunny was only the Puritan 'corrector' of the work – the original text, which was really only slightly amended, was written by a Jesuit named Parsons. In fact, Parsons was still alive to publish a perturbed response to Bunny's corrections in a new edition of his original work, also written for an English audience.[65] Thus, the recusant Catholic publishing efforts sometimes had great effect beyond what their legal proscription might suggest.

Where then, does realist mysticism fit within the overall development of English devotion? The narrow context is within a movement of the 14th

---

[63] Augustine Baker, *Sancta Sophia* I, 86-87, in Helen C. White, *English Devotional Literature [Prose]* (New York: Haskell House, 1966) 126.

[64] *The Correspondance of Isaac Basire, D.D. Archdeacon of Northumberland and Prebendary of Durham, in the Reigns of Charles I and Charles II with a Memoir of his Life*, ed. W.N. Darnell (London, 1831) 21, in White, *English Devotional Literature*, 142.

[65] For nature of the disputes, see White, *English Devotional Literature*, 145-49.

century whose authors are often referred to as the 'English Mystics.' The principal writers are Richard Rolle, Walter Hilton, Julian of Norwich, Margery Kempe, and the anonymous author of *The Cloud*. Admitting the diversity of their writings, certain common theological and especially experiential themes tied them together. They owed much to Dionysius the Areopagite as well as Augustine as he was formalized by the Victorines,[66] for whom contemplation was 'a half-intellectual, half-devotional, grace-enlightened penetration of Christian truth, the normal if somewhat uncommon result of long ascetic and mental preparation.'[67] While the neo-platonist tendencies of the movement as well as the more dramatic bodily manifestations (the physically experienced raptures described by Rolle and the public shouting of Kempe) offered little to impress a Puritan, it is not without reason that 'some Calvinist theologians from the low countries have castigated the Puritans as "the English mystics" and deprecated their spirituality as "the cultivation of a soft-life of feeling."'[68] Can the Puritans meaningfully be understood as seventeenth-century reincarnations of the English Mystics? While likening the Protestant English Puritans to the Catholic English Mystics is not a comparison often heard today, surprisingly, it was an easy comparison to derisively make for continental Calvinists, who were otherwise the theological allies of their brethren across the English Channel. And, in fact, certain shared themes between the movements are significant.

For example, Julian of Norwich's *Revelations of Divine Love* has an affective and trinitarian emphasis that may not have been repeated in quite the same way until the Puritan era, and even perhaps until Owen himself. Julian vividly describes her vision of the wounded head of Christ, red blood trickling from under the thorns, and yet the effect of this image on her is not to produce mere guilt nor resolution to go and suffer likewise (as would be the conclusion in *The Imitation of Christ*). Rather,

> in the same Shewing suddenly the Trinity fulfilled my heart most of joy...For the Trinity is God: God is the Trinity; the Trinity is our Maker and Keeper, the Trinity is our everlasting love and everlasting joy and bliss, by our Lord Jesus Christ. And

---

[66] Hugh of St. Victor (d.1142) and Richard of St. Victor (d.1173) hailed from the Abbey of St. Victor in Paris. They contributed to the development of the theology of meditation through allegorical studies of scripture (Richard) and attempts to broaden Bernard's concentration on the sacred humanity of Christ as the object of contemplation to include other created things (Hugh).

[67] David Knowles, *The English Mystical Tradition*, in *The Westminster Dictionary of Christian Spirituality*, ed. Gordon S. Wakefield (Philadelphia: Westminster Press, 1983) 130.

[68] Gordon S. Wakefield, 'English Spirituality,' in *The Westminster Dictionary*, 132.

this was shewed in the First [Shewing] and in all: for where Jesus appeareth, the blessed Trinity is understood.[69]

For Julian, the work of the economic Trinity is best understood, and more than that, the Trinity's redemptive love for sinners most powerfully felt, when watching the sufferings 'pressed on His blessed head who was both God and Man.'[70] Seeing the God-man crucified for her is what ushers her into the communion with the all the Persons of God as she senses the weight of the whole Godhead's saving love for her in that act. Certainly the unifying theme of this book is devotion to the Passion of Christ, a theme which is a shared trait of all the English Mystics. Unique with Julian though is that the operation of such meditation centers on how the Passion incites her to return love to the whole Trinity, whom she sees has willingly gone to such lengths to save her through the cross, and with such love comes the sheer delight in being granted intimate access to such a God as this. Thus, the joy that Jesus experiences in redeeming her is met by her own joy in response. Owen will focus similarly on the Son's 'purchased grace' and the believer's heartfelt 'returnal' for that grace.[71] Julian's imagined conversation with Christ goes as follows:

> THEN said the Lord Jesus Christ: Are thou pleased that I suffered for thee? I said: Yea, good Lord, I thank Thee; Yea, good Lord, blessed mayst Thou be. Then said Jesus, our kind Lord: If thou art pleased, I am pleased: it is a joy, a bliss, an endless satisfying to me that ever suffered I Passion for thee; and if I might suffer more, I would suffer more.[72]

Although in other places there is much language describing her response to Christ's love, the overall emphasis seen here is not on herself or her duty, but rather on what Christ himself has done, how his love for her makes him eager to suffer in order to obtain her, and how the Trinity's pleasure in saving her is behind it all. In addition, we see the suffering of Christ at Calvary in terms of its devotional effect on believers, which approaches the spiritual use of the *historia salutis*. The culmination of all of these themes is in her 'Sixteenth Revelation,' which is simply an unparalleled account of grace-centered trinitarian devotion:

> AND the Lord opened my spiritual eye and shewed me my soul in midst of my heart. I saw the Soul so large as it were an endless world, as it were a blissful kingdom...and I understood that it was a worshipful City. In the midst of that City sitteth our Lord Jesus, God and Man... a most majestic King, most worshipful Lord;

---

[69] Julian of Norwich, *Revelations of Divine Love*, ed. Grace Warrack (London: Methuen and Co., 1901) 9.
[70] Julian of Norwich, *Revelations*, 9.
[71] II.154ff.
[72] Julian of Norwich, *Revelations*, 12.

and I saw him clad majestically. And worshipfully He sitteth in the Soul, even right in peace and in rest...[and] the place that Jesus taketh in our Soul He shall never remove it, without end, as to my sight; for in us is His homliest home and His endless dwelling. And in this sight he shewed the satisfying that He hath of the making of Man's Soul. For as well as the Father might make a creature, and as well as the Son could make a creature, so well would the Holy Ghost that Man's Soul were made: and so it was done. And therefore the blessed Trinity enjoyeth without end in the making of Man's Soul...[and I] knowing, by reason, that his dwelling is in the worthiest place, thus I understood in verity that our Soul may never have rest in things that are beneath itself...yet may it not abide in the beholding of its Self, but all the beholding is blissfully set in God that is the Maker dwelling therein. For in Man's Soul is His very dwelling; and the highest light and the brightest shining of the City is the glorious love of our Lord, as to my sight. And what may make us more to enjoy God than to see in Him that He enjoyeth in the highest of all His works?...and He willeth that our hearts be mightily raised above the deepness of the earth and all vain sorrows, and rejoice in Him.[73]

OWEN'S METHOD FOR MEDITATING ON THE TRINITY

There is no evidence that Owen read Julian, though even had he done so it is not surprising, given his intended audience, that he would not have quoted her (after all, it would have been illegal for him even to purchase her writings). Certainly her claim to direct revelation, her asceticism, and her Marian devotion would have given him caution. Yet, knowingly or not, Owen the trinitarian is carrying on, in some sense, an old Augustinian, mystical, even Julian tradition when he speaks of glorifying and enjoying the trinitarian God who has first enjoyed him, who loved him enough to save and personally indwell him. Most notably, both he and Julian emphasize the pleasure that God experiences in being Savior and how this pleasure produces a like reaction in those who are being saved. Her themes became his themes, albeit with a much more elaborate covenantal scheme that further explains how God worked out this saving love in the history of redemption.

An example will show this similarity, as well as how Owen goes much further to enumerate the way each person of the Trinity is differently appropriated in nearly the same actions Julian describes. In doing so we will also find ourselves near the heart of his theology of devotion. Like Julian, Owen speaks of the sense in which the Trinity takes up a kind of personal communion with the human soul by communicating to it Christ, who then reigns within it. Redemption, in fact, involves for him the 're-enthroning of the Person, Spirit, Grace, and Authority of Christ, in the hearts and consciences of men.'[74] There is a particular order of this divine communication, however, which follows from the order of

---

[73] Julian of Norwich, *Revelations*, 168-69.
[74] I.5

subsistence within the Godhead: The Father's wisdom, love, and grace is the fountainhead, the person and mediation of the Son are its substance, and the Holy Spirit follows by applying the Son's personal and mediatory glory by infusing into the believer 'light,' 'life,' and 'power.'[75] Another way he says this is that the Father gives the Son to the Christian, in the form of two 'unions' – first, as the Son's incarnation unites human nature to divine nature, and secondly, as Christ takes the believer's person into a mystical union with his own person. Because Christ's nature is itself a divine/human union, by extension, the mystical union with the believer thus unites her to the divine nature itself: 'it is not enough that he hath taken our nature to be his, unless he gives us also his nature to be ours.'[76] The result is a 'mutual inbeing' of Christ and his people, language strikingly similar to the Greek *perichoresis* principle used to describe the inter-penetration between the divine *hypostaseis* themselves.[77] Owen's point in articulating this is more to stir the heart than to inform the mind. In fact, he is ruthless toward those who fail to follow the doctrine of the Trinity's *opera ad extra* to its true end, which is to enflame the heart with love for God.[78] Somehow in the believer's meditative concentration on these truths about the Trinity she will find the essence (and the transformative power) of true worship. He says regarding the above workings, 'And here is the glorious truth of the blessed Trinity, – which by some is opposed, by some neglected, by most looked on as that which is so much above them as that it doth not belong unto them, – made precious unto them that believe, and *becomes the foundation of their faith and hope*.'[79] And why can such a view of the Trinity in action become the foundation of the whole of the Christian's faith? Because, 'in a view of the glorious order of those divine communications, we are in a steady contemplation of the ineffable glory of the existence of the nature of God in the three distinct persons of Father, Son, and Holy Ghost.'[80] Ruminating on the Trinity in action brings one into the presence of a glory of God that is revealed nowhere else. This is all helpful evidence that for Owen the doctrine of the Trinity is not just a doctrine to be believed as a mark of orthodoxy, but is primarily a truth which provides a worshipper with the only fully Christian answer to basic questions like, 'why is God glorious?' and 'how do you know he loves you?' God is never more glorious than in his triune conspiracy to re-enthrone Christ in someone's heart, and is never shown more loving than in the great favor this is to the one he lovingly

---

[75] I.363
[76] I.366
[77] I.367
[78] I.396-402
[79] I.363, emphasis mine.
[80] I.363

overtakes. Owen here sounds somewhat like Julian, but with an even greater dependence on the public saving work of the Trinity as a meditative object.

In all of this, though, there is still something vague about the exact connection between a believer's mental understanding of these distinct works of the divine persons within and in behalf of her soul, and the kind of rapturous love of God and unshakable faith that he says cannot be attained any other way (and Owen is clearly convinced that meditation on these truths is the only means to such spiritual fruit). The vagueness of Julian seems less problematic because she is simply writing about her own experiences, and only secondarily as some kind of guide to normative spiritual practice. Owen, on the other hand, is writing devotional theology, and is telling us that this theology should set the pattern for everyone's Christian practice.

For example, what exactly is the connection between meditating on the Trinity in action and actual growth towards Christian maturity? The best way to understand this may come by examining Owen's answer to another related question in which he is more specific: how is meditating on Christ transformative for the believer? These are related questions, of course, because for Owen the prime *ad extra* act of the Trinity is to communicate Christ to the believer (through the two phases of incarnation and mystical union, as above). Thus, to meditate on the glory of Christ as Redeemer is to meditate on the most important work of the Trinity. Owen urges meditation on Christ in three aspects, but only the first will be considered for present purposes: meditation on the glorification of Christ's human nature in heaven.[81] The effects of such meditation are clear to him, for 'apprehending Christ in his glory is' not only 'the remedy for spiritual decays,'[82] but 'our apprehension of this glory is the spring of all our obedience' and is also the controlling object of Christian affection because of Christ's consuming beauty.[83] How is this contemplation so effective? Two reasons seem to rise to the surface. The first is that since the Spirit's work is to fashion believers into the image of Christ's human nature, the believer's own transformation begins as she fills her mind with thoughts of the now glorified human nature of Christ. In other words, one slowly becomes what one fills one's mind with, or in keeping with his language, one becomes what one 'apprehends' or gazes upon. The connection between beholding and transformation comes also in the scriptural language 'we all, with open face beholding as in a glass

---

[81] The three aspects are (1) the glorification of Christ's human nature, (2) his mediatory exaltation, and (3) the exercise of his office from heaven, cf. I.239-53. For practical purposes, these all overlap for Owen, meaning that by the time his finishes his full exposition of the first, he has very little left to say about the other two.

[82] I.459-61

[83] I.243

the glory of the Lord, are changed into the same image, from glory to glory, even as by the Spirit of the Lord'[84] in which Owen slightly stretches the word *katoptridzo* to mean 'diligently inspecting' as a distant object through a telescope.[85]

More deeply, a consideration by the worshipper of the very hypostatic union by which Christ's human nature is united to divine nature is especially powerful. On one hand, 'diligently inspecting' the Son of God's condescension to take on human nature impresses the believer's mind with the prototype of all Christian self-denial, for human obedience is similarly acting in self-denying submission to the will of the Father.[86] On the other hand, the hypostatic union presents to the mind a glorious mystery that exalts God's ineffable wisdom in salvation. Owen nowhere makes such heavy use of the concept of mystery as when he is trying to convey the way in which contemplating the uncontemplatable – Christ as fully God and fully man – raises the human mind to new heights of both delight in God, and progress in sanctification.[87] Somehow, such lofty thoughts of such an inexplicable union, yet a union made real by the Godhead as an act of love for those who would be saved because of it, moves the soul to humble worship and new sensations of appreciative delight. And everywhere that Owen describes the value of meditating on Christ, he uses the language of 'enjoyment.' In the last analysis, the enjoyment of Christ is what drives out the enjoyment of sin, for the former causes the believer to lose his appetite for the latter. The late-born Puritan Thomas Chalmers would express the same idea with the title of a sermon on the secret of dislodging fleshly appetites, 'The Expulsive Power of a New Affection.'

In all of this, what is organically related to a realist tradition is the way in which Owen describes how meditation on the three-in-one God (or Christ) without use of sensate images or devotional objects produces a change within the affections. At the same time, unique to Owen is the much more in depth analysis of how the details of theology – in this case, classic christology and even the Reformed 'Covenant of Redemption' – produces such change. Contrary to the claims being made against high-Puritan spirituality, however, the point of such doctrinal exposition is always to deepen pleasure in God as he is more profoundly discovered to be a Trinity *pro nobis*. These themes will be unfolded in Chapter Six.

WALTER HILTON'S *SCALE OF PERFECTION*: TOWARDS SUCCESS

Hilton's *Scale of Perfection* stands perhaps as the defining theological treatise of the movement of English Mysticism. Hilton spells out in much

---

[84] 2 Cor. 3:18
[85] See Goold's word study, I.222.
[86] I.332
[87] I.221ff, 312ff

detail what would have been the underlying and often unspoken assumptions of Julian of Norwich and the author of *The Cloud*. Of greater interest is that Hilton's work stands as 'the first book, or the first pair of books, written in English to cover the whole field of the spiritual life, integrating this closely with the doctrine of the Trinity.'[88] Hilton's own sources for his comprehensive work are primarily the three greats whom Abbot Cuthbert Butler describes in his *Western Mysticism*:[89] Augustine, Gregory the Great (who as a pastor simply popularized much of Augustine), and Bernard of Clairvaux. Great emphasis should be placed especially on Augustine's *De Trinitate*, in which the doctrine of the Trinity is related to creation and redemption. To have used such respectable and orthodox sources specifically serves a secondary polemic purpose of Hilton's work. By the time he wrote *The Scale* there existed throughout Europe the increasing problem of 'Free-Spirit' devotional movements that were rejecting perceived limitations of scholastic theology in favor of extremely experiential and immediate forms of communion with God. In response, other writers were trying to define themselves against such radical trends. Suso, Tauler, and Ruysbroeck, for example, while certainly inspired by Eckhart in some ways, nonetheless also tried to avoid his more famous excesses in their own devotional theology. Evidence suggests that by Hilton's day, fear was growing that the Free-Spirit movements might spread to England, and it is possible that Hilton was himself motivated to forestall such a possibility, as well as to create a practical theology of the contemplative life that could be proved to have very orthodox credentials.[90] So in Hilton we find another rarity in the history of devotion: the attempt to weld explicitly orthodox theology, a trinitarian theology no less, to a model of spiritual practice.

What features of this contemplative orthodoxy paved the way for later theologians of the seventeenth century? Following Augustine, Hilton believed that the human soul is a created trinity (*trinitas creata*) reflecting the uncreated Trinity of the Godhead. Power, wisdom, and love are attributes appropriated to the divine persons as they disclose their activity to humans, though these attributes are not necessarily peculiar to any of the three individually. The human soul, in kind, has three faculties which correspond and answer to the divine persons: (1) the memory (*memoria*) which really means something like 'awareness,' (2) the understanding (*intelligentia*) which Hilton refers to as 'the reason,' and (3) the will (*voluntas*) (or love). Through the Fall, these faculties of the soul fail to remain trained on the members of the Trinity in the following ways.

---

[88] John P.H. Clark and Rosemary Dorward, introduction to Walter Hilton, *The Scale of Perfection* (New York: Paulist Press, 1991) 33.

[89] Cuthbert Butler, *Western Mysticism* (London: 1922).

[90] Cf. J. Bazire and E. College, *The Chastening of God's Children* (Oxford, 1957) 51ff, in Clark and Dorward, *Walter Hilton, The Scale of Perfection*.

Humans (1) have lost their memory of the Father, that is, they have no intuitive awareness of the Father or spontaneous conformity to his law; (2) their reason is no longer responsive to the Son, who, as the Word, is the essence of reason; and (3) love has become disordered and restless and no longer answers to the Holy Spirit.[91] The concern of Hilton is to describe how the soul can be renovated so that its own trinitarian structure is re-tuned to that of the Holy Trinity. In this regard, it is helpful to note that Hilton himself never called his work *The Scale of Perfection* – in fact, another early title from British Library MS Harley 2397 is *The Reformyng of Mannys Soule*.[92] While perhaps this is still not Hilton's own title, it seems to better express the purpose of the work as a tool to re-image the human soul according to its own inherent trinitarian nature, rather than as some kind of a stepladder to moral perfection or mystical ecstasy.

How is this trinitarian redemption accomplished for Hilton? From God's side, by grace, while from the human perspective, through the act of contemplation – a habit which has three parts. The first stage of contemplation is rational knowledge of basic Christian truths (close, it seems, to the scholastic concept of *notitia*). The second, by contrast, is experiencing affection for God, including almost physically manifested feelings of devotion for him (feelings which might include even unpleasant sensations of dread when God's pure majesty is in focus).[93] The third part, the highest, is called 'true contemplation,' which holds the rational and affective elements of the first two parts together. The affection for God at this third and highest stage is described less now in terms of bodily sensations (and here surely Hilton is criticizing Richard Rolle) and more as an affective response to truths about God which produce a more internal and settled joy in God. For Hilton, this final form of contemplation is of highest value since it is less fleeting than mere sensations and is rather a true reflection, however dim, of the glorified state where a believer will have both full knowledge and full joy together. In fact, this level of contemplation (which is available to all Christians, including those with secular vocations, even if perhaps less regular among such)[94] is what is meant when he describes the soul as *unitas spiritus* with Christ, a state, for Hilton as well as Augustine and Bernard, where knowledge and love are held together:

> The third part of contemplation... lies both in cognition and in affection: that is to say, in the knowing and perfect loving of God. That is when a person's soul is first

---

[91] See Hilton, *Scale* I.45; and Bazire and College, in Hilton, *Scale*, 36.
[92] The earliest manuscripts (Cambridge University Library Add, MS 6686 and York Minster Chapter Library MS XVI K5) bear no title at all.
[93] Hilton, *Scale* I.5
[94] Hilton, *Scale* I.9

cleansed for all sins and reformed to the image of Jesus...afterward he is visited and taken up from all earthly and fleshly affections, from vain thoughts and imaginations of all bodily things, and is as if forcibly ravished out of the bodily senses; and then is illumined by the grace of the Holy Spirit to see intellectually the Truth, which is God, and also spiritual things, with a soft, sweet burning love for him – so perfectly that by the rapture of this love the soul is for the time united and conformed to the image of the Trinity. The beginning of this contemplation may be felt in this life, but the fullness of it is kept in the bliss of heaven ... God and the soul are not two, but both are one – not in flesh, but in one spirit – and certainly in this union that marriage is made between God and the soul which shall never be broken.[95]

The Bernardian influence is strong here with the marriage analogy regarding God and the soul. The passage also might seem to suggest that an ecstatic emotional process is at work. But remember that for Hilton, to be 'ravished out of the bodily senses' is not his way of saying that his senses were somehow overwhelmed with feelings for God. He means almost the opposite, that this highest contemplative experience of God was a true ravishing, but *not* of the sensate variety that some ravishings produce. Evident here is a kind of realist disapproval of particulars such as bodily sensations of ecstasy as ends in themselves. Hilton is thinking of himself as a conservative with this description, trying to show that one does not need to become a reckless enthusiast in order to have the deepest experience of God. But, on the other hand, neither will anyone be properly ravished who simply remains in the realm of historical faith or mere doctrine. This fruit of 'true contemplation' is the highest pinnacle of Christian experience, yet will be rare, and, when it occurs, should spur the worshipper on to thoughts of heaven where in a future day God will be known in this way without interruption.

Hilton succeeds at avoiding the doctrinal excesses of Eckhart's brand of realism, yet we still find little in the way of a dealing with salvation history for its use to the worshipper. Our two criteria prove to be rarely held together, for the recurring sense in the Western tradition is that the pinnacle of emotive or devotional response includes deep knowledge of God but not, apparently, knowledge mediated through the events of the scriptural record. Quite the opposite seems to be the ideal: the knowledge which leads to the highest enjoyment of God will be unhampered by mediating objects in the embodied world of creation. Perhaps in its nervousness about particulars, even the more theologically orthodox realism of Hilton is unsure of the meditative value of the particulars of the Son's work while in union with a particular human body in the particular land of first-century Palestine. And, even while Hilton speaks much about the goal of contemplation as a reformation of the soul into the image of

---

[95] Hilton, *Scale* I.8

the Trinity, we might ask whether or not he could not have just said 'image of God.' One wonders if the ancient creedal statements about the essence and relations of the divine persons (statements with which Hilton would no doubt have agreed) could be proved untrue without harming the system of meditation he offers. There is not a clear sense that the trinitarian meditation of which he speaks relies in any significant way on the processions or missions of a triune God. Perhaps even the particularity of a God in three distinct persons with distinct missions is an ungainly fact for those who are theologically orthodox but who remain philosophically realist is their approach to Christian worship.

THE *DEVOTIO MODERNA*: REALIST MYSTICISM GOES MAINSTREAM

Between the 1380's and 1430 a school of lay monastics developed in the eastern Netherlands, eventually spreading widely throughout Germany and the lower Netherlands (Belgium). The New Devout, as they became known, gathered their adherents into residential houses, the number of which grew to several hundred, and attracted the suspicious eye of church authorities who found them hard to categorize. On one hand, their orthodoxy seemed acceptable, yet they preferred to freely associate rather than make vows or apply to be recognized as an official order. They supported their local parish congregations, yet held their own separate public meetings. Even Luther later approved of the New Devout house located in Hereford in 1532 and saved it from the closure required of other religious houses.[96] While the organized movement of the New Devotion finally died out, the writings it produced were fantastically long-lived and widely read among very diverse Christian groups. Oberman makes an explicit connection between the *devotio moderna* and various groups including the English Protestants: 'the Modern Devotion has continued to survive under many other names such as Jansenism or Puritanism, and it fed into that resurgence in vitality which we vaguely call "reform Catholicism."'[97] If he is right, what exact thematic connection is there between the New Devotion and Puritan devotion? And, does Owen's particular version of Puritan devotion strengthen or weaken that proposed link?

Certainly the most famous work connected to the *devotio moderna* is *The Imitation of Christ*. But before getting to the direct themes of that book, it will be helpful to see the broader teachings of the movement as represented by some of the more foundational though lesser known writings. The founder of the movement, Geert Grote (1340-1384) set the

---

[96] For a full review of the incident and Luther's letter, see Robert Stupperich, 'Luther und das Fraterhaus in Herford,' in *Geist und Geschichte der Reformation, Festgabe H. Ruckert zum 65 Geburtstag* (Berlin, 1966) 19-38.

[97] Heiko Oberman, preface to *Devotio Moderna: Basic Writings*, ed. John Van Engen, New York: Paulist Press, 1988) 3.

theological and methodological tone for what would come. Grote bucked the trend in his day and became a realist, converting from the nominalism that he had been taught at the University of Paris. He believed therefore that particular things had an essence that transcended the things themselves and any particular image or sensation the things might provide to an observer. A separate religious problem for him was that true knowledge of God could only come through knowledge of his transcendent essence, which is not directly knowable. So, if God can neither be directly known, nor known indirectly through created particulars, then what hope is there to know him at all? Because Grote was more bound to Scripture than Eckhart, he believed that sensual images of particulars, and especially the sensual images described in the Scriptures (for example, the image of Jesus laying in a manger) must be somehow important for the believer to come to a knowledge of God. We might say then that Grote advocated a kind of scripturally qualified realism. The challenge he faced was to reconcile the seeming contradiction (for realists, especially) of using sensual, biblical, and particular images as a way of gaining fellowship with the transcendent reality of God.[98] Grote becomes interesting for our present thesis because he seems to advocate a new role in spirituality for particulars, perhaps even the historical particulars of the biblically attested events of saving history.

One treatise that deals with the problem of how particulars might help one gain knowledge of a transcendent God is 'On Four Classes of Subjects Suitable for Meditation: A Sermon on the Lord's Nativity,' an essay on the philosophy and psychology of meditation. Grote's main point is that while images are a divinely ordained means by which humans receive divine truth, they do a disservice to someone who does not allow them to take her beyond their particularity toward the universal they signify. God has constructed humans so that spiritual desire and spiritual knowledge are expressed and received through the senses. Meditating on the physical picture of Jesus' nativity, for example, was an unavoidable and proper way to commune with God through the truths about him that the nativity scene reveals. However, Grote-the-realist said that such image-revealed truth fails to have its full transformative power, and in fact can be dangerous, unless it leads the worshipper to universal truth beyond its particular sensual impression. This way of being discontent with the mere sensual value of meditation is what keeps the *devotio moderna* from fulfilling the stereotype of a mystic as a dreamy-eyed, experience-driven contemplative – a more difficult stereotype for an Eckhartian to avoid. In fact, Grote's insistence that any sensual mental

---

[98] I suggest, therefore, that while Grote admits to the a necessary role for particulars in his model of devotion, he remains essentially a realist with nominalist features rather than the other way around.

images of scriptural scenes should ideally effect a transformation of personal character explains the hallmark of Grote's model of meditation: we mentally replay biblical stories for the final purpose of changing our own conduct. A classic example of what we might call Grote's 'criteria of conduct' is his reservation about the danger of meditating on physical images of the crucified Christ,

> lest we spend too long in pursuit of a simple image of a nude Christ, without clothes or attire, with no garment of splendor or fortitude or righteousness or light...therefore the flesh is to be permeated with divine forms. When he comes in his glory what will it profit the damned to have seen the flesh of Christ and been transfixed? What did it profit Herod or Pilate or the Jews to have seen Christ with their eyes when they did not follow his precepts?[99]

Contemplation of a particular image like a physical crucifix has value, but a crucifix on its own actually fails to capture the fullness of theological truth about the crucifixion. Merely gazing at a nude figure on the cross does not itself connect the worshipper to the invisible glory and splendor of what was actually being effected at the crucifixion of Jesus – that is, the incarnate second person of the holy Trinity conquering sin and death. Dare we suggest that Grote wants to protect the full value of the historical particular as well as the doctrinal truth that such an event is meant to reveal? To put Grote's concern another way, only soaking the mind in the image for what it directly communicates, the mere particular sensual image of that day at Calvary, will actually leave the worshipper open to the final condemnation of Christ because the worshipper has failed to achieve the true end to which the image of Calvary is pointing him. This so-called worshipper is really more like Pilate who saw the image of the suffering Jesus yet did not let the universal truth behind the image penetrate him enough to change his conduct. For Grote, the change of conduct is the ultimate measure of the legitimacy of a meditative technique.

Some of this does have a Puritan aroma to it – especially, of course, the perceived danger in using physical images in worship. Owen's way of analyzing this danger is to say that physical images are only attractive to people when, through their own unbelief, they fail to see the transformative power of Christ as he is experienced in the historical gospel story and New Covenant promises:

> Having a spiritual light to discern and behold the glory of Christ, as represented in the glass of the gospel, they have experience of its transforming power and

---

[99] Geert Grote, 'A Treatise on Four Classes of Subjects Suitable for Meditation: Sermon on the Lord's Nativity,' in John Van Engen, ed., *Devotio Moderna: Basic Writings*, 101.

efficacy, changing them into the likeness of the image represented unto them, – that is, of Christ himself...but this spiritual light was lost among men, through the efficacy of their darkness and unbelief; they were not able to discover the glory of Christ, as revealed and proposed in the gospel, so as to make him the present object of their faith and love...What shall these men, then, betake themselves unto? Shall they reject the notion in general, that there ought to be such a representation made of Christ unto the minds of men, as to inflame their devotion, excite their faith, and stir up their affection to him? This cannot be done without an open renunciation of him, and of the gospel as a fable. Wherefore they will find out another way for it... by making images of him of wood and stone, or gold and silver.[100]

The problem of images for Owen (apart from their often direct violation of the second commandment) is that they fail to really serve the cause of devotion – they lack the power that only the spiritual truths of the gospel story have to transform the worshipper. Yet Owen is still in favor of a 'representation made of Christ' in some sense, as it is made unto the mind's eye rather than the physical eye. Grote's warning, of course, would apply even to *thinking* about an image of a crucifix in a wrong way, while Owen usually is taking aim at physical images placed in churches as a substitute for gospel preaching. It seems to me, though, that Owen's perceived limitations of a 'wooden Jesus' also apply to a mental picture of Jesus that is adored apart from the conscious meditation on the spiritual truths about what his death meant and means. In other words, Owen wants the story of Christ's passion to be preached in order for its transformative power to be released, that is, the particular events of the story should be explained as to their theological meaning, their redemptive-historical placement, and most of all, their personal implication to the life and conscience of the listener. What is fascinating, however, is that Owen's iconoclasm is only relative to his over-riding concern that the soul be affectionately captured by the love that Christ has demonstrated for it. Owen's deep suspicion of religious formality, liturgies, and those who make public worship a theatrical 'pageant of religion,'[101] with all the attendant physical images, is especially the hallmark of those like himself who occupied the Independent branch of Puritanism. Yet Owen takes one notable exception to what he thinks is the occasionally misappropriated iconoclastic zeal of his friends: 'Others there are who abhor these idols, and when they have so done, commit *sacrilege*. As they reject images, so they seem to do all love unto the person of Christ...but the most superstitious love unto Christ – that is, love acted in ways tainted with superstition – is better than none at all.'[102] He goes on to admit his doubts about the heart condition of those who seem

---

[100] VIII.552
[101] I.167
[102] I.160

so intent on opposing images that they fail to realize that the Scriptures themselves present, in a sense, an image of Christ to us for the purpose of exciting the reader's love to the beauty of Christ. And is it not, after all, appropriate that the basic human susceptibility to the power of images would have been placed in us by God to the end that we become inflamed by them in love for our comely Redeemer, especially when we gaze at the images of the Redeemer that Scripture paints?[103] Owen is suspicious of the misuse of images, even if for different reasons than Grote. But both men want the theological meaning of Christ's historical Passion to be held before the believer in order to transform her in some way, and both seem to suggest that meditating on the event of such a death has a unique power to effect the soul as it captures the imagination.

The *Devotio Moderna*'s Tendency Toward Moralism

In this area of relative agreement between Grote and Owen, one significant difference begins to show itself. While both are skeptical of misused images because of their lack of transformative power, Grote is referring to a behavioral transformation, and Owen to a transformation of affections. It is this moralizing tendency of the *devotio moderna* that keeps it from being in the same nuclear family as Puritan devotion – even if it is in some sense in the same extended family. According to John Van Engen, 'The New Devout accepted a relatively sobering view of man as overwhelmed with evil passions – not much different in practice from that of the Protestant Reformers – but they went on to work so much the harder toward perfect love and harmony as their goal...this much talk about progress...could sometimes become wearisomely moralistic.'[104] And in fact, a shared Augustinian view of human depravity by both the New Devout and the Puritans is answered in very different ways by each movement. The New Devout fought depravity with a call to personal interior reform (over and against the prevailing late-medieval strategy, which was to rely on the redeeming power of particular sensate things like sacraments). The Puritans, on the other hand, sought the solution to their depravity in the personal interior purity of Christ himself, that is, the personal righteousness of Christ as it is forensically applied to them through a personal union (all of which would have seemed to the New Devout like a convenient strategy to avoid real personal transformation of one's own).

And in a related contrast, the New Devout's great emphasis on interiority, which is organically connected to the realist emphasis on the spiritual and transcendent that exists beyond physical particular truths, shows its distance from the Puritan solution to sin, one focused on the

---

[103] I.160

[104] John Van Engen, introduction to *Devotio Moderna*, 30-31.

external world of particulars. In other words, according to the Puritans, the individual Christian's law-breaking is covered by Christ's active law-keeping, on her behalf, as Christ was obeying God's law in the what might be called the historical world of sensate particulars of first-century Palestine. That is, the Puritans (at least those who drew their doctrine from Protestant scholasticism) believed that God declared them righteous actually because of Christ's real world obedience during his thirty-three years on earth. This is not to say that there is no deep interiority to the Puritan devotional models as well. Interiority is certainly a stronger theme with them than the original Reformers, yet the nature of their interior project was to become cognitively and emotionally renewed by an ever deepening awareness of the particular saving acts of Christ done for them, while outside them.

Some of the words of the New Devout themselves may help illustrate these different strategies. The treatise 'John Brinckerink on the Holy Sacrament' asserts an almost proto-Calvinist view of the sacraments when the author writes, 'If we do not receive our dear Lord spiritually, we may also never receive him sacramentally to our salvation.' But he then explains that what he means by his expression is not at all the same 'receiving' that the Reformers or Puritans would later understand as \ resting in Christ's merit: 'This is what it is to receive our dear Lord spiritually: *to persist in all those things that our dear Lord would have us do*, carefully to note whether or not all that we do is born of God, always to see our dear Lord in them and to resist all those faults that create a barrier between God and us...'[105] So, for Brinckerink, to 'receive' the Lord is primarily to stir up our obedience to the Lord. According to Luther's paradigm, this is a classic example of confusing law and gospel, for it describes the benefit that Christ offers the believer as like unto the benefit that a trainer provides an athlete: he prods the runner to improve his skills so that he may finish the race on his own. This is in contrast to the Reformation understanding which portrays Christ finishing the race himself on behalf of the runner.

The impression one gets in reading widely in the *devotio moderna* literature, however, is more varied. Sometimes the movement seems like a direct precursor of the Reformed and Puritan desire to anchor personal devotion on the objective work of Christ *pro nobis*, while at other times it seems a highly strenuous system that views the gospel story as merely the most powerful way to energize the believer toward greater obedience. It is perhaps because the *devotio moderna* was a broad movement that resisted a formal or official theology that such tensions were able to coexist, which allows us to guess that Luther might have been attracted to the

---

[105] John Brinckerink, 'John Brinckerinck on the Holy Sacrament,' in Van Engen, *Devotio Moderna*, 232, emphasis mine.

certain elements which he agreed with, perhaps without encountering the movement's contrary tendencies.

There are certain recurring technical phrases within the literature which help shed additional light on the dominant and sometimes contending themes within the *devotio moderna*.[106] Discussing a few of these phrases has the added benefit of making sure we let the movement speak for itself rather than imposing on it a grid that is alien to it. One very common principle is *resolutio/intentio (een goede opzet maaken)* which meant 'to make a good resolution' as it applied to the decision either to join a congregation of the brothers and sisters, to pray enough, to work enough, or to energetically train in virtues. This emphasis on religious determination was not balanced with nearly as much, if any, teaching on the sovereignty of God above the human will, and as a result there are records of several sisters who were so filled with worry about constantly choosing the right devotional path that they suffered anxiety, depression, or even left the houses. Another principle, *profectus virtutum (in doegeden voert gane*; 'progress in the virtues') sounds a similar theme about what is the final measure of devotional effectiveness. By such an emphasis on moral progress they self-consciously separated their brand of mysticism from that of even some of their favorite authors, such as Bernard, Suso, and Ruysbroeck, who they believed wrongly placed mystical union or the experience of being ravished by God as their final goal.

Counterbalance: The *Devotio Moderna*'s Affective Use of Gospel Imagery to Engage the *Historia Salutis*

The principle of *exercitium (oefning)*, on the other hand, has a very different focus. While the spiritual 'exercise' to which the principle refers is applied to various habits of Christian disciplines, it is most commonly used to refer to a certain meditative technique. Particularly, the *exercitium* was working at the habit of systematically replaying the life and passion of Christ at certain set times of the day and attempting to absorb and relive the story oneself. There is an unresolved modern debate about whether or not this practice was the beginning of the 'methodical meditation' technique that the Jesuits became known for,[107] and perhaps this debate should be extended to include the possible tie to similar strains within Puritan devotion. Certainly this emphasis is rare in its devotional application of the *historia salutis*.

---

[106] See treatment of these and other phrases in Van Engen, *Devotio Moderna*, 28-35.

[107] P. Debongnie, *Jean Mombaer* (Louvain-Toulouse, 1928); and M. Smits van Waesberghe, 'Origine and developpement des Exercices spirituels avant saint Ignace,' *Revue d'ascetique et de mystique* 33 (1957), 264-72, in Van Engen, *Devotio Moderna*, 321.

Consider, for example, passages from *On the Life and Passion of Our Lord Jesus Christ and Other Exercises*. These somewhat lengthy quotations are highly significant for demonstrating the often unacknowledged though admittedly rare emphasis within the movement to connect the details of the plot-line of Christ's Passion to the believer's growth in affective appreciation of the redeeming grace she has received. For each day of the week, the author describes three guided meditations for use at three times during the day – the first upon rising in the morning, the second while hearing mass, and the third when the refectory bell rings for the meal. The first meditation is always on a scene from Christ's early ministry, the second from his Passion, and the third, it seems, on the godly examples of great saints. On Monday the worshipper is to think about

> the last supper which our Lord had with his disciples: how humbly he washed their feet, how after that paschal lamb he consecrated his own most holy body and blood...call to memory some of the special and most loving words from that meal so as to grasp in your heart how much he showed them there...break and chew upon those words with all your strength...now throw yourself to the ground and with the loud voice of your heart and folded hands cry out and say, 'O grieving Lord, how shall I repay you for all you have given me? I will accept the cup of salvation.[108]

On Tuesday,

> Consider, brother, how that sweet and holy little boy was wrapped in vile rags, laid upon straw in a manger, announced by angels to shepherds...raise your voice now in praise and sing with the angels, "Glory in the highest to God" (Lk. 2:14). Then meditate upon the arrest of the Lord, how humbly and freely he who created the heaven and the earth allowed himself to be bound for your sake.[109]

On Wednesday the gaze turns to

> how the boy Jesus was circumcised on the eighth day and how while still so young his holy blood was poured out for you, whereupon he was called Jesus. To this name all spirits, in heaven, on earth, and in hell, bend their knees. When therefore you hear or sing this sweet name of Jesus, reverently bow your head because it is by virtue of this name that you will be saved...Next contemplate how our Lord Jesus was stripped of his clothes, stretched out against a pillar and bound there, wounded and scourged from head to foot, and then how he poured out his holy blood so copiously that those punishing him were able to wash their feet in it, the very blood he had once received from the Virgin, and how he alone, man and God, was born without spot or sin from the pure Virgin Mary and yet willed to be so bitterly wounded and punished for your sake. Thinking upon this punishment and all the other points of his passion, lament deeply and continuously that you are able to

---

[108] Van Engen, *Devotio Moderna*, 191.
[109] Van Engen, *Devotio Moderna*, 192.

> suffer so little for him, and ardently ask that you be ever grateful for all his pain and suffering so that his precious blood may not be lost on you.[110]

And on Friday afternoon,

> consider then all the other things that took place on the cross, beneath the cross and around it, and with all your strength think diligently upon them, as if you stood beneath the cross, *gazing upon and seeing each particular* ... Look into the face of your Christ and see his whole body livid, covered with blood and his five open wounds. Enter them in your heart and have your sins washed in the blood flowing from them. Join your heart to his and be kindled with the fire of his love; taste how sweet is your lord, your spouse and lover.[111]

This sample of the *exercitium* method is powerful in the way that it almost never indulges in the use of what the Modern Devout are often (rightly) accused of doing: reducing all scriptural imagery to its usefulness in improving behavior. Instead, the purpose of 'gazing upon each particular' is, with few exceptions, to make the reality of Christ's life and passion somehow real to the believer as a vivid reminder of his saving love for her, apart from her ability to ever repay Christ's passion. Even Jesus' circumcision is experienced as a foretaste of his later more 'copious' shedding of blood for her on Calvary. The shocking imagery of Friday's meditation on the marred face of the crucified Christ is not to inspire mere guilt or a general humility, but to move the believer to, in a sense, appropriate the wounds of Christ for her own cleansing from guilt. And to what end? The final goal seems to be the renewal of delight and pleasure in communion with the Lord who has so served her. This method is not what the New Devout are known for, yet the example shows the diversity and promise of their exercises. Instead of particular biblical images put into the mind in order to affect the will, they are aimed to first move the affections. In fact, the word *affectus* (*begheerlichheid*) occurs many times throughout the literature when describing the goal of desiring God and delighting in what delights him. This idea is very near the heart of Owen's method, and Puritan devotion in general: letting the truth of Christ's historically demonstrated saving love penetrate the heart, which, in turn, will move the will. Near the end of the treatise are words to this exact effect that might have as well been written by John Owen or Richard Sibbes:

> what is sweeter, what more secure, more pleasing to God, and more consoling to a simple dove than devoutly to tarry in the cleft of the rock, that is, in the wounds of our Lord Jesus Christ? The sweet Lord, your loving spouse, allows you not only to

---

[110] Van Engen, *Devotio Moderna*, 193.
[111] Van Engen, *Devotio Moderna*, 194, emphasis mine.

tarry daily in them, to find delight and rest, but also with that charity by which he was wounded and died, to live each day unto death.[112]

And so, the discipline is to apply daily to one's mind the fact of the wounds that Christ suffered in one's own behalf, to revel in the security and sweetness which those wounds provide, and to then let that sensed love of Christ emanate outwards to other people.

The Imitation of Christ

This balance of mind, affections, and will is not present, however, in certainly the most famous and influential work of the movement, which must be considered in some depth. *The Imitation of Christ* is generally considered to be written, or at least compiled, by Thomas à Kempis (1380-1471), though other theories abound, cases being made for the English mystic Walter Hilton, Grote himself, Bernard of Clairvaux, and even Augustine.[113] Thomas, who was born in the town of Kempis near Cologne, joined a branch of the *devotio moderna* movement that became a legally authorized religious order with a rule, a constitution, and a papal bull – it was called the Windesheim Congregation of the Canons Regular. In 1413 Thomas was ordained as a priest, and two years later hebegan writing what is almost universally acknowledged to be the most widely read book in the history of Christian devotion. By the end of the sixteenth century, the number of printed Latin editions numbered just over one-hundred thirty, and by the end of the seventeenth century, more than two-hundred eighty.[114] So, while the book was over two-hundred fifty years old by the time Owen reached mid-career, it was still gaining in popularity and influence. Interestingly, English translations in the Puritan era were published by both Roman Catholics and Protestants and were thus appreciated by constituencies who seemed to agree on very little else. Amazingly, this thoroughly medieval book of mystical devotion survived the storms of religious controversy in England and remained a popular classic all the way through the seventeenth century. One of the harder questions surrounding this phenomenon is why the Protestants remained so attracted to it. For our purposes, the book illustrates what can happen to a devotional system that has an underdeveloped doctrine of God and a virtually absent sense of God's own saving deeds.

---

[112] Van Engen, *Devotio Moderna*, 203.

[113] A. Ampe, *L'imitation de Jesus Christ et son auteur* (Rome, 1973); and *Thomas à Kempis en de moderne devotie* (Brussels, 1971); Stephanus G. Axters, *De imitatione Christi: een handschrifteninventaris bij het vijfhonderdste verjaren van Thomas Hemerken van Kempen* (Kempen-Niederrhein, 1971); and L.M.J. Delaisse, *Le manuscrit autographe de Thomas à Kempis et 'L'imitation de Jesus Christ* (Brussels, 1956). Listed in Van Engen, *Devotio Moderna*, 316.

[114] White, *English Devotional Literature*, 81.

The *Imitatio Christi* is a very practical manual, and it is of interest to our study of trinitarian devotion that at its outset the book links the doctrine of the Trinity to Christian practice: 'What good does it do to speak learnedly about the Trinity if, lacking humility, you displease the Trinity?'[115] With this kind of check against vain or speculative theologizing about the Trinity, Owen would have heartily agreed, but much of what follows would have utterly frustrated him. The first sentences, in fact, declare quite openly that the reason a believer is to study the life of Jesus is in order that he may learn to imitate his life and habits. For the Puritan mind, this already somewhat moralistic beginning would seem like the first crumbling of what becomes an avalanche of works-righteousness in the rest of the book. For reasons that will be soon be made clear, the devotional model of *The Imitation of Christ* is almost a polar opposite of the Puritan method in general, and even more so that of Owen. An easily comparable topic between Owen and Thomas à Kempis is that of mortification and vivification, the believer's effort to resist the old self and nurture the new self which has been regenerated by the Holy Spirit. For Owen, the engine behind putting-off sin and putting-on righteousness is the believer's meditation on the affective and behavioral implications of the Father's love which sent the Son of God to the cross to bear her sins. Thomas, on the other hand, in a chapter entitled 'On Resisting Temptation' (Bk.1, Ch.13), advises that 'little by little, in patience and long-suffering you will overcome [sin],... in temptations and trials the progress of a man is measured; in them opportunity for merit and virtue is made more manifest.'[116] Here is the *devotio moderna* emphasis on the Christian's strong 'resolution' as the prime *modus* in gaining victory over sin. However, this is truly the *devotio moderna* at its most moralistic pitch, for with the method as here described, the success one gains by use of personal resolution seems almost the sole determiner of spiritual progress. To say that the added incentive to resist sin is the opportunity for merit, which temptation creates, is to go further than most all other writings of the movement in giving moral vigor such an optimistic forecast for success, as well as in giving a direct promise of divine reward. As for vivification, the 'Practices of a Good Religious' (Bk.1,Ch.19) suggests the following morning prayer: '"Help me, O Lord God, in my good resolution and in Your holy service. Grant me now, this very day, to begin perfectly, for thus far I have done nothing."...As one's intention is, so will be one's progress.'[117] As the day begins, the worshipper should consider that his moral slate is blank. Yet, as the hours wear on, her success in personal righteousness is dependent primarily on

---

[115] Thomas à Kempis, *The Imitation of Christ*, trans. Aloysius Croft and Harold Bolton (Nashville: Thomas Nelson Publishers) 2.

[116] Thomas à Kempis, *The Imitation of Christ*, 12-13.

[117] Thomas à Kempis, *The Imitation of Christ*, 18.

the will, with her intention being the prime determiner of success. The role of God is not absent in this endeavor, but is conceived as a more general help to the believer to carry through on what she has resolved to do. One historical question that has faced the student of English devotional history is how John Wesley's preaching on the believer's moral perfectibility could gain so many quick adherents even by 1740, just a generation after the last famous Puritans preachers were dying out. The trajectory of this kind of thinking within the *Imitatio*, however, certainly is toward at least a kind of moral perfectionism. And in light of the vast use which Thomas's work still enjoyed, a fertile seedbed in the mind of many of the Christian populace would have been prepared for the doctrine that Wesley would later develop more systematically. Wesley, as it turns out, praised the *Imitatio* and suggested that his followers meditate on it daily and even translated his own abridged version of it for the use of English Methodists.[118]

Such a strong stress on personal effort rather than on reliance on God's grace, whether grace manifested through the cross, the agency of the Spirit, or however, certainly suggests a moralistic extreme within the *devotio moderna*'s own breadth. But this emphasis is continued even further by Thomas à Kempis, surprisingly, in sections of the book that deal directly with more hopeful themes, such as divine grace, friendship with Jesus, and the place of the cross in the life of the believer. The chapter 'Loving Jesus Above All Things' is a string of exhortations to love him better, to love him more exclusively, and a warning that failing to love him will bring one to loss. Absent is any reason to love Jesus that is rooted in his own worth or inherent 'loveliness,' a word which by contrast is repeated to the point of cliché in Puritan writings. The following chapter, 'The Intimate Friendship of Jesus,' makes no mention of specifically how Jesus has been a friend to the believer, but lays the stress exclusively on how the believer should seek to avoid being a poor friend to Jesus and by doing so offend him: 'you may quickly drive him away and lose his grace, if you turn back to the outside world.'[119] In the most hopeful interpretation of this, Jesus is only as committed to the believer as the believer is to him. One might expect some relief in the chapter entitled 'Appreciating God's Grace,' yet even here grace seems almost conditional on one's appreciation of it: 'the gifts of grace cannot flow in us when we are ungrateful to the Giver, when we do not return them to the Fountainhead. Grace is always given to him who is duly grateful...'[120]

---

[118] John Wesley, *The Christian's Pattern, or an Extract of the Imitation of Christ* (Nashville: Abingdon Press, 1954).

[119] Wesley, *The Christian's Pattern*, 44.

[120] Wesley, *The Christian's Pattern*, 47.

The *Imitatio Christi* eventually treats the devotional use of the crucifixion in the chapter 'Few Love the Cross of Jesus,' yet here too the emphasis is not on the worshipper loving Jesus for the sake of his death, but on encouraging the believer to take up her own cross in order to imitate the sufferings of Jesus. The *imitatio* principle of the book's title is hereby explained: imitating Christ is suffering like Christ as a sign of love for him. To use the image of Jesus' crucifixion in this way, primarily as a devotional call-to-arms for believers to suffer their own crosses, is almost the direct opposite of Puritan (and even most Roman Catholic) manuals on devotion, which instead use thoughts of the cross to remind the believer of what Jesus has suffered for her. 'Many revere his miracles; few approach the shame of the cross,'[121] does not mean for Thomas the shame of the cross as it offends human pride that the Son of God must die to atone for one's flaws, or the shame of declaring that one's Lord was crucified and seemingly died a failure, but it means the shame of undergoing one's own suffering and humiliation as a lover of Christ. It is not that a Puritan would deny the call to suffer for Christ, yet the energy to fulfill such a call tends to be rooted in the believer's coming to terms with the value of Christ's own shame that he experienced in her behalf. Owen treats the topic of why believers should undergo shame for Christ's sake in the following way:

> here lies the foundation of our reason: – If the Lord Jesus Christ, the Son of God, – being engaged purely out of his own love in a work for us poor, vile, sinful worms of the earth, whom he might have left justly to perish under the wrath of God...underwent all these shameful things, and never had a recoiling thought to draw back and leave us to ourselves; have we not an obligation of love, gratitude, and obedience, not to be ashamed of those few drops of this great storm that may possibly fall upon us in this world for the sake of our Lord Jesus Christ?...Oh, that we would persuade our hearts in every duty that this is our state,-- that Jesus Christ stands by, and saith, 'I am not ashamed of you!' God stands by, and saith, 'I am not ashamed to be owned to be your God.' Is this not great encouragement?[122]

So, the Christian's ability and motivation to endure under shameful hardships comes when she is persuaded that the shameful hardship that Christ endured was motivated by his saving love for her. More than that, such a passage is an example of Owen's virtual inability to make great summary statements about Christian duty without a reference to the Trinity. We have no direct mention of the Spirit here, but Owen does manage to slip into the end of this passage that this compelling 'shameless' love comes from not just the Son, but from the Father himself, the very one whose wrath is appeased by his own designs through

---

[121] Thomas à Kempis, *The Imitation of Christ*, 49.
[122] IX.232-33

Christ. Thinking such thoughts melts the affections and results in determination of the will to suffer one's own crosses. This method provides a revealing glimpse of how trinitarian activity can inform various aspects of Christian living. If the topic is how to suffer for Christ, the method for gaining motivation and energy would be to meditate on the distinct love of the Father and the Son that the crucifixion suggests, then to let these thoughts melt the affections toward gratitude and increase one's resolve. The public actions of the Trinity can thus act as the ground for even motivation to suffer well.

Because the *Imitatio* was so well received by various branches of the church over many centuries, we would be surprised if it completely neglected to comment on what Christ actually accomplished on the cross. There is the admission that the path to eternal life was pioneered by Jesus, that, 'He Himself opened the way before you in carrying His cross, and upon it He died for you.' Yet, such thoughts are swallowed up by this human-centered conclusion which would have sent chills up the Puritan spine: 'Behold, in the cross is everything, and upon *your* dying on the cross everything depends.'[123] It appears here that the imitation of Christ is of greater weight than Christ himself. Surprisingly, it has been claimed that Thomas's work should be placed within the Augustinian tradition, and beyond this, that he evidences 'a belief that we are saved by God's grace through faith in Christ alone – and not through our works' as a forerunner of Reformation doctrine.[124] But certainly this is a claim without evidence. To the contrary, this work is too optimistic to be really Augustinian, for while it takes seriously the presence of sin, it is confident in human ability to resist sin if one will only try hard enough. And, as for grace, more often than not it is presented as a reserve of assistance for the believer in her efforts, but definitely not as God's monergystic gift of salvation. The Puritan theology of sanctification, then, was a rebuttal to this exhausting book, not its heir.

Nowhere did Owen respond directly to the *Imitatio* or even mention its author. Owen's placid nature (compared to his contemporaries) when it came to controversial writing means that he often failed to name names when students of history would most like him to have been explicit. The closest he came is to say,

> some men speak of the imitation of Christ, and following his example...but no man shall ever become 'like unto him' by bare imitation of his actions without that view or intuition of his glory which alone is accompanied with a transforming power to change them into the same image.[125]

---

[123] Thomas à Kempis, *The Imitation of Christ*, 50, emphasis mine.
[124] See introduction to Thomas Nelson edition, pp. vii-x.
[125] I.304

In Search of Trinitarian Spirituality

Again, it is the 'view' or representation of Christ's love to the mind which then melts the affections and finally produces a change of resolve. As well, the following text certainly could have functioned as a rebuttal to the *Imitatio Christi*, but equally likely it is a response to the mortification strategies of Arminians, whose similar optimism about the will's ability to resist sin produced, in Owen's mind, a merely vain moral coaching against temptation and sin:

> If it be inquired how the mind may be freed and cleared of these perplexing, defiling imaginations...I say it will never be done by the most strict watch and resolution against them, nor by the most resolute rejection of them. They will return with new violence and new pretences, though the soul hath promised itself a thousand times that so they should not do.[126]

This strikes a genuinely Augustinian note. The fallen mind, because of its depravity, will evade the best resolutions of the will to reform it. In fact, it might be said that if Augustine was impressed by the pervasiveness of personal sin, Owen is more awed by its combination of craftiness and power: when the fully-restored will takes a muscular blow at it, sin only shape-shifts to a more powerful manifestation.

Excursis: Owen's Mechanics of Meditating on the Cross

But the real thing that takes Owen further away from Thomas than Augustine and even Luther is his *use* of the cross, as was very briefly mentioned above. And, in 1688, a treatise of his was posthumously published, with the abbreviated title 'The Dominion of Sin and Grace; Wherein Sin's Reign is Discovered...How the Law Supports It; How Grace Delivers From It, By Setting Up Its Dominion in the Heart,' which functioned to further his cross-centered method. As one might expect, Owen believes in the absolute dominion of sin over the lives of non-believers. Believers, on the other hand, have experienced the conquest of that dominion by Christ, who replaces it with his own loving dominion over their hearts. The sober fact of Christian experience, though, is that the old dominion of sin often temporarily regains the upper hand, sometimes leading the believer to even doubt that Christ has come into him. The solution, that is, the means by which the believer can mortify the indwelling sin that antagonizes him, is through the duty of daily exercising faith on Christ as crucified. When Rom. 6:6-13 speaks of the 'old man' being crucified in Christ, Owen understands this to mean not just that sin of the old self is punished in Christ's death, but that the power of the old self is also killed. How does this translate into a spiritual method? The believer's act of faith in the crucified Christ not only transfers the sin-atoning benefits of the cross to him, but is also the organ

---

[126] VII.522

by which sin-beating power from Christ also flows into him. Therefore, not only does justification come by faith in Christ crucified, but so also does the power of sanctification.

Why does 'looking' at Christ muster actual personal holiness in the life of the faithful observer? Partly because it causes 'holy mourning' over how our ongoing sin caused Jesus to suffer: 'the more believers are exercised in this view of Christ, the more humble they are, the more they are kept in that mourning frame which is universally opposite unto all the interests of sin, and which keeps the soul watchful against all its attempts.'[127] Not only that, but imagining the crucifixion and knowing that Christ was on the tree in order not only to atone for sin but also to subdue sin in us, gives us the motive to righteousness that our will needs: 'shall we keep that alive in us which he died for...? Can we behold him bleeding for our sins, and not endeavour to give them their death-wound?'[128] Meditating on the cross, for Owen, may not be the only tool to which the believer has recourse (he also deals with the use of prayer in this treatise), but it is the primary tool, and is entirely indispensable for holy living. In this counsel, Owen sees himself as pointing to a very different source of spiritual energy than other devotional teachers offer. The spiritually weak

> know not how to make use of Christ crucified to this end, nor how to set themselves about it. Other ways of mortification they can understand. The discipline and penances assigned by the Papists unto this end are sensible; so are our own vows and resolutions, with other duties that are prescribed; but as for this way of deriving virtue from the death of Christ unto the death of sin, they can understand nothing of it.[129]

So, Owen is not just opposing penances as we might expect, but even the usefulness of 'vows and resolutions' in the effort against sin – no other method has the transformative power that the cross has when the Spirit makes it vivid in the mind's eye of the believer.

In terms of other Protestant scholastic thinkers, Owen is in the company of many when he claims that moral progress comes by faith in the same way that justification does. Yet, many of the standard Reformed works are simply much more vague about exactly the psychological mechanics of sanctification which Owen is at such pains to draw out. The Westminster Confession's chapter 'On Sanctification' says that 'they who are effectually called, and regenerated, having a new heart, and a new spirit created in them, are further sanctified, really and personally, through virtue of Christ's death and resurrection, by his Word and Spirit

---

[127] VII.527
[128] VII.528
[129] VII.528

dwelling in them...the several lusts thereof are more and more weakened and mortified.' So, Christ's death is the ground for holy living, and the means are Word and Spirit – but we are still left wondering how these all really drive sanctification. How exactly, on the level of the believer's consciousness, do these realities make their impact on holy living? The expression '*through virtue* of Christ's death' is unspecific. The next chapter in the Confession, on 'Saving Faith,' again asserts the doctrinal claim friendly to Owen that the 'principle acts of saving faith are accepting, receiving, and resting upon Christ alone for justification [and] sanctification,' yet without additional elaboration as to faith's relationship to sanctification. The modern Reformed systematician Louis Berkhof seems to acknowledge this common vagueness within the tradition by admitting that much of sanctification really takes place at a 'subconscious' level by the immediate operation of the Holy Spirit – that is, moral improvement often happens without the believer's own mind being directly involved.[130] Interestingly, one notable precedent for Owen's more concrete psychology of grace occurs not in late Reformed scholasticism but in Ursinus, who was somewhat of a transitional figure between the first-generation Reformers and the later scholastics. His Heidelberg Catechism, question 43 asks, 'What further benefit do we receive from the sacrifice and death of Christ on the cross?' and answers, 'That by virtue thereof our old man is crucified, dead, and buried with him; so that the corrupt inclinations of the flesh may no more reign in us, but that we may offer ourselves unto him a sacrifice of thanksgiving.' As stated, this is still vague. But Ursinus elaborates in his commentary on the Catechism by saying that the death of Christ is in two respects the 'efficient cause' of salvation – the first in respect to God as Christ's death merits the remission of sin (i.e. the cross justifies sinners). But the second efficient cause of his death is in respect to justified sinners; those

> who believe that Christ obtained for us righteousness and the Holy Spirit, cannot be otherwise than grateful to him, which is done by commencing to walk in newness of life. *The application of the death of Christ, and a proper consideration of it, will not suffer us to remain ungrateful; but will constrain us to love Christ in return...the desire to obey God can never be separated from an application of the death of Christ.*[131]

Here is the logic of the death and resurrection of the cross: thoughts of the work of Christ argue the believer toward personal holiness as they soften him to the commands of the one who has already given him everything in his justification.

---

[130] Louis Berkhof, *Systematic Theology* (Grand Rapids: Eerdmans, 1939) 534-35.

[131] Ursinus, *Commentary on the Heidelberg Catechism* (New Jersey: Presbyterian and Reformed, 1852 reproduction) 227, emphasis mine.

THE TWO NOMINALISMS AND JOHN OWEN

Only a few words will be said about the significance of the nominalist *via moderna* and its theologically very different cousin the *schola Augustiniana moderna*. The simple point is that both of these theological schools produced corresponding devotional methods that were still present in seventeenth-century England, and both relied on a particular doctrine of God. While, philosophically, both of these late versions of scholasticism were united in their opposition to the realism of the Thomists and Scotists, they were actually near opposites when it came to doctrines of sin and grace. To its critics, the *via moderna* was simply Pelagian in its view of salvation, and became known for its phrase *facienti quod in se est Deus non denegat gratiam*, 'God will not deny his grace to anyone who does what lies within him.' Interestingly, William of Ockham, perhaps the *via moderna*'s most famous philosophical author, [132] was investigated for suspected heresy by the same Pope John XII who had also condemned Eckhart, though obviously on different grounds. But while Eckhart and other realists have left us with more widely recognized examples of mysticism, that is, of three ascending stages whereby one eventually pierces through the lower earthly regions to a transcendent intuition of God, there remains a way in which even the nominalistic *via moderna* should be understood to have produced its own mystical tradition which stands in opposition to realist mysticism.

The case of Jean Gerson (1363-1429) illustrates this difference. Gerson, chancellor of the University of Paris beginning in 1395, was the prime voice of the *via moderna* when it came to the mystical and contemplative life. Yet, like any nominalist, he made a distinction between God's *potentia absoluta* and his *potentia ordinata*. Thus, since God cannot be known in his absolute nature or potential, the contemplative must focus on the ordinary channels that God has determined to reveal himself. The mystical climax therefore is not an arrival at higher knowledge, which is unattainable, but is a higher affectionate response to what is already revealed. This is a very different kind of mysticism, for it 'is concerned with union with God through the ecstasy of love. The ecstatic soul does not lose its being in the Being of God as a drop of water is dissolved in a cask of strong wine, but retains its identity at the very moment it becomes one spirit with God through conformity of will.'[133] Through heightened senses of love for God, one's will becomes united to his. It is this union of the will, in contrast to an essential union of the soul with the divine in the speculative mysticism of Eckhart, that makes *via moderna* mysticism unique. There is much here for a Puritan to like,

---

[132] Others include Pierre d'Ailly, Robert Holcot, Jean Gerson, and Gabriel Biel.

[133] David Steinmetz, 'Jean Gerson,' in *The Westminster Dictionary*, 173. The image of the drop of water dissolved in a cask of wine is from Eckhart.

especially in the *potentia ordinata* emphasis, which would seem to draw the believer back to Scripture, the covenants, and redemptive history as a means of communing with God, rather than immediate contemplation without such God-ordained particulars. The humble assessment of what is cognitively possible for an epistemic pilgrim, a *viator,* to know about God as well as the emphasis on renewed affections driving the will are also positive connections to Protestant emphases on God's incomprehensibility in himself and his substantial knowability through the normal channels of his self-disclosure.

However, it is ultimately the place given to the will that eventually drove off from the *via moderna* those who were more Augustinian, including those of the *schola Augustiniana moderna* and their Puritan progeny. Gabriel Biel, the *via moderna*'s greatest theological author, was aware of the reigning medieval view that baptism sacramentally infuses the *gratia gratum faciens* (the grace that makes one a friend of God) which is necessary for salvation and which is then is built upon and nurtured by such exercises as *lectio, meditatio,* and *oratio*. However, Biel said that these exercises were the means by which a person can produce within herself such of a love of God, the *gratia gratum faciens,* actually before God infuses such grace himself: 'to be saved, one has to fulfill the law, that is to love God with all his heart...In this way if he does his very best, he will receive immediately at the moment he reaches the point of love for God above everything else this gift of sanctifying grace.'[134] Biel goes on to describe the *gratia gratum faciens* as the birth of Christ in the soul[135] and even states that there is in a sense an inhabitation of the Trinity in the soul of the earnest believer. However, as Oberman notes, 'one is forced to conclude that this communion with Christ is psychological in nature and anthropocentrically determined: it is not an operation of the Holy Spirit but of the spirit of man.'[136] It is in light of this that a judgment can be made about the sometimes suggested proto-Protestantism of Biel. While it is true that he commonly speaks of the doctrine of justification in terms of 'acceptation,' this should not be understood in a forensic sense, as tempting as that interpretation might

---

[134] '*Et hec aliquo modo est nobis in precepto, aliquo modo non. Non est in precepto quantum ad eius infusionem, nam slius dei est eius infusio. Est autem in precepto quantum ad nostram preparationem et eius conservationem: ad scl. faciendum quod in nobis est ut infundatur... Sed quomodo illam charitatem tam necessariam adquirere possumus? Respondetur breviter quod immeditissima ac ultima dospositio ad eam est...actualiter diligere dominum ex toto corde etc.*' from Biel's *Sermones Dominicales de Tempore,* quoted and trans. by Heiko Oberman, *The Harvest,* 348

[135] Biel, *Sermones de festivitatibus christi,* 50 G, (Hagenau, 1510), in Oberman, *The Harvest,* 349.

[136] Oberman, *The Harvest,* 350-51.

be.[137] The acceptation of God of which Biel speaks is not God's declarative act or imputation of righteousness, but a description of the internal habit of grace that brings the Trinity into the soul, after the worshipper succeeds in preparing for and making himself worthy of such an arrival.[138]

Interestingly, the stronghold of the *via moderna* in the fourteenth-century was the University of Oxford, which was also where the first major backlash against the movement began. Thomas Bradwardine, who was later to become the Archbishop of Canterbury, published *De causa dei contra pelagium*, implicating his Merton College colleagues for reviving Pelagianism and also articulating his own soteriology, which revisited the grace-centered emphases of Augustine. On the Continent, Gregory of Rimini further developed these views at the University of Paris and within his own Augustinian Order. This *schola Augustiniana moderna* as it is now known, remained philosophically committed to nominalism while affirming, against the *via moderna*, that human nature is hopelessly captive to sin, that all of the resources for salvation lie outside of the believer, and that God's grace alone can justify. McGrath and Oberman, among others, have debated the degree to and timeframe within which Martin Luther might have been exposed to this school. Yet, regardless of the final answer to such questions, Luther was early on steeped in the *via moderna* and the writing of Biel, but eventually rejected the theology of such in favor of something much closer to the thinking of Bradwardine and Rimini.[139] And the case that Calvin was influenced by the new scholastic Augustinianism is even stronger, suggested by his doctrine of double predestination, his heavy use of Augustine,[140] and even a debatable possibility that when Calvin was at the University of Paris

---

[137] H.S. Denifle, *Luther und Luthertum*, Vol. I (Mainz, 1906) 594.

[138] Biel, *Lectures 31 B* (Basel, 1510), in Oberman, *The Harvest*, fn. to p. 354.

[139] Heiko Oberman, 'Headwaters of the Reformation: Initia Lutheri – Initia Reformationis,' reprinted in *The Dawn of the Reformation: Essays in Late Medieval and Early Reformation Thought* (Edinburgh, 1986) 39-83; and Alister E. McGrath, *The Intellectual Origins of the European Reformation* (Oxford, 1987) 108-15.

[140] Other more controversial evidences of the new Augustinianism in Calvin are his epistemological nominalism, and his voluntarist rather than intellectualist view of the grounds of human merit and the merit of Christ. The voluntarist position is that moral acts have a meritorious value in the eyes of God only to the degree that God chooses to value them, not because of any inherent value (as the intellectualist position holds). Interestingly, even Oxford *via moderna* writers used the voluntarist reasoning to explain why their own view of human merit was not really Pelagian, since the good works they advocated were really not inherently worthy of merit. Calvin, who was no friend of the *via moderna*, used voluntarism to describe how Christ's death was assigned by God, in God's own good pleasure, a value that allowed it to cover the sins of the many (contrary to Luther, who believed that the sacrifice of the God-Man, inherently, had the value to make it efficacious).

he may have been taught by the Scot John Major who would have introduced him to Augustine, Bradwardine and Rimini.[141]

Even more explicit, however, is the connection between Owen and this school, and his direct appreciation of especially Bradwardine, whom he refers to by name as many as one-third the number of times as Owen refers to Calvin himself.[142] Owen indeed was influenced by late medieval scholasticism – one could easily make the case that he shares the philosophical nominalism of other past scholastics who favored Aristotle over the realism of Plato. Yet he is highly critical of the theological nominalism of Biel (among others), who he believes was guilty of 'opening a way to the Socinian error' in his own day by his assertion that acceptance from God did not require the punitive satisfaction of Christ.[143] Additionally, he finds Biel and Ockham at fault for their inadequate view of the grace of regeneration which for them was merely a kind of moral persuasion that 'is able only to excite and draw out the strength which we have' already in ourselves.[144] Theological nominalism, in its original writings and in later generations who repeated the same errors, presented in Owen's mind a risk to the health of devotional purity in his own England. Nathaniel Mather, who wrote the preface to one of Owen's posthumously released discourses on the Holy Spirit, directly credits Bradwardine as not only heroically resisting such scholastic Pelagianism in his own day, but beginning a chain reaction against the perennially recurring Pelagianism in England, a resistance that had been maintained by the early Puritan works of Twisse and Ames (and now at the end of the chain, he implies, by Owen).[145] Late-era Puritans like Mather could therefore see a continuance of the *schola Augustiana moderna* up to their own day as a necessary rebuttal to the worst kind of late scholasticism, yet with merely a more theologically accurate brand of grace-centered scholasticism as the needed agent of restoration. Most of Owen's use of Bradwardine actually comes in what is arguably his own most pastorally-motivated work, *The Doctrine of the Saints' Perseverance*. Owen is at pains to restore in his people the confidence that the same Spirit who provided them habitual grace of regeneration will certainly preserve them in obedience to the end. The counter position, taken in Owen's day by John Goodwin and Henry Hammond, is roughly that believers are responsible to maintain their own salvation, without the direct aid of

---

[141] Karl Reuter, *Das Grundverstandnis der Theologie Calvins* (Neukirchen, 1963); and *Vom Scholaren bis zum jungen Reformator: Studien zum Werdegang Johannes Calvins* (Neukirchen, 1981).

[142] IV.353; VIII.11; XI.21, 22, 63, 68, 69, 70, 71.

[143] II.369. He also here assigns some of the blame to Aquinas.

[144] III.309

[145] III.353

God.[146] As Owen saw it, the present fight within the Catholic Church has resulted in a defeat of the more Augustinian Dominicans who lost their case when Pope Innocent X issued a bull in 1653 (the same year Owen finished his own book) in favor of the more semi-Pelagian views of the Jesuits. Essentially, the battle was over spiritual comfort, and Owen saw its first historically significant melee in Bradwardine's bid to clean up the Pelagianism at Oxford and his successful attempt to convince the pope then of the rightness of his position. While Owen is bitterly opposed to many aspects of medieval scholasticism, in Bradwardine he finds one who rightly used his scholastic methodology in defense of the truths that afford believers lasting comfort, while magnifying the glory of God as the preserver of salvation in his elect. No doubt feeling connected to the man who held essentially the same post at Oxford that he himself did at the time of his writing, Owen was able to use these glowing words that he reserved for very few:

> Among the schoolmen, there is none of greater name and eminency, for learning, devotion, and subtilty, than our Bradwardin, who was proctor of this university in the year 1325, and obtained by general consent the title of Doctor Profundis...concerning the grace of God, and his sovereignty over the wills of men...Bradwardin in his days cried out so earnestly for the defense of God and man against the Pelagian encroachment.[147]

Owen sees himself as a modern day Bradwardine, carrying on his cause for a new generation at Oxford and England at large. For Owen, theological precision about how one is saved – a thoroughly triune grace that freely regenerates and acquits the believer – is required if real rest in God is to be attained, as well as proper motivation to worship God and do his work.

What we have discovered in our historical search are occasional moments of interaction with the Trinity in a history of salvation, yet often the philosophical realism that pervaded such systems made this a tenuous connection that was not fully developed. Theological orthodoxy in a doctrine of God was not absent from the most promising of the medieval traditions of devotion, yet again, it would be difficult to claim that such devotional systems drew significantly from many of the features of the long established theological trinitarianism of the church. Most of the time, we find a form of devotional unitarianism which happens to address God in the mere language of Father, Son, or Holy Spirit, but makes little reference to either ontological or economic distinctions amongst the *hypostaseis*. Philosophical nominalism might seem to offer a promising antidote to the realism of these systems and their downplaying of history,

---

[146] For editorial reference to the more obscure Hammond, see IX.27.
[147] IX.69,70

yet most nominalists ended up advocating a Pelagian view of the human will. Prior to Owen, Bradwardine seems the most promising nominalist because of his theological orthodoxy, but he was too busy fighting to recover an Augustinian doctrine of sin to write much about devotional concerns. If Owen was able to carry some of Bradwardine's theologically orthodox nominalism into the realm of devotion, his efforts would be especially promising in light of our two criteria. We now turn to the theological underpinnings of Owen's trinitarian spirituality.

CHAPTER 4

General Features of Trinitarian Spirituality

One might expect that a spirituality with a highly trinitarian foundation must at some point face the problem with which the doctrine itself contends – how to make sense of the simultaneous three-ness and one-ness of God. Applied to the field of Christian devotion, this problem raises some of the following questions: Do we address our prayers to the unified divine *ousia* or to the three *hypostaseis* distinctively? If distinctively, how should one praise, petition, and offer thanks to the Son differently than the Father or Spirit? And how far may one go in addressing each divine person distinctively without functionally becoming tri-theistic? At this point, John Owen becomes a particularly helpful conversation partner, for these were his own concerns, and he was as much interested in doctrinal orthodoxy as he was devotional practice. Yet, for Owen, true Christian devotion requires the believer to engage in a surprisingly differentiated relationship with each person of the Trinity. Certainly if this claim is within bounds of orthodoxy, a devotional model that is uniquely trinitarian might result. I suggest that without a claim at least something like Owen's, Christian devotion will not easily be able to escape the charge that it is practically unitarian (even if not fully so theologically). But is Owen's reliance on such seemingly strong distinctions within divine activity (and distinct human responses to each *hypostaseis*) really warranted by Western orthodoxy's emphases on divine unity? This chapter will explain and evaluate Owen's basic thesis in light of our first criteria of historic orthodoxy which Owen's assertions might at first seem to challenge. The stakes are somewhat high, for if Owen is found to violate this tradition, it would appear that a trinitarian spirituality different from the mild versions we have already examined may be impossible, at least in the West.

The Dilemma of God's Incomprehensibility and the Solution of Salvation History

Fundamental to Owen's spirituality is the conviction that the believer cannot deeply respond to the Christian God without some level of propositional knowledge about God's trinitarian essence. What is at first striking about such a presupposition is Owen's apparent assumption that

God is, somehow, highly knowable – even knowable in his tri-unity. Outside his Reformation tradition, which asserted the unknowability of God-in-himself, a schema of spirituality so dependent on divine ontology might not be so surprising, but this is a claim made by a man who catechised his parishioners in Fordham with the following questions from his own catechism: 'Do we know God as he is? No; his glorious being is not of us, in this life, to be comprehended,'[1] and in another place:

> Can we conceive these things as they are in themselves? Answer: Neither we nor yet the angels of heaven are able to dive into these secrets, as they are internally in God; but in respect of the outward dispensation of themselves to us by creation, redemption, and sanctification, a knowledge may be obtained of these things, saving and heavenly.'[2]

Owen is making the classic Reformed scholastic distinction between archetypal and ectypal theology, that is, between the partial, mediated knowledge of God possessed by angels and humans, and God's own perfect knowledge of himself. Yet it might still be surprising that in other places he can expect the Christian to know so much about the Trinity (compared to what other devotional writers required) while here he simultaneously teaches about God's inherent unknowability. Two causes have been suggested for his teaching on the incomprehensibility of God.[3] On one hand, God is ungraspable because human rationality and mental capacity cannot lay hold of the immensity and infinity of God's perfections such that 'in itself, the divine nature is hid from all living, and dwelleth in that light whereunto no creature can approach.'[4] We may even detect whispers of the negative theology (*via negationis* or *via negativa*) of Plotinus, Dionysius, and the realist tradition when Owen says, 'What we deny of God, we know in some measure – but what we affirm we know not; only we declare what we believe and adore.'[5]

However, Alan Spence rightly suggests that Owen's somewhat Aristotelian epistemology provides another source of his doctrine of incomprehensibility.[6] Owen held that 'our knowledge of things is more by their operations and proper effects than from their own nature and formal reason. Especially is it so in divine things, and particularly with respect unto God himself.'[7] In other words, things in general, and

---

[1] I.471

[2] I.473

[3] Alan Spence, 'John Owen and Trinitarian Agency,' *Scottish Journal of Theology* 43 (1990), 157-59.

[4] I.45

[5] I.66

[6] Spence, 'John Owen and Trinitarian Agency,' 158.

[7] III.38

especially God, are known by our experience of their activity rather than by some intuition of their essence. However, contrary to others who have argued for Owen's slavish dependence on Aristotle rather than Scripture, it is only fair to listen to Owen's own reasons for such an empirically-driven theology.[8] Owen preempts Aristotle by showing evidence for his view from an older source, Psalm 19:1, 'The heavens declare the glory of God, and the skies proclaim the work of his hands,' as well as the New Testament follow-up, 'since the creation of the world God's invisible qualities – his eternal power and divine nature – have been clearly seen, being understood from what has been made...'(Rom. 1:20). Such a contention, that we know God by our experience of his actions, places Owen in the center of the extremes of his two most regular opponents. Quakers claimed to have an immediate knowledge of God through an 'inner light' which provided a purer knowledge than both inspired Scripture or creation itself could offer (such as what is revealed through the natural theology of Ps.19 and Rom. 1), while the Socinians furthered a program of religious rationalism which especially rejected a doctrine such as the Trinity because it could not possibly be derived by unaided efforts of human reasoning. Contra Quakerism, Owen says that 'as to the being of God, and his subsistence in the Trinity of persons, we have no direct intuition of them, much less comprehension of them,'[9] while to the Socinians he replies, 'the subsistence of his most single and simple nature in three distinct persons, though it raises and ennobles faith in its revelation, yet it amazeth reason which would trust to itself in the contemplation of it – whence men grow giddy who will own no other guide, and are carried out of the way of truth.'[10]

We might say that Owen chides the Quakers for naïveté and the Socinians for pride. The latter sin is surely the worse of the two for him, for Owen seems to acknowledge that the believer's desire to encounter God face-to-face is actually proper, even if it is an impossible hope to requite at this stage of redemptive history. Moses' request to see God's unmediated glory is evidence that such an impulse is devotionally proper (Ex.33:18):

> Glorious evidences [God] gave of his majestical presence, but no appearance was made of his essence or person. Hereon Moses desireth, for the full satisfaction of his soul, (as the nearer any one is unto God the more earnest will be his desire after the full fruition of him,) that he might have sight of his glory – not of that created

---

[8] Alan Clifford and R.T. Kendall make such a critique of Owen; however, Carl Trueman (cf. *The Claims of Truth: John Owen's Trinitarian Theology* [Carlisle: Paternoster Press, 1998]) and Alan Spence are able to agree that Owen uses Aristotelian categories without necessarily abandoning scriptural sensitivity.

[9] I.67

[10] I.65; see also Haykin, 'John Owen and the Challenge of the Quakers.'

glory in the tokens of his presence and power which he had beheld, but of the uncreated glory of his essence and being.[11]

To compare Moses' goal to that of Quakerism, Owen might say that what the Quakers claim they have – direct unmediated knowledge of God's essence – they really do not, nor can any finite creature. But, like Moses, they are at least right to have the desire.

Owen's response to his opponents is to advance a nearly empiricist program of religious knowledge, as Spence puts it, an 'alternative epistemology' which says that we 'come to know the nature of God through his effect on the world of our experience.'[12] In his commentary on Hebrews 1:3, Owen discusses what God had revealed about himself in the early stages of redemptive history:

> But this God, invisible, eternal, incomprehensibly glorious, hath implanted sundry characters of his excellencies and left footsteps of his blessed properties on the things that he hath made; that, by the consideration and contemplation of them, we might come to some such acquaintance with him as might encourage us to fear and serve him, and to make him our utmost end.[13]

Owen is referring to the 'sundry characters' which appear in creation and providence, but which are, in the end, inadequate to bring a person into fellowship with God by themselves. They lack effectiveness specifically in that they are unable to provide the degree of knowledge of God that would be needed for God to become the highest object of human affection (as well as the object of saving faith, love, fear, and obedience).[14] The deeper disadvantage of this partial knowledge is that when God is lesser known by his creatures, he is lesser glorified by them, nor do they come into full enjoyment or 'fruition of him'[15] (and thus, in the Westminster Catechism's way of thinking, the entire 'chief end of man' could never be fully realized).

Does this mean the 'alternative epistemology' of God-revealed-through-experience provides only a meager yield? Not according to Owen, since God had planned a particular historical event that paid an inestimably higher dividend than his previous self-revelations. Here is where, I suggest, the *historia salutis* proves its worth as the way for a believer to gain new depth of knowledge about God – knowledge that is not obtainable any other way, and knowledge that seems particularly relevant to worshipping a God who is distinctively triune. The perfect

---

[11] I.66
[12] Spence, 'John Owen and Trinitarian Agency,' 158.
[13] XX.99
[14] I.69
[15] I.69

representation of God, for Owen, is ultimately found in the historical incarnation of God-the-Son. Christ is the complete image, not of everything that God is, but of that of himself, which he offers to us as the object of our faith.[16] It is likely that though Christ's historical coming was an eye-witness experience only for some, Owen would have believed that the inspired and inscripturated record of Christ's coming makes him a God-revealing experience for anyone who has eyes to see and ears to hear. But, more significant for our purposes, Christ's coming in history provides an experience of God that specifically delivers knowledge of the Trinity itself – and not just as a doctrine *per se*, but truth about God for the sake of our added pleasure in God. It appears that this is the basic progression: the 'new creation' (2 Cor. 4:6) that came as a result of Christ's work is new because, unlike the original creation, the fullness of many of God's attributes is now laid bare before humanity. One such new, clear revelation in Christ is that God exists as three in one: 'There was no one more glorious mystery brought to light in and by Jesus Christ than that of the Holy Trinity.'[17] The manner in which Christ alerts us to God's triune nature is not primarily by giving direct theological propositions about the immanent relations (though Jesus implicitly makes such claims when, in the Gospels, he refers to his dealings with the Father and the Spirit), but when his work shows how God is salvifically at work 'for us, in us, and toward us' as the accomplishment of all divine persons working together (Owen cites Eph.1:4-12).[18] In other words, the Trinity is at last revealed in order to show the sinner clearly how it is that God predestined and then put into action his plan to redeem his people. God's ultimate purpose in revealing himself as triune is therefore to deepen his communion with his people by affecting their hearts with what he has done on their behalf:

> This revelation is made unto us, not that our minds might be possessed with the notions of it, but that we may know aright how to place our trust in him, how to obey him and live unto him, how to obtain and exercise communion with him, until we come to the enjoyment of him.[19]

We might say that a greater and deeper experience of God is now available since, in effect, Christ has drawn back the curtain to show the saint the full nature of God's love for him: the genius of the Father's eternal loving plan revealed to Adam and Eve partially in the *protoevangelium* and then increasingly through successive covenants with Abraham, at Sinai, and with David; the Son's full proclamation and

---

[16] I.69
[17] III.158
[18] III.158
[19] III.158

willing payment of the plan's cost in his state of humiliation and Passion; and the Spirit's multi-faceted application of the Son's merit beginning at Pentecost. Comparatively, non-trinitarian worship looks shadowy and one-dimensional. In this light, it would seem that the doctrine of the Trinity might be the most devotionally suggestive of all Christian doctrines for the way in which it triangulates God's gracious intentions and accomplishments. This is especially so as the Trinity is understood not *in se* but through the lens of its own self-disclosure in historical emplotment. There are aromas of Grote and even the *Imitatio Christi* in this emphasis on knowledge-of-God for the sake of changing the human heart and conduct, but the difference is that the trinitarian plot-line announces, and calls the believer back to, what God has already accomplished and provided in actual fact. Communion and even obedience is deepened out of a fairly spontaneous human response to God's elaborately planned and executed rescue mission (not a mere moral call-to-arms or appeal to duty) and such human responses are even, in a sense, given by God with the aim that we would be restored first to an especially pleasurable personal communion with him.

Owen's Dual Affirmation and the Point Where Speculation Yields to Devotion

But is it logically consistent for Owen to simultaneously affirm the indivisibility of divine work as well as the distinctness of the Son's and the Spirit's personal projects? The legitimacy of this dual affirmation hangs on the validity of a distinction Owen sees in external trinitarian activity: 'we must consider a *twofold operation* of God as three in one. The *first* hereof is absolute in all divine works whatever; the other respects the economy of the operations of God in our salvation. In those of the first sort both the working and the work do in common and undividedly belong unto and proceed from each person.'[20] So, beyond a general kind of unity in all of God's external actions, a second type of trinitarian activity includes 'those operations which, with respect to our salvation, the Father, Son, and Holy Spirit do graciously condescend unto,'[21] and in these cases a real distinction exists between each person's work. The pre-incarnate work of the Son, for example, is undivided from the work of the other persons because in such activity the Son is operating purely on the basis of the same divine nature which he shares with the Father and the Spirit. At this point it is still important to note that the Son's pre-incarnate work, as well as all other non-redemptive work accomplished by the Father and the Spirit, can still be appropriated to one individual person

---

[20] III.198
[21] III.198

without, in Owen's mind, positing a real distinction in their agency. In other words, the different subsistences of the persons within the immanent Trinity leave their special imprint on God's external work, but not in such a way, for example, that the work of creation can be credited to the Father and not to the Son. This way of recognizing some level of hypostatic agency was always allowed for by the Western doctrine of appropriations, and so here Owen is surely uncontroversial. However, the kind of distinction in operations that Owen believes the doctrine of appropriations recognized is less dramatic than the much more substantial distinction of activity that he believes takes place when each member of the Godhead takes up his unique role in the project of saving sinners. The work of redemption proves to be a very different kind of work that stretches the otherwise proper boundaries of the doctrine of appropriations. That the Father and the Son, somehow, had different involvement in creation is in some sense very different from the deeper distinction of their activity when the Son leaves the Father's side and humbles himself to take human nature so that he can act as mediator between the Father and human beings. If God's salvific work reveals a whole new category of distinction between the labor of the Father and the labor of the Son, then we are also justified to look for unique ways in which the Spirit is also at work in salvation (and such is Owen's project in much of his massive treatment of the Spirit – over one thousand pages in the Goold edition of his work, and thus, a much deeper analysis than he gives to either the Father or the Son). According to Spence, Owen holds together his dual affirmation of the divisibility/indivisibility of divine action by making the claim that,

> the indivisibility of the external divine operations applies to the trinitarian persons only as they are considered as divine persons absolutely and not as they condescend to their particular offices in the work of our salvation.[22]

Here now is a link between salvation history and trinitarian agency that I propose will become very useful as a foundation for devotional acts, for only by attending to the drama of redemption will the believer see how her God is an irreducible Trinity. Even given such a promising formulation of trinitarian agency, an Owen investigator is left wanting a more thorough explanation of his somewhat novel assertion. What is the exact difference between the distinction in divine involvement that the doctrine of appropriations allows in any of God's works, and the distinction Owen saw in God's works of redemption? To say that the former distinction (that is to say, between each person's role in the work of creation) is rooted in the order of divine subsistence still does not identify the heart of the difference, for even the latter distinction in redemptive work must still be based, at some level, on the order of

---

[22] Spence, 'John Owen and Trinitarian Agency,' 168.

subsistence. To put the question another way, if the Son and the Father can be said to have such exclusive roles in salvation, then what within God's ontology prevents us from identifying the same kind of exclusive roles in creation? Must we say that when the Spirit hovered over the primordial waters in Genesis 1 that he was not as uniquely at work as when he appeared at Pentecost? Why would God's ontology effect his work in creation in a different way than his work of redemption?

Ultimately, it appears that Owen does not answer these questions. Possibly, in a spirit like Calvin's who resisted the temptation to press too far into the secret councils of the divine decree, Owen may simply have wanted to avoid speculation about the divine essence. In fact, it would be hard to imagine him further connecting the distinctions in hypostatic saving actions to essential distinctions in the Godhead without, truly, brushing very close to at least mild tritheism. Certainly, for Owen, Socinianism would have been a ready example of the sad result when human reason demanded mathematical exactness about the Godhead. He would not likely risk the similar mistake of backing his way into a violation of Nicene and Chalcedonian orthodoxy by risking answers to questions about God's work to which scripture does not even allude.

An additional and more explicitly stated reason that Owen stops looking for answers may be that he has already gone far enough to secure his primary goal whenever he speaks about the Trinity – the goal of providing food for devotion, not for mere notional knowledge. After he describes the order of the accomplishment of salvation as 'made necessary from the order of subsistence'.[23] of the Father, Son, and Holy Spirit, he reminds us that the point of his whole discussion is that 'this instructs us in the way and manner of the *communion* we have with God by the gospel; for herein the life, power, and freedom of our evangelical state do consist.'[24] A Christian's acts of devotion mirror the acts of grace extended to him in the trinitarian economy:

> as the descending of God [the Father] towards us in love and grace issues or ends in the work of the Spirit in us and on us, so all our ascending towards him begins therein; and as the first instance of the proceeding of grace and love towards us from the Father is in and by the Son, so the first step that we take towards God, even the Father, is in and by the Son. And these things ought to be explicitly attended unto by us, if we intend our faith, and love, and duties of obedience should be evangelical.[25]

How can prayer 'explicitly attend' to such realities? From what follows in chapter five, it is clear that Owen wants the Christian to begin her

---

[23] III.198-99
[24] III.199
[25] III.200

communion with God in a kind of prayerful appropriation of the Spirit, whose unique gift is to deliver the fruits of the Son's mediation. Aware and thankful that the Son's merits are her sole credentials, she then moves prayerfully toward the Father, desiring to experience his love. In a sense, the Christian's devotional duty is to speak to the divine persons in the corresponding way that each person is himself active in the Godhead's project of redemption. It appears that in Owen's dual affirmation, the 'one-ness' of God theologically anchors all devotion as to a unified divine nature, while the 'threeness' of divine agency forms the actual structure and rhythm of prayer. Just as in our own proposal, a link appears between God's threeness and God's public saving work, and does so in such a way as to fundamentally program devotional response. The threeness of God, especially evident in his threefold *activity*, is what really promises to shape devotion to a trinitarian God.

But how well does such a sharp threefold distinction in divine activity in salvation projects fit within traditional orthodoxy? Certainly, this is a somewhat novel emphasis in the West – but is it too novel to satisfy our first criterion? If so, then what we have said about the particular usefulness of salvation history for the devotionalist is also called into question, and also, it seems, the real possibility of a thoroughgoing trinitarian devotion itself. All to say, if the *hypostaseis* cannot be prayerfully addressed respecting what the drama says about their distinct roles in salvation's accomplishment, then we may be stuck with a practically unitarian devotion after all.

Owen and the History of One-ness vs. Three-ness

Spence suggests, rightly, I believe, that Owen's clear dual affirmation (the general works of God being indivisible, while the saving works being more divisible) overcame an impasse in traditional trinitarian thinking. Drawing on James Mackey, Spence argues that the problem of an overly strict emphasis on divine unity (vs. tri-unity) began as early as, surprisingly, the Cappadocians.[26] Mackey's argument is worth considering since it is rare in recent discussions to fault the Cappadocians for a problem that is usually blamed on Augustine and his *failure* to appropriate Cappadocian thinking.[27] To defend the propriety of using the *homoousios* with reference to the Spirit, the Cappadocians argued that the Spirit's deity is proven by Scripture's nonchalant attribution of his work to other persons of the Godhead. This tendency to ground the proof of

---

[26] Spence cites James Mackey, *The Christian Experience of God as Trinity* (London: SCM Press Ltd., 1983) 149-52.

[27] Colin Gunton, *The Promise of Trinitarian Theology*; and John Zizioulas, *Being as Communion: Studies in Personhood and the Church* (Crestwood, New York: St. Vladimir's Seminary Press, 1985).

the Spirit's deity in biblical texts which focus on the Spirit's outward work finally culminated in Gregory of Nyssa's formula, 'the one-ness of their nature must needs be inferred from the identity of their operations.' The result was that the best biblical ground for the distinctions between the persons, the *opera ad extra*, was pressed into service for the very opposite argument – the different outward works were now used to prove the unity of the divine essence. Henceforth, in order to draw distinctions between the persons, the Cappadocians were forced to resort to using aspects of the subordinationist model for the Trinity, which the *homoousios* doctrine had been formulated to replace.

The unfortunate and explicit development of the doctrine of the indivisibility of the actions of the persons, though, begins with Athanasius, who asserted that the divinity of the Spirit could be demonstrated by his unity with the work of the Word: 'For not that the Spirit is separate from the Word, but by being in the Word, he is in God through him.'[28] Basil of Caesarea further pressed this link between the Spirit's divinity by saying that 'in all things the Holy Spirit is inseparable and wholly incapable of being parted from the Father and the Son.'[29] His evidence for close connection between the Spirit and the Son was that the Gospel accounts regularly mention the presence and involvement of the Spirit in various earthly actions of Christ. Since by this time, the *homoousion* had already been recognized in regard to the Son, any close linkage between the Spirit and the Son therefore functioned to vouch for the Spirit's divinity as well. The theme developing was an apologetic for the Spirit's divinity based on the *opera ad extra* of the Spirit and the Son. Gregory of Nazianzus continued this tradition:

> But now the swarm of testimonies shall burst upon you from which the Deity of the Holy Ghost shall be shown to all... Look at the facts: Christ is born; the Spirit is His Forerunner. He is baptized; the Spirit bears witness. He is tempted; the Spirit leads Him up. He works miracles; the Spirit accompanies them. He ascends; the Spirit takes His place.[30]

In Spence's argument, the action of the Spirit in Gregory's thought is only closely linked with that of the Son, but not yet inseparably identified with it; the Spirit and the Son still remain distinct agents even though they

---

[28] G.A. Egan, *The Armenian version of the letters of Athanasius to Bishop Serapion concerning the Holy Spirit*, Studies and Documents 37 (Salt Lake City: University of Utah Press, 1968), 205, in Spence, 'John Owen and Trinitarian Agency,' 168.

[29] Basil, *de Spiritu Sancto* xvi 37, *The Nicene and Post-Nicene Fathers*, second series, vol. 8 (Grand Rapids: Eerdmans, 1978) 23, in Spence, 'John Owen and Trinitarian Agency,' 168.

[30] Gregory of Nazianzen, *Orations* xxxi 27, *The Nicene and Post-Nicene Fathers*, second series, vol. 7, (Grand Rapids: Eerdmans, 1983) 327, in Spence, 'John Owen and Trinitarian Agency,' 168.

are involved in the same type of work. It took Gregory of Nyssa to finally take Cappadocian thought to the damaging next step. He warns, 'Suppose we observe the operations of the Father, of the Son, of the Holy Ghost, to be different from one another, we shall then conjecture, from the diversity of the operations, that the operating natures are also different.'[31] So, Gregory argues that if we insist on a difference of operation then we will be forced to conclude that there is a difference in divine nature. Since this is an obviously false conclusion, we must resolve that, since the Son and the Spirit have the same divine nature, their external actions can in no way be divided.

The resulting doctrine of the absolute indivisibility of divine actions finally 'became a part of Western orthodoxy primarily through the work of Augustine, who consistently developed some of its implications.'[32] Indeed, the doctrine that Gregory of Nyssa seems to have merely backed himself into is stated in bold affirmations by Augustine: 'just as Father and Son and Holy Spirit are inseparable, so do they work inseparably.'[33] It is through this principle that Augustine interprets the tough New Testament passages which seem, at the surface, to prove the possibility of independent actions amongst the divine persons. For example, of the several occasions when the Father's voice is heard during Jesus' ministry – Jesus' transfiguration on the mountain, his baptism, when the Father assures Jesus that he will glorify his own name (Jn.12:28 'I have glorified it, and will glorify it again.') – Augustine quickly makes the qualification, 'Not that the voice could be produced without the activity of Son and Holy Spirit (the triad works inseparably); but it was produced to manifest the person of the Father alone.'[34] So, even apparently distinct actions of one member are really the action of all members working together, even if only one member is uniquely manifested (as per the doctrine of appropriations).

Further, for Spence, 'Augustine was also unwilling to grant reality to the *ad extra* acts of the divine persons towards one another,'[35] illustrated most vividly in the Scripture's affirmation that the Father sends the Son into the world. Since the sending of the Son is a divine act, for Augustine it is not just an act of the Father but of all the divine persons. This would perhaps awkwardly suggest that somehow the Son also prays to himself when he prays to the Father, and that along with the Father he also sends himself into the world. Spence concludes that 'for Augustine and those within his trinitarian tradition any relation between the divine persons

---

[31] Basil, *Letters*, d. 189 6, *The Nicene and Post-Nicene Fathers*, second series, vol. 8, 231, in Spence, 'John Owen and Trinitarian Agency,' 168.

[32] Spence, 'John Owen and Trinitarian Agency,' 170.

[33] Augustine, *On the Trinity*, 70.

[34] Augustine, *On the Trinity*, 110.

[35] Spence, 'John Owen and Trinitarian Agency,' 170.

which has respect to the economy of salvation is ruled out'[36] and quotes Barth as a modern representative of that tradition:

> Can we really think of the first and second persons of the triune Godhead as two divine subjects and therefore as two legal subjects who can have dealings and enter into obligations one with another? This is mythology, for which there is no place in a right understanding of the Trinity as the doctrine of the three modes of being of the one God...[37]

It is easy to see from this why Barth would have difficulty with Covenant Theology, especially its Covenant of Redemption, which shows the Father entering into a *pactum* with the Son – that those for whom the Son suffered would be granted to him. Perhaps, however, Barth's virtual modalism in this passage goes further than Augustine would have himself. Augustine seems not to deny that the Father and the Son can enter into relations with each other, but merely that any difference between their actions must be explained by the doctrine of appropriations and not by suggesting that the Father and Son are two absolutely independent actors. Spence, of course, rightly identifies Augustine's heavy reliance on appropriations when he cites an example from *De Trinitate*: 'Since, then, that the Son should appear in the flesh was wrought by both the Father and the Son, it is fitly said that He who appeared in that flesh was sent, and that He who did not appear in it, sent Him.'[38] The one potential mistake of this critique, however, is to turn the first half of a statement such as this into proof that Augustine opposed any unique operations among the divine persons, for he at least acknowledged that the Father did not himself 'appear in the flesh.' There is a temptation in Owen scholarship to find in Owen a radical figure who challenges an entrenched monolithic view of God that the West has suffered with since Augustine. But to say this may be to overly define Owen in relief to Augustine. Certainly Owen recovers 'three-ness' themes in a way that makes him perhaps the most explicitly trinitarian writer of his community. Certainly he pushes the limits of the doctrine of appropriations to show just how diverse are the divine works in the economy of salvation. And certainly, he does these things in ways that Augustine did not. However, we must be careful not to pit Owen against Augustine in all cases merely because of the latter's tendency to argue for divine unity.

---

[36] Spence, 'John Owen and Trinitarian Agency,' 171.
[37] Karl Barth, *Church Dogmatics*, IV/1, 65, in Spence, 'John Owen and Trinitarian Agency,' 171.
[38] Spence uses a different translation: Augustine, *On the Trinity*, pt. II, vol. 9, *The Nicene and Post-Nicene Fathers*, first series, vol. 3 (Grand Rapids: Eerdmans, 1980) 50.

Though Augustine stresses the unity of action (based on unity of will), he is not beyond showing the various ways each person was involved in the sending of the Son. For example, he believes that the Holy Spirit is somehow uniquely responsible for the 'conception' aspect of the incarnation.[39] As for the exact manner in which the Father sent the Son, we cannot be sure, he admits, except to say that 'whichever way it was done'[40] it was done by the Father's word, that is, the Word – the Son himself. The exact mechanics of the sending are thus hidden from us, allowing us only the conviction that, somehow, 'it is by the Father and the Son that the Son was sent.'[41] The 'whichever way' vagueness of Augustine's view of the unity of divine action prevents us from saying that his firmness about the unity of the divine will would altogether rule out Owen's recognition of the 'two-fold operation of God' as has been described earlier.[42]

Augustine has become a somewhat embattled figure of current trinitarian scholarship, and the outcome of such battles impinge on the question of to what degree Owen was bucking Western trinitarianism, on which Augustine has clearly had profound influence. The most expert critic of Augustine's doctrine of the Trinity was Colin Gunton, a modern trinitarian scholar of great insight who, with some danger of oversimplification, posited the forgotten Cappadocian view of the Trinity as the remedy to the malaise of Western theology caused by Augustine. One area of concern for Gunton was the historical development within the church of views about the ontology of divine personhood. The scriptural testimony about a God who is somehow three-in-one raised the question for the ancient church of the identity of the inherent nature of a *hypostasis*. The Cappadocians settled on the discovery that personal being is constituted by its relationality or communion with other personal beings, a point that Gunton says Augustine missed altogether.[43] The Godhead is comprised of truly three persons, 'beings whose reality can only be understood in terms of their relations to each other, relations by virtue of which they together constitute the being (*ousia*) of the one God.'[44] Two things are thus accomplished:[45] on one hand, it is now possible to distinguish between the one-ness and three-ness of God, for

---

[39] Augustine, *On the Trinity*, 103
[40] Augustine, *On the Trinity*, 103
[41] Augustine, *On the Trinity*, 103
[42] III. 198
[43] Gunton, *Promise*, 83-99. Gunton also frequently credits John Zizioulas, in particular his *Being as Communion*.
[44] Gunton, *Promise*, 71-72.
[45] Noted by Brad Green, 'Did Augustine's Trinitarian Theology Lead the West Astray?: A Look at a Contemporary Trend in Theology,' paper delivered at 51st meeting of the Evangelical Theological Society, November 17-19, 1999, Danvers, Massachusetts.

'the Christian God can be thought of as triune without loss to his unity,'[46] while secondly, 'a new ontology is developed: for God to be is to be in communion.'[47] In contrast, Augustine's ontology, it is said, was largely derived from Aristotle's view that each thing has both a substance, which determines its identity, as well as accidents, which are its non-essential properties. The result is that the essence of God for Augustine was a timeless substance which underlies the three persons as accidents, rather than the *ousia* being the communion of the persons itself.

Without doubt, Gunton's analysis is immensely helpful in its reappraisal of themes long-forgotten in the West, though Brad Green rightly suggests that Gunton is perhaps too hard on Augustine for the following reasons.[48] First, Augustine dedicates considerable space in *De Trinitate* to discussing the issue of 'missions,' that is, the sendings of the Son and Spirit for redemptive purposes.[49] Since, for Augustine, the temporal missions reveal the eternal processions in the Godhead, the economic Trinity therefore reveals the immanent Trinity, and, therefore, the very ontology of the Godhead. So, Augustine is clear about a threeness of persons that is truly basic to the Godhead. Edmund Hill has similarly noted in Augustine that, 'The sendings of the Son and the Holy Spirit reveal their eternal processions from the Father (and the Holy Spirit's procession as well), and thus reveal the inner trinitarian mystery of God.'[50] So while in some cases the problem may have been overstated by Gunton, it is true that Owen provides a contrast against a tendency in the West to relegate distinct hypostatic operations to a place only within the immanent Trinity rather than in public acts in salvation history. Owen's epistemology moves him toward this point prior to any direct exegesis of classical trinitarian texts: knowledge of the ineffable God comes only mediately, that is, through his observable actions rather than through intuition or reason.[51] Owen thus follows Basil's declaration, 'we know God from his operations.'[52] And yet, perhaps going even beyond the Cappadocians, Owen was convinced that it is only by seeing the distinction between the external works of the Father, Son, and Holy Spirit that we know God to be fully triune, since the distinction in activity not only testifies to the triune unity of God but to his triune diversity.[53]

---

[46] Gunton, *Promise*, 39.
[47] Gunton, *Promise*, 39
[48] Green, 'Augustine's Trinitarian Theology,' 1-18
[49] Augustine, *On the Trinity*, book ii ch.2 and near the end of book iv.
[50] Edmund Hill, *The Mystery of the Trinity* (London: Geoffrey Chapman, 1985) 89, in Green, 'Augustine's Trinitarian Theology,' 15.
[51] Spence, 'John Owen and Trinitarian Agency,' 171
[52] Basil, *Letters*, esp. 234 1, *The Nicene and Post-Nicene Fathers*, second series, vol. 8, 274.
[53] Spence, 'John Owen and Trinitarian Agency,' 172

Three direct and related consequences of such a high view of the Trinity in action are found in Owen's soteriology, his famous work in pneumatology,[54] and his christology.[55] Soteriology itself becomes expressively, outwardly trinitarian when it is recognized that God not only plans for the salvation of his people in an immanent transaction as per the Covenant of Redemption of Reformed scholasticism, but also as God procures and applies salvation in distinct public works of the Father, Son, and Holy Spirit. Owen's high pneumatology is also no surprise, for though the Spirit is ultimately indivisible from Father and Son, he is a distinct person engaged in his distinct redemptive tasks and can therefore be related to by worshippers as such. An unqualified indivisibility doctrine, by contrast, has a more difficult time explaining why the Spirit is not merely an undifferentiated force or impersonal agency.

To notice a real distinction between the work of the Spirit and the Son, in addition, effects christology by describing Christ as one who was filled with the fulness of the Godhead in the person of the Son, and who also received the Spirit for his earthly life and work. This means that Christ must be interpreted in both incarnational and inspirational categories, that is, in relation to the Son and the Spirit respectively.[56] Spence's observation of this dual affirmation is tremendously helpful, for it shows the value of Owen's firmness about distinctions in divine operations for the rest of theology, and by extension, devotion. The historical and conceptual placement of such an Owenian 'two-sided' christology is between the patristic era's dominant use of merely incarnational categories in which to describe Christ – at the expense of seeing Christ as dependent and empowered by the Spirit to accomplish his mediatorial tasks – and the Antiochene model, which understood the value of Christ's anointing by the Spirit, but did so in such a way as to sometimes conceive of the eternal Word's relationship to Christ's humanity merely in terms of indwelling and inspiration, thereby endangering the doctrine of the incarnation, and thus, the unity of the person of Christ himself.[57] Conclusions about the value of this two-sided christology will be made in chapter six. Interestingly, Owen's high economic trinitarianism thus guards a high christology and a high pneumatology by preventing the work of either the Son or the Spirit from collapsing under the other. In all, while Owen's trinitarian theology remains clear about God's unity, it sees a distinction in divine operations, not merely in the immanent Trinity, but in the public works of God in redemptive history. The more a believer sees distinct acts of each person of the Godhead as it executes the

---

[54] Vols. III and IV

[55] Vol. I especially

[56] Spence, 'John Owen and Trinitarian Agency,' 172.

[57] Spence, 'John Owen and Trinitarian Agency,' 172-73; and Spence, 'Inspiration and Incarnation,' 52-55.

plan of salvation, the more she is aware of how she has been loved by each person, and can return that love in equally *hypostasis*-specific ways.

Connecting Theology to Doxology: What is Communion with God?

To speak of 'communion with God' is a common phrase in the history of devotional practice, and the way various traditions define the phrase is illustrative what it considers the heart of its aims. But if the doctrine of the Trinity is true in its historical formulation, and if this Trinity is known primarily through its particular self-disclosure in saving events, how might a basic definition of communion with God be properly affected? Answering this question will give a broad definition to the goal of Christian devotion from the perspective of our two criteria. Owen's logic is worth following for the way he tries to describe communion with God, for it is more adequately trinitarian than other traditions we have examined.

The central work in which Owen expounds his ideas about the Trinity is a treatise published in 1657, the title of which perfectly states the work's unique thesis: *Of Communion with God the Father, Son, and Holy Ghost, Each Person Distinctly, in Love, Grace, and Consolation; Or, The Saint's Fellowship with the Father, Son, and Holy Ghost Unfolded.* In common with other works of Reformed dogmatics, this work contains, to some degree, a theology of *ad intra* trinitarian relations.[58] More significantly, however, the author contends that each person of the Trinity relates in a distinct way to the individual believer. What this means is that any movement of God towards his people, whether it be through propositional revelation, through the grace of regeneration, justification, or sanctification, through divine intercession, or whatever, all movement of God towards his elect may be profitably designated as flowing *primarily* from one of the Father, the Son, or the Holy Spirit. Each person of the Trinity thus relates to the Christian 'distinctly.' As has been mentioned above, Owen interprets these distinctives in stronger terms than in the standard doctrine of appropriations. The purpose here is to explain and analyze Owen's claim that the believer relates in a different way to each divine person, and to ascertain the nature of those differences.

Owen breaks new ground in two ways – first, by emphasizing the Trinity as the foundational substructure upon which is constructed almost the entirety of Christian soteriology, and second, as will be explained more fully in this section, by showing how the Christian's devotional

---

[58] Cf. Musculus' *Loci Communes*, Vermigli's *Loci Communes*, Beza's *Tabula Praedestinationis*, Ursinus' *Doctrinae Christianae Compendium*, Zanchius' *De Tribus Elohim*, and Perkins' *A Golden Chaine*.

response to God takes on a distinctively trinitarian shape. These are the features that properly designate Owen as perhaps more explicitly trinitarian than other Western theologians who might have essentially agreed with his basic soteriology and doctrine of God. For Owen, all of God's redemptive activity is trinitarian, and all of the Christian's communion with God is correspondingly trinitarian.

Before a defense can be made of the possibility of human 'communion with God' as particularly triune, it will be helpful to understand what Owen means by the phrase. To speak very generally, communion describes the joint participation of two or more persons in a common nature, condition, or action.[59] All human beings, for example, have a kind of *communion of nature* with one another in the sense that they share in 'flesh and blood' (Heb. 2:14). In a different sense, a *communion of condition* occurs when two persons simultaneously experience the same existential state. Christ, for example, shared such communion with the two thieves with whom he suffered crucifixion. Further, those who celebrate the worship of God together can be said to have a *communion of action* 'in the gospel' (Phil 1:5).

Communion with God, however, is entirely unique and must for that reason actually *exclude* certain elements of the general definition. The main reason for this, perhaps, is that while a human being has natural communion with other humans with whom she shares a common nature, there is nothing natural about her communion with God. Why? Human nature, as fallen, is sinful and corrupted. The thought of approaching God will thus *naturally* lead to 'terror and apprehensions of death at the presence of God,' not, certainly, to safe personal dealings with him.[60] It is not just that human-nature and divine-nature are separate principles, but that they are, in the current state of affairs, sharply opposed to one another. Furthermore, Owen is sure that there is no overlap between even the existential states experienced by a human and God. Thus, humans can have no communion of condition with him. Owen is presumably referring to the transcendence and impassability of God, who could not share in the ever-shifting conditions inherent in spacio-temporal existence. At this point, of course, he is speaking of God prior to the incarnation, an event which, as we shall see, opens up entirely new possibilities for divine-human communion. In general, though, the chasm between God and fallen humanity cannot be overestimated.

Owen goes as far as to cite Aristotle to show that the infinite disparity between God and man prevents friendship between the two.[61] The reference is from *Nichomachean Ethics*, and its meaning to Owen

---

[59] II.8
[60] II.8
[61] Aristotle, *Nichomachean Ethics*, book viii, ch.7. cited in II.8.

becomes clear as we translate a slightly broader passage than his original citation:

> in all friendships, where one party is superior, the affection also ought to be proportionate... this is evident if there is a great distance between the parties in virtue, or vice, or wealth, or anything else: for they are then no longer friends, and they do not even expect it. This is most evident in the case of the gods, for they are most superior in all goods...they who are very inferior do not presume to be friends with them.[62]

For Aristotle, the degree of affection between two friends ought to be proportional to how much they have in common. Specifically, this meant that the friend with greater status should be loved more than he himself loves the lesser. What makes one person greater than the other is sometimes civil authority (a king vs. his subject), sometimes familial authority (a father vs. his son), but can also be a quality of the personality itself, i.e. virtue. In Aristotle, Owen found a pagan author who understood the ultimate delimiters of friendship between God and humanity: authority and virtue – for God has both these qualities, *ad infinitum*, beyond his creatures. The emphasis for Owen, however, was on what we might call the 'virtue defeater' more than the 'authority defeater' for friendship, for while in some sense God's kingliness prevents him from being approached as one would approach a neighbor, the central miracle of the gospel is about how particularly unvirtuous subjects are still given a kind a free access to his throne.

So, while God and humanity stand ontologically distant from each other, the main roadblock to their communion is ethical. There is nothing here of the future Deistic concept of a God who is distant and unreachable merely because he decides to be, as per one deist's declaration about God's refusal to meddle with his own world: 'it is greatly improbable that God should especially interpose to acquaint the world with what mankind would altogether do without.'[63] Rather for Owen, God is distant because the covenant-breaching impurity of humanity has required it. Adam and Eve, while in the Garden, were the first to dismiss God – and they did so knowingly. Since then, humankind carries on this tradition of breaking the Covenant of Works because of humanity's corrupted nature. Humanity either stubbornly suppresses what knowledge of God may be naturally available,[64] or in keeping closer

---

[62] Based on R.W. Browne's translation, *The Nichomachean Ethics of Aristotle* (London: George Bell and Sons, 1875) 215-16.

[63] Thomas Chubb, *Deism Fairly Stated* (London, 1744) 35, in John Leland, *A View of the Principal Deistical Writers That Have Appeared in England in the Last and Present Century* (London: T. Tegg and Son, 1837) 204.

[64] Rom. 1:18ff

to the precedent of its Edenic predecessors, flagrantly denounces God, as it were, to his face.

Perhaps the main point of the entire Bible, for Puritanism, was that despite this major derailing, friendship with God can be regained. The Son of God, in his incarnation and death, fulfills the Covenant of Works with his own obedience to the Father, purchases the right for sinners to be renewed in their communion with the Father, and then distributes this gift by means of the Holy Spirit. Later, we will explore Owen's view of the diverse mediatorial role of Christ as not just the purchaser of redemption, but as the 'personal' source of salvific grace as well. In short, the Bible is all about how Jesus Christ has solved the crisis of communion. This may prompt the question, if communion with the Father comes through Christ and, more particularly, to those who exercise faith in Christ, then what of the pious Israelites who lived prior to Christ's coming? Was intimate relation with God impossible before Christ came to lead the way in? For Owen, the experience of communion with God is, in fact, described in the Old Testament, yet the details of its christological source and shape are only revealed in shadows. While real, the experience of communion with God then would have been less full. Abraham was indeed the 'friend of God,' David a man 'after God's own heart,' Enoch 'walked' with him – all enjoyed authentic communion and fellowship with God; however, they were all lacking what Owen will continually call both 'boldness' and 'liberty' in their access to God.[65]

But, the *way* that this boldness and liberty with God are regained through Christ's death and resurrection becomes programmatic of the ongoing rhythm of the renewed relationship itself. We might say that the doctrine of justification contains the seeds of the experience of sanctification and ongoing delight in God. The mode of God's redemptive victory to regain communion with sinners is at once triune and public, so, I suggest, a system of devotion something like Owen's is valuable because it never strays from worshipful appreciation of this triune agency and the public events that secured friendship with God in the first place. In a sense, the trinitarian source of salvation as well as its public historical mode of accomplishment are mutually reinforcing principles – if the worshipper dwells on one emphasis for long, the second soon comes along with it. In historical terms, the peak human experience of re-connection with God can only come after Christ has, at the occasion of his death and resurrection, opened a new entrance into the Holy of Holies where the Father dwells. After Christ opens that entrance, he then reveals it to sinners by sending the Holy Spirit to illuminate darkened minds and to regenerate deadened human wills. This is the Puritan gospel to which Owen would have subscribed: humans who are

---

[65] Owen cites 2 Cor. 3:15-16; Eph. 3:12.

estranged from the Father may be reconciled to him by the Son's merit, through the direct work of the Holy Spirit applying that merit to them. The possibility of the believer's experiencing a fuller communion with God thus coincides with God's fuller self-revelation as the Father, Son, and Holy Spirit who have various roles in the economy of salvation. As the history of redemption progresses from the Old to the New Covenant, God increasingly reveals himself more fully as triune, and the greater the degree of closeness to God is made possible. To know the Trinity is to know soteriology, and to know soteriology at the climax of its historical revelation (Christ's death and resurrection) is to discover how God can be personally approached with greater boldness and liberty. If all of this is historically and theologically true, then it seems fitting that the Christian response to such a salvation would make reference to these elements, and that it would be a somewhat arbitrary omission if it did not.

Because Owen spends most of his time expounding the nature of communion after Christ's advent, his base-line definition of communion with God incorporates within it the theological density of the New Covenant. Thus, the vivid experience of knowing God is never divorced from the nuanced Covenantal Theology which explains how God made such an experience possible. In other words, experiencing God is not done immediately, mystically, or as a result of the believer's success at what some later writers have called 'spiritual disciplines,' but rather as a result of a monergistic covenant where the Father, Son, and Spirit work in holy conspiracy to pull rebellious sinners toward union with themselves. While Owen shares some similarities with other devotional writers who had emphasized the experiential element of religion, he always seems to be mixing subjective spirituality with scholastic theology. While at one moment he is exhorting worshippers toward near rapturous delight in Christ, in the next he is explaining Christ's role in the *ordo salutis* and how the *ordo* itself is driven by the accomplishments of Christ while in Palestine and afterward from his heavenly session. Within paragraphs he will happily dart between such poles, from a sonorous description of the beauty of Christ to a defense of crucial distinctions between special grace and common grace, from the comeliness of the Savior's countenance to the distinction between Christ's federal relationship to the Father and that between sinner and the Father. So, we have in Owen a truly vibrant spirituality, one deeply informed by a doctrine of God and an elaborate system of salvation's covenantal emplotment and public accomplishment. Simply put, for Owen, one cannot stray very far from thoughts of the historically played-out covenants between the triune God and his people without losing sight of the motives and goals of prayer and devotion.

The Enjoyment of Communion Flows from the Fact of Union

It is no surprise, then, that Owen's basic definition of communion with God is itself theologically precise, and should be seen as somewhat of a rebuttal to elements of medieval mysticism: 'Our communion, then, with God consisteth in his communication of himself unto us, with our returnal unto him of that which he requireth and accepteth, flowing from that union which in Jesus Christ we have with him.'[66] The significant phrase here is *flowing from that union*. Not just anyone may enter into the presence of the Holy One, but only those who have been qualified by virtue of their union with Christ. Communion is grounded upon union. In fact, Owen's regular usage of the term *communion* should always be understood to encompass the concept of union as well.[67] This is an essential feature within Owen's devotional theology: a person is first savingly united with Christ, and only then moves on to experience any real communion with the triune God. This is not to say that union and communion will be separated in time as if communion were some 'second blessing' which builds upon an earlier experience. Rather, the point is one of logical precedence: only the soul which the Holy Spirit has united to Christ and his merits will have the prerequisite needed to experience God's friendship.

This ordering is crucial. The fact that union with Christ actually *precedes* any communal experience of God represents a reversal of the medieval ordering of things and is what makes Owen a distinctively Protestant devotionalist. For example, Owen's *Greater Catechism* follows the logic of the classically Protestant *Westminster Confession* in describing the origin of union as a 'free, gracious act of Almighty God, whereby in Jesus Christ he calleth and translateth us from the state of ...sin...into the state of grace and union with Christ.'[68] What the human performs to effect this uniting with Christ is 'nothing at all, being merely wrought upon by the free grace and Spirit of God, when in ourselves we have no ability to any thing that is spiritually good.'[69] However, now united to Christ, the believer has possession of Christ's Spirit and thereby grows in knowledge and love of God through the process of sanctification. In other words, only since he is graciously united to Christ (through justifying faith) is he made free to commune with God, and even to seek deeper experiences of such communion.

The medieval order had placed these stages in reverse, placing union as only the top and final rung in a stepladder of increasingly pure levels of communion with God. It has been noted that since Gregory of Nyssa

---

[66] II.8
[67] Sinclair Ferguson, *John Owen on the Christian Life*, 75.
[68] I.486
[69] I.486

(330-c.395), a man sometimes known as 'The Father of Christian Mystical Theology,' had distinguished three stages in the spiritual pilgrimage – purification, enlightenment, and then union with God – his ordering had become standard.[70] To translate Gregory's stages into seventeenth-century parlance would be to say that the spiritual pilgrimage begins with 'sanctification' and grows toward 'illumination' before reaching the goal of union. Bonaventure (whom Pope Leo had called the 'Prince of Mystics') elaborated upon Gregory's program in his *Threefold Way*. For him as well, the *culmination* of spiritual experience is 'the way of Union, and in that the Bridegroom is received.'[71] For the Puritan, however – and Owen in particular – union with Christ is not the end but the beginning of Christian life. Gordon Wakefield retorts that the Puritans also thought of three stages, 'but these are justification, sanctification, and glorification.'[72] Wakefield is right, but even still, for Owen, the soul's union with God must come even before these: it is the Father first uniting a person to Christ and his excellencies which paves the way for these three experiences. The Puritan Walter Marshal likewise says that union with Christ is the first work of saving grace in the heart so that even faith itself, being a gift of grace, 'cannot be in us before the beginning of [union], but rather it is given to us, and wrought in the very working of the Union.'[73] Faith, which results in justification, is merely an instrument whereby one may actively receive and embrace Christ, who has already come into the soul to take possession of it as his own habitation. Because of the noetic effects of sin, the fallen soul would never even strive to be united with Christ – Christ must first come in, as it were, uninvited. This is what Owen refers to when he speaks of regeneration (which causes the union of the soul with God) as something which not only is 'not any act of our own' but even 'excludes the will of man from any *active interest* herein.'[74] When Christ unites himself with the soul, he bestows the gift of faith. Then, and only then, do such further benefits as justification, sanctification, and ultimately the glorification of the sinner follow along.

Another difference between Owen and the medieval devotional tradition relates to the quality of the believer's experience of God, especially as it describes what heights the worshipper might expect to attain. The Puritans suggested that while a believer is living on earth, she

---

[70] R. Tudor Jones, 'Union with Christ: The Existential Nerve of Puritan Piety,' *Tyndale Bulletin* 41 (1990), 186-208.

[71] Quoted in R. Tudor Jones, 'Union with Christ,' 191.

[72] Gordon S. Wakefield, *Puritan Devotion: Its Place in the Development of Christian Piety* (London: Epworth, 1957) 160.

[73] Walter Marshal, *The Gospel Mystery of Sanctification* (London, 1692), quoted in Wakefield, *Puritan Devotion*, 160.

[74] III.336

may indeed have real communion with God, and even have it in a more bold and more liberal way than her Old Covenant brethren. Yet, they believed, communion in the here and now will always be partial and incomplete. It is not until heaven is attained that the believer's experience of God reaches its zenith. The beatific vision reported by the medieval mystics is therefore not attainable until the 'poor reflection' (1 Cor. 13:12) of God that can be had in this world finally gives way to the next world where, and only where, 'we shall see face to face.' There, God will radiate his glory toward the believer in an intensity that is now unimaginable, as the believer, for the first time, is able to return God's advances with a total self-abandon. Owen's declared purpose for writing about the doctrine of communion, in fact, is to stir up in the reader an increased longing after this fullness of God's salvation which will only at a later time be made fully manifest.[75] In the end, this emphasis on the 'not yet' of the believer's experience of God seems to do more justice to the historically unfolding nature of salvation. While Jesus inaugurated his Father's kingdom, the Holy Spirit has brought only the firstfruits of that kingdom into the believer's experience. It would seem that the overly eschatologically-realized spirituality that plagued some of the medieval devotional writers could have been minimized by a closer adherence to our present location in the timeline of salvation. When Christians seek to worship a God who is not just ontologically trinitarian, but trinitarian in the particular actions that the New Testament describes surrounding the inauguration (not consummation) of Christ's New Covenant, the balance between the 'already' and 'not yet' of communion with God is much more easily attained.

Distinct Communion with Each Divine Person

Even if the possibility of communion with God is truly held out in scripture, Owen must still prove his central thesis. The believer does not simply commune with God, nor even with God-who-is-triune. Owen contends that biblical communion involves a believer relating in distinct ways to each person of the Trinity. In some sense, the believer's relationship with the Father is different than his relationship to the Son or the Spirit. Though this is a much harder point for which to assemble biblical proof-texts, Owen had to make the attempt if his ideas were to gain currency amongst a Puritan audience to whom his promotion of distinct relations with each hypostasis would have appeared novel, given the emphasis on divine unity in the West. And, for our purposes, we must test Owen's assertion for its basic orthodoxy.

---

[75] II.9

To satisfy his own biblical criteria, Owen needs to be able to cite texts which indicate that a believer has three somewhat distinct relationships with God. Perhaps his favorite single text in this regard is an English translation of 1 John 5:7, 'There are three that bear record in heaven, the Father, the Word, and the Holy Ghost.' In the context of 1 John, the 'record being born' is that of the sonship of Christ and the salvation of believers in his blood. Thus, according to the verse, the Father, Son, and Holy Spirit each distinctly testify to the believer's salvation through Christ, and respectively, the believer receives this testimony from each divine person as a comforting assurance of his acceptance by God. Unfortunately, it is almost certain that, unbeknownst to Owen, he is working here with a corrupted Vulgate text, as no Greek manuscripts before the sixteenth century list the three persons of the Trinity here. Certainly, this is a significant failing for Owen's argument since this verse was one of his favorite lines of defense. Yet his broader argument is strengthened when he interprets 1 Cor. 12:4-6. Paul, in speaking of the distribution of spiritual gifts to God's people, ascribes the gifts distinctly to each person of the Trinity: 'There are diversities of gifts, but the same Spirit...differences of administrations, but the same Lord...diversities of operations but it is the same God.'[76] This verse is more convincing when making the point that, at least in some sense, separate emanations of grace flow from the divine persons.

But what about the believer's 'returnal' of God's grace that Owen requires for the circuit of communion to be completed? This point is also significant for our thesis, since we wish to discover how a doctrine of God properly shapes the human response to that God. Is there really a connection between a three-fold grace and a three-fold devotional response? Ephesians 2:18, as compressed a statement as it may be, is part of the reason to think so: 'For through Christ we have access by one Spirit unto the Father.' Thus, the Christian's access to God, that is, that wherein he acts out communion with him, is *dia Christou, en pneumati*, and *pros ton patera*. Owen garners increased support for trinitarian communion by two other foundational verses: 2 Cor. 13:14, 'The grace of the Lord Jesus Christ, and the love of God, and the fellowship of the Holy Ghost be with you all,' and John 14:23, 'If a man love me, he will keep my words: and my Father will love him, and we will come unto him, and make our abode with him.' Such texts seem to accomplish most of what Owen needs them to, and he will return to them whenever he needs to show evidence of trinitarian communion. In my estimation, Owen's case could have been better made had he cited any of a number of other

---

[76] For the argument that in the New Testament, 'Lord' usually refers to Christ and 'God' to God the Father, see Arthur W. Wainwright, *The Trinity in the New Testament* (London: S.P.C.K. Press, 1975) 41-91.

texts that explicitly establish a believer's fellowship with only one of the divine Persons, and thus made his argument for fellowship with the Three from cumulative evidence.[77]

That somehow a believer is given two-way personal access to the triune God is adequately established as a biblical claim. However, the nature of this communion may yet seem a bit abstract. What exactly takes place when a person, to use Owen's above definition, receives God's 'communication of himself' and responds with her own 'returnal unto him'? At one level, the divine/human relationship is analogous in many ways to certain kinds of communion between two humans. Owen relies heavily on such metaphors. Human marriage is his favorite: in the next chapter, we will explore the great degree to which Owen squeezes as much as is allowable out of the husband/wife relationship in the Song of Solomon. In a sense, if one wants to know what communion with God is about, she should study her relationship to her spouse (or at least, what such relationship might *ideally* be like). Ultimately, though, communion with God is not the same as human marriage but is an absolutely unique experience that will be, says Owen, first shaped by God's standing as the ruler of his universe. In other words, before marital love can be used to describe a human's relationship to God, another human response to God must be considered primary: the worship of a divine Lord. Therefore, all metaphors derived from everyday human relationships have severe limitations in describing what it means to know God. God gives fatherly love, yes, but of such a magnitude and unflagging steadiness that close comparisons to the love of a human father become embarrassing. Like a forgiving friend, the Son cancels the believer's past relational debts – but beyond normal friendship this forgiveness extends even to the divine judicial sphere in which an acquittal means the escape of eternal condemnation and release into the loving arms of the Judge himself. The Spirit is in many ways like a human 'counselor,'[78] yet prior to offering encouragement to his counselees,[79] he must first bring them from spiritual death to new life.[80] Certainly, Owen's is a devotional theology 'from above.' That God has given of himself in these ways means that the only appropriate 'returnal' will be to render to him utter worship.

The final theological argument that humans must approach God in his three-ness is that God himself has first approached his people from three personal vantage-points, a fact made most clear by a look at events in redemptive history. Owen regularly feels the need to justify the ground of his distinction between the divine persons, presumably so that a human

---

[77] For example, Rev. 3:20 invites the reader to specific communion with the Son, while 2 Cor. 8:14 strictly mentions only fellowship with the Spirit.

[78] Jn. 16:7

[79] Rom. 8:16

[80] Jn. 3:5-9

who desires to offer trinitarian worship will better know how to address each divine Person. The following schema is used by Owen in only a few places, yet is a very helpful substructure to keep in mind before we delve into the specific intricacies of the *ad extra* work of the Trinity and the proper worship that is derived from it. Basically, the graces that God bestows come from 'the Father by way of '*original authority*,' the Son as he distributes grace from a '*purchased treasury*,' and the Holy Spirit by way of '*immediate efficacy*.'[81] Thus, it is the Father who determines *that* he will redeem and *whom* he will redeem, and that the process of redemption will push forward on his own 'life-giving power.'[82] And in keeping with Owen's monetary metaphor, it is the Son's bank account (of his own active and passive righteousness) from which the Father makes the withdrawals that purchase sinners for himself. It is the Spirit who finally applies redemption to the individual as a sort of efficient cause, actually illuminating, regenerating, causing faith and repentance, and then sanctifying the believer.

For Owen to prescribe that believers worship each *hypostaseis* according to these distinctions does not, in the end, do real violence to even Western emphases on divine unity. Why? Because the nature of individual communion is such that 'the person, as the person, of any one of them, is not the prime *object* of divine worship, but as it is *identified* with the nature or essence of God.'[83] It may be said that it is the God-ness of each hypostasis that is being worshipped, not the hypostasis considered independent of God's essence, if that were possible. For Owen to say that 'the person, of any one of them, is not the prime object of divine worship' is perhaps his deliberate reminder that for all of his rigorous efforts to show 'distinct' communion with the persons (to which we now turn), he still affirms the essential unity of the Godhead, even as an object of worship. The closing chapter will have some final analysis about Owen's orthodoxy in this regard. We turn now to examine the exact nature of the believer's relationship with each hypostasis, and to what degree Owen is able to link a doctrine of God to spiritual practice.

---

[81] II.16
[82] II.17
[83] II.18, emphasis is Owen's.

CHAPTER 5

Owen's Communion with the Father, Son, and Spirit

This chapter is, in a sense, an extended case study of how both of our criteria, when taken together, can produce certain positive results for Christian devotional practice. While some of Owen's material that will be examined builds the case that he in fact satisfies our criteria, the larger aim is to let Owen illustrate how attendance to a rich doctrine of God in both essence and action can be constructive of profound devotional practices that one really cannot arrive at any other way. This chapter analyzes Owen's devotional method as it applies to the believer's life with the Father, Son, and Holy Spirit, respectively. In the first section, we will see Owen's theological claims about the Father's disposition toward believers as a template for a certain kind of devotional response, one that, I suggest, is not possible without relying on prior doctrinal confession. The overall burden of my thesis, to show how a theology of God can directly program a spirituality, will thus find promising resources in Owen's form of devotionally exercised Protestant scholasticism. Present in all the following sections is evidence that when theology is done in a redemptive-historical mode, devotional application flows quite organically. Perhaps more surprisingly, the flavor of devotion drawn from such emphasis on the quite technical nuances of Covenantal (or Federal) Theology tends to be highly oriented to the transformation of human affections for God. Owen's Federalism, pregnant as it is with emotive exchanges with the triune God, requires a re-assessment of a theological tradition that has been largely ignored for its service to spiritual practice. In fact, Federal Theology may prove to have certain unique advantages for connecting a doctrine of God to private worship. We now move to look over Owen's shoulder to see how these connections might be made, and what fruit result when our original criteria are met.

Communion with the Father

Owen writes that there are various 'mediums'[1] by which a believer may commune with each divine Person. Probably the best way to understand 'medium' as used by Owen here is as that through which God and a

---

[1] II.18

human being may have a sort of personal exchange. A medium is a carrier of relationship – that upon which personal dealing builds itself. A milkman and his customer may have a very shallow relationship, but what little relationship they have is mediated by the milk. Smiling, he delivers the bottles into the hands of his customer; the customer returns by offering payment, and perhaps a friendly greeting. At whatever depth these two may be said to know one another, it is the milk itself which can be credited, to use Aristotelian terms, as the 'instrumental cause.'

There are a variety of media by which a human may have fellowship with God, and these will be explained in detail below as we consider the believer's relationship with each person. Yet while Owen may seem slavishly scholastic in the cumbersome outlines by which he dissects these media, he disclaims any exhaustiveness in his own system. He limits himself to media which he sees declared in the gospel message. By declaring these limits on his own system, Owen may be leaving room for the existence of additional carriers of relationship that may be found in creation. Psalm 19 reads, 'The heavens declare the glory of God, and the skies proclaim the work of his hands.' So described, the created order itself seems to perfectly fit Owen's definition of a medium of communion, for in the cosmos one may partially apprehend the character of the Creator. But Owen bypasses such promising tributaries in his more narrow search for media of communion that arise from the plan of redemption. Does this mean that Owen downplays the legitimacy of natural theology as a way to know God? No, for elsewhere his assertions regarding human responsibility to God will depend on the inexcusability of ignoring God's clear testimony to himself found in the natural world.[2] It seems that while natural theology has its place for Owen as a revealer of God, it does not yield the quality or degree of personal exchange with God that would warrant the language of 'medium.' By this emphasis we see the scope of Owen's doctrine of communion to include primarily redemptive motifs rather than creational ones.

The reason for his narrowed salvific focus comes back to the close relationship Owen sees between the Trinity and the full message of God's redemptive plan: God is most *gloriously* revealed when he is viewed through the lenses of the gospel. That is, when the Godhead is appreciated as the Father who determines to redeem, as the Son who accomplishes redemption, and as the Spirit who subjectively actualizes redemption in the believer's life, he appears more wondrous than in any other manifestation. Certainly the created world bears valuable testimony to certain of the divine attributes, but only in the gospel of trinitarian

---

[2] III.24; V.25,26; IV.87

redemption can a person gain the full realization of how God is fully God *for* us.³

The medium therefore through which the saints most eminently have communion with the Father is love. Specifically, it is the Father's 'free,' 'unmerited,' and 'eternal' love which brings God and the sinner into a reconciled relationship. Since, for Owen, all the media that induce communion exist in order to open up a two-way dealing between God and his people, this love of God is that by which God first delivers himself unto the sinner, and secondly, that love which invites the return of the sinner's own response to God.

The believer is to view the Father, above all else, as one who delights in and cherishes her. This discovery of God as being wholly beneficent is the 'great discovery of the gospel.'⁴ The Old Covenant could not reveal such things, for its purpose was to reveal the unapproachable holiness of God and the impossible task of unholy people to commend themselves before him. The true depth of the love of God becomes clear only in the gift of Christ, who shows to what length God is willing to go in order to reclaim his people. Love is the first thing that should come to mind when the believer asks herself, 'What does the Father think of me?'

To say 'God loves you' has become somewhat of an epigram in more contemporary Christian history, yet few have ever credited the Puritans with beginning this trend. To the contrary, seventeenth-century English preaching is sometimes caricatured as being as severe and bad-tempered as the God whose message it believed it was proclaiming. The Puritan practice of drawing out biblical law to its furthest implications for Christian duty has left the impression on some that, for the Puritans, God's law eclipsed God's love.⁵ It cannot be denied that the Puritans were scrupulous about the law of God – when Richard Rogers was lecturing at Wethersfield, Essex, someone told him, 'Mr. Rogers, I like you and your company very well, but you are so precise,' to which Rogers replied, 'O Sir, I serve a precise God.'⁶ However, Owen stands contrary to assumptions about the stern God of English Puritanism: The Father's primary attribute which he reveals to the saints is the greatness of his love, not the precision of his justice. 'God is love' in 1 John 4:8 is taken by Owen as a summary statement of the Father's inherent nature as

---

³ Catherine Mowry LaCugna should be credited for helping to bring this phrase back into the discussion of the economic Trinity, cf. *God For Us*.

⁴ II.19

⁵ Cf. Ernest Kevan's refutation of this caricature in *The Grace of Law* (Ligonier, Penn.: Soli Deo Gloria, 1993).

⁶ Quoted in Ryken, *Worldly Saints: The Puritans as They Really Were* (Grand Rapids: Zondervan, 1986), 5.

well as the primary medium through which his people experience him.[7] To put it more directly, it is the Father's 'infinitely gracious, tender, compassionate, and loving nature...[in which he] dispenseth himself unto us.'[8] In order to correctly shape one's thoughts regarding the primacy of God's fatherly love, understanding one of the broader themes of 1 John becomes crucial. The remaining verses of chapter four use the Father's sending of the Son as proof of his love. This gives Owen the grounding for a claim that is rarely so clearly expounded in later treatments of Covenant Theology: The Father does not first love his people because of Christ's mediation, rather, Christ's mediation is the outworking of the Father's prior love. For Owen, the love of the Father is the impetus for the whole of the plan of salvation, including his sending of the Son.

The impression sometimes taken away from discussions of the Covenant of Redemption (that is, the covenantal agreement between the Father and the Son that the Father would give the elect to the Son if the Son would in return die for them) is that the Son is the prime source of divine love towards humanity. The image of the Father becomes that of a frustrated parent who has thrown up his hands at his children's waywardness and no longer delights in them – helpless and embittered, he leaves it to someone else to save them from the consequences of their rebellion. No sixteenth- or seventeenth-century covenantal theologian would describe the covenant in quite this manner, but such an understanding may have been somewhat common in the popular mind, if the urgent tone of Owen's writing is any indication. Previous theologians and preachers, men with whom Owen was doctrinally very close, commonly emphasized the *purchased* access by which believers may only safely approach God – access which Christ purchases when he expiates the Father's wrath by his own suffering. Indeed, Owen himself spent a great deal of time explaining Christ's 'purchased grace,' but not until he had first made his point about the Father without respect to the Covenant of Redemption. The 'purchased treasury' of the Son must not come before the 'original authority' of the Father.[9] To fail to see the Father's love as logically prior to the Son's incarnation and death will do real damage to the psyche of the worshipper, in addition to being simply untrue. God the Father will seem to have no inherent love for the believer; his love will be only a contractual approval which he must render since the Son has paid the agreed ransom. The believer's relationship to God will sadly resemble that between a woman and her husband who gives her roses on her wedding anniversary, but then adds, 'Since it is our

---

[7] The following verse makes clear that 'God' in vs. 8 refers to the Father in particular, not God 'essentially.' Cf. II.19

[8] II.19

[9] II.16

anniversary, I felt it was my solemn *duty* to give you these.'[10] The roses may smell sweetly, but her own affections toward her husband are not stirred because she senses that his love flows mainly from obligation. Communion with God so suffers because the 'returnal' of human affections to a contractual Father is near impossible. Owen, though always affirming the intra-trinitarian Covenant of Redemption,[11] insisted that the Father's love is not conditional upon it, but rather conditions it. The psychological effect of this on Christian devotion is profound: says the believer, 'The Father has loved me enough to send his Son to redeem me,' not, 'because the Son has redeemed me the Father must now love me.'

Would not this unmediated love of the Father prior to the cross make Christ's redemptive work less necessary? Rather boldly, Owen said in his interpretation of John 16:26-27[12] that the love of the Father is free and eternal, and 'there is no need of any intercession for that.'[13] Yet, Christ's intercession remains of utmost importance. Because of the work of Christ, the Father will now send all the gracious *fruits* of his love – the graces of justification, adoption, sanctification, the Spirit to indwell the believer, etc. By this design, there can truly be no *communication* of God's love to the believer outside of the sin-bearing mediatorial work of Christ, yet the love of God itself is shown to be truly spontaneous and uncaused. There is real reason for the believer to exult in the love of the Father, and this without de-emphasizing the work of the Son. Owen's interpretation of John 16 found earlier support from Zanchius, the Continental Protestant who, when it came to John 16, said that Jesus here is flatly denying that his petition to God the Father aims to unite the apostles to the Father. Instead, Christ desires to persuade the apostles that not only he, but the Father himself *already* 'embraces them with maximum love.' Zanchius will take Christ to mean that since the Father has made up his mind to gratify and benefit the disciples he 'has a need of absolutely no one – and not of his very own Son – through such an intercession.'

Without hearing such Federalists like Zanchius and Owen on this point, it is not hard to imagine how critics of Protestant scholasticism in general would imagine that the Covenant of Redemption makes God into an emotionally distant Father-by-contract. Yet if such spontaneous love for the elect actually conditions the covenant, as Owen and Zanchius say, the portrait of the Father is changed entirely, and an equally spontaneous devotion to such a Father becomes natural and obvious. Thus, one must

---

[10] Credit to John Piper for this illustration in *Desiring God* (Sisters, Oregon: Multnomah Books, 1986).

[11] XIX.77, 84; XXII.230

[12] 'I say not unto you, that I will pray the Father for you; for the Father himself loveth you...'

[13] II.20

admit that a doctrine of God that is fundamentally informed by a truncated version of the Covenant of Redemption might well do damage to the believer's view of the Father's love for her. Yet the version of the Covenant of Redemption that Zanchius, Owen, and others articulated did not have this problem, for it recognized from the start the pre-mediatorial love of the Father, a love which put such a covenant into action as a means of satisfying both God's love and his justice. Such a doctrine of God has the advantage of recognizing love at the forefront of God's character (rather than making him a mere contractual strategist) while not downplaying his justice and wrath over sin, qualities which motivated Father and Son toward an immanent covenant that was finally played out in the Son's earthly mission. In light of such knowledge, the believer is moved toward both love and fear, gratitude and reverence. While such responses might be produced in other ways, the organic relation between them and such a doctrine of God is striking and attractive in its simplicity.

Responding to the Father's Love: Receiving and Returning

In order to complete the love-communion with the Father, believers must simply determine to receive his love. To do so is, in fact, the definition of faith. It is necessary to keep in mind, however, that while the Father's love is its own source, it is a love mediated through the Son. So too must the human response to the Father be routed through Christ. In this way, the Son is truly the proper and primary object of the Christian's faith, not the Father *per se*. So, when a person has faith in Christ directly, she is then brought by him into the presence of the Father where she can, as it were, behold his glory and see and receive his love. Two of Owen's own analogies help clarify this spiritual transaction:[14] the sun is the source of light, yet one does not experience the light of the sun apart from its beams. Put another way, cold refreshment can be found in a stream, but the stream serves only to relay the benefits of the spring. Jesus Christ, in respect of the love of the Father, is the beam, the stream, whereby all of the believer's light and refreshment comes, yet through whom she experiences the Father's own loving disposition toward her.

Owen's unique quality is that he turns the above theological description of the mechanics of divine love into an actual spiritual exercise. Christian growth takes place when this circuitry of divine love (from the Father, through the Son, to the believer, then back again in reverse order) is traced by the believer in her own mind. The specific goal at this point is that the believer convince herself, and actually *repeatedly* convince herself, of the Father's loving favor for her, and that this favor descends down to her through Christ. When she views the Father as

---

[14] II.23

benign, kind, tender, and unchangeably loving, she is lifted from some of the storms inherent to life in a fallen world and up to another world of serenity and quiet. In this framework, the experience of Christian growth can be described in terms of the following succession of events: The human soul, when it does not sense the love of the Father, realizes that it can find no rest. Christ has come, though, to announce a way of rest for the soul by revealing the Father as *supremely loving*. Christ provides the soul access to the Father's love, which has, in fact, been toward the believer for eternity and can now, for the first time, be experienced through the Son. When the soul trusts in Christ to deliver it to such love, it is brought into the very bosom of God. There the soul is soothed as it basks in the Father's love – it has at last found its repose. Again, repose in the Father's love becomes the experiential goal of Christian living. In fact, the whole of Owen's practical theology (which describes the majority of his published works) is designed to explain the further intricacies by which a believer may not only attain but, in fact, deeply enjoy, the experience of reclining in the bosom of the Father. As multi-faceted as communion with a trinitarian God will be shown to be, this ultimate love-rest with the Father is always its *telos*. If there is a 'spiritual discipline' to be drawn from Owen's Federalism, this is it – to work hard to convince oneself of the Father's determined love. Yet this is no simplistic task, since the whole diverse structure of biblical covenants and trinitarian agency itself tell the believer how that love is historically expressed by God and can be returned by sinners in lives of worship and obedience.

Though the believer has the duty to love God, this fact does not take away from love's pleasantness and spontaneity, for it remains 'an affection of union and nearness, with complacency therein.'[15] Further still, loving God logically precedes and grounds all moral obedience. Here is the progression: the soul apprehends the Father's love toward it and is thus itself raised to return that love. This love of the Father now motivates all further observance of the Father's commands. Thus, communion with the Father, though in essence full of the bliss and joy of direct personal encounter, necessarily draws the believer toward godly behavior. For Owen, any lesser motivation to obey God's law than an organic reaction to a sense of the Father's love is a false and threadbare spirituality.

Although Owen's circuitry of communion emphasizes love as the basic and shared medium between the Father and the worshipper, he will make a qualitative distinction between the Father's love and that of the believer to prevent overstating the similarities between divine and human love. This is what the monism of Eckhart and the whole realist tradition was

---

[15] II.24

never quite equipped to do, since in their view the individual worshipper is subsumed by God's own essence. The most illustrative difference between divine and human love for Owen flows from the basic difference in ontology between the Father and the finite sinner. The love of the Father is like himself: constant, tireless, and incapable of either growth or diminution. Our love, on the other hand, reflects our finite and fallen nature and will variously surge or wane, grow more intense or become fickle. The Father's love is constant in that those whom he loves, he always loves. When the immutable God chooses to fix his love on a person, his love for her is also immutable. In fact, his love for her is also eternal, for there is no temporal cause by which it could be brought either into or out of temporal existence. The implication is that no act of the beloved can have any effect to either heighten or lessen God's love for her.

Since Luther, the Reformed tradition had emphasized that justification is granted by God's grace, not human merit; God's favor descends on a person apart from human striving. Owen takes Luther's point to the next logical step: after God justifies a person, the believer is *still* unable to cause God to increase his love for her by anything she does. And the complementary truth is even more crucial to Christian living: a Christian is powerless to make God love her *less*. No amount of post-conversion sinning can diminish in any way God's favor and delight in her. Can God really love his people in the midst of their sinning, or – more radically still – can he love them to the same degree when they are sinning as when they succeed in the strictest obedience? Owen said 'yes,' yet expected that some would think his answer absurd. But, he said, if the love of God were any more changeable than God himself, no flesh could be saved.[16] If the Father's pleasure were contingent to any degree on inherent or infused goodness within us (even after our justification), no one would ever meet his minimum qualifications. Owen anticipates the more modern expression, 'God loves the sinner but hates the sin' when he declares that God loves 'his people, not their sinning.'[17] What ultimately prevents this love-language from slipping into anti-nomianism is what he will later say about the Son's mission as a redeemer. This is another advantage of a practical trinitarianism rooted in historical, covenantal accomplishment: if we understand the costly work of the Son to have once-and-for-all undone the guilt and damage of sin, we are quite free to speak unhesitatingly about the love of the Father without fear of wrongly softening God. An infinitely loving Father is a correct picture of God, yet this is a Father whose retributive justice once prompted the tragic self-offering of God the Son. The roles the divine members each play in

---

[16] II.30
[17] II.31

redemption prevents an imbalance in devotion, and, in this case, allows the Father's love to be spoken of in exalted terms without the otherwise real threat of anti-nomianism.

The Meditative Technique Regarding the Father

Owen wants Christians not only to be good theologians, but also to apply their theology in such a way that they encounter the Father in loving communion. To call this 'technique' is not to reduce the divine/human relationship to a series of simple steps, but to recognize that something beyond mental assent is required for doctrinal belief to yield its greatest fruit. One may even be regenerate yet have only vague and irregular acquaintance with 'the light of His countenance.'[18] This relationship, like all others, must be worked at in order to be enjoyed – and enjoyment of God is at the heart of humanity's created purpose.[19] Following Owen's general thesis about trinitarian communion, separate meditative exercises will be described as the believer approaches each divine person. And, for reasons that will be described, the believer must begin with a proper approach to the Father lest she assuredly skew her relationship to both Son and Spirit.

Puritans followed the view that the psyche is tripartite in its faculties, composed of the mind, will, and affections. Having informed the mind of the fact of the Father's love, Owen essentially prescribed that the believer 'roll'[20] certain of these doctrines in the mind until they make impact on the affections.[21] Once the mind fixes upon a truth, the inclination then judges its value, import, or desirability. When the inclination assesses that a certain fact is important, it moves the will into action. For example, when a person's mind perceives that a closed door lies in her walking path, her will responds by ordering her hand to extend itself and turn the doorknob. This is a mundane illustration, but proper, for the will is the aspect of the inclination which deals in the sometimes trivial daily actions called forth by commonplace facts. The affections, however, become engaged when the inclination has been more strongly impacted by a perceived reality. If the woman understands that her beloved awaits her beyond the door, she will still open the door, but will do so with glee and

---

[18] *Westminster Confession of Faith* 18.3. The chapter also describes the believer's duty to the 'right use of ordinary means' in order to attain the peace of assurance of salvation.

[19] *Westminster Shorter Catechism*, question 1.

[20] A common word for Owen and other Puritans when describing the devotionally necessary subjective response to religious truth claims.

[21] Jonathan Edwards, who admits to being influenced by Owen, collapses the will and affections to one basic faculty of the soul which he calls the 'inclination' (*Religious Affections*, ch.1).

expectation. The affections are strong judgments about facts, whether strongly approving or strongly abhorring. Owen's aim is that the believer's intellectual recognition of the Father's love would go beyond merely affecting her will (by which theological truths would motivate only toward a sense of religious duty, but little more) to stirring her affections in a way that she experience a strong sense of the awe and peace that divine favor should instill. While shallow critiques of Protestant scholasticism charge that the movement was primarily concerned to fill the believer's mind in order to change her will, Owen provides evidence that right doctrine finds its victory only when it first changes the human affections.

But how does one get doctrine into the affective compartment of the soul? Given that the mind has been convinced through biblical testimony that God is indeed 'full of love,' the believer must now 'eye' the Father as love. Owen's terminology is vague, but to 'eye' a truth involves fixing the mind on it in such a way as to draw forth its most searching implications; it is not simply to 'see' a fact by way of recognizing its propositional content, but to gaze upon it as one would an object of beauty. Though Owen is ultimately aiming at the affections, he does not try to capture them directly – the mind remains the only portal by which the devotionalist can reach the affections. Here again, Owen's method is different than realist mysticism, for he is sure that active thinking cannot be bypassed on the way to fuller experiences of communion with God. The effect is to keep the locus of devotion on the object rather than the human subject. God and his love remain the center of attention, not the believer's own heart as she tries to raise herself to spiritual enjoyment. What Owen avoids by this structure is the same thing that plagued certain medieval writers – a steep slope towards sentimentalism. For Owen, emotional response to God is a proper goal of Christian living, yet the response is always limited and shaped according to the way that biblical revelation first informs the mind. Owen's method here is closer to the *lectio divina* discussed earlier, with its meditative focus on scriptural truths as a stepping-stone toward encounter with God in *contemplatio*. But Owen's version of the *lectio divina* method is intellectually centered on truths about trinitarian redemption, a focus that distinctively colors the affective encounter with God that results.

To raise our affections toward the Father we must then gaze on both the one who loves as well as the quality of his love. We must dwell on the fact that the God who loves us is actually, in himself, without any outside relational needs – the Father has within the Godhead a relationship with his Son and Spirit that is enough to delight him for eternity. The fact, then, that God goes outside of his own trinitarian community to seek his saints shows that he has not only his own satisfaction in mind, but our good as well.[22] Recognizing this is an important corollary of Reformed theology that is, in practice, sometimes eclipsed by the otherwise correct assertion that God created the world in order to glorify himself. Such thoughts might seem to compete: does God call the elect to salvation primarily so that they will give him glory or because he loves them and seeks their eternal bliss? The former assertion, that people exist for God's benefit, was a distinctive of the Calvinist tradition as it sought to vindicate God's prerogative in election, and thus it appeared regularly as the subject of Puritan preaching. However, Owen proved that his own assertion about the Father's purpose to fill his elect with joy lay within the domain of Reformed orthodoxy as well: God was, by definition, in no need of being glorified by anything in creation since he was already infinitely glorified across his own eternal, immanent, trinitarian relations. Without philosophically settling the issue of priority between these two assertions, Owen tells believers that they are right to think that God's love for them is rooted in his loving nature, not merely as an accidental means by which God gains glory for himself. And, though God's loving nature is the ground, his love-acts are utterly voluntary, never necessary. When a broader sweep of Owen's theology is taken in, it becomes clear that God's glory and the happiness of the elect are two sides of the same coin. In fact, God is particularly glorified as his people experience his love. How? When God loves his saints and gives them hearts that return that love, the cycle of communion is completed. The elect thrill to his unmerited favor, and God is pleased and glorified because their delight, far from being conditioned on God's gifts or benefits, is focused on God himself as the giver. God is glorified because the saints find their ultimate enjoyment in him above all other persons or things. Of course, this kind of joy in the Father's love is not possible without reference to his identity within the immanent Trinity.

The Four Adjectives of Fatherly Love:
Free, Distinguishing, Unchangeable, Eternal

Meditating on the Father as one who is, within the Trinity, the Great Lover (of his Son) and the Greatly Beloved (by the Son), but who yet extends himself to love his saints, will result in the worshipper being assured of the degree of voluntary determination with which the Father approaches her. Certainly God must be deeply motivated to love his people if he voluntarily extends his love beyond the boundaries of his own trinitarian relations. Four qualities of his love rise up as particularly fruitful when meditatively considered.[23] Owen has suggested some of these qualities

---

[22] II.33
[23] II.33

elsewhere as theological truths, but his subjective application of them shapes his spiritual method. In loving fallen creatures who, in their fallen state, will never return his love with anything near the perfection of the love of the Son, the Father's love for the saints is proved to be 'free.' Ironically, had Christians deserved God's love they would inevitably value it less, for it is difficult to be thankful for that which one is due. Conversely, believers who discipline themselves to mentally dwell on the "freeness" of his love will soon find within themselves newfound appreciation for their accepted status before the Father. Still, God has not chosen to love all people in this way. His salvific love is 'distinguishing' – the 'Jacobs' who receive it are further humbled when they see the 'Esaus' who are equal to them in sin, but, for reasons that are locked up in the Father's secret counsel, have not been objects of love's mercy in the same way. While some might object to this kind of Calvinistic particularism on other grounds, it is not hard to see how it is equipped to induce wonder and humility at the level of the affections. For God's love to be so clearly without driving cause in the believer herself, it must also be unsusceptible to other outside influences and is thus 'unchangeable.' The believer may rest confident that though her own love for God fluctuates daily, his love for her never will. Something which is unchangeable by temporal events and is rooted in the eternal character of God is therefore itself 'eternal' – God has always known each saint by name and forever has had a design for their happiness in him. Thus, the worshipper should meditate upon God's love particularly as it is free, distinguishing, unchangeable, and eternal. These are qualities of Fatherly love particularly systematized by Protestant scholasticism's *ordo salutis* as well as its doctrine of God, not to mention illustrated by the loving deeds of God in redemptive history. Such rich theological undergirding to the relatively simple assertion, 'The Father loves you,' replaces vagueness with particularity, abstract attributes with real world divine action, and thus increases the possibility that meditating on such a divine attribute will really move the heart of the worshipper to adoration and a 'returnal' of such love.

Of these four qualities of Fatherly love, 'eternality' proves to be particularly fruitful for the interests of human communion with the Trinity. Interestingly, Owen draws proof of the eternal love for his elect from Proverbs 8:30-31, a text which traditionally had been interpreted to speak instead of the Son's exulting in the Father's pre-creational love for him. Owen did not disavow this reading, but briefly adds to the traditional view by asserting two things. First, generally speaking, what the Father loves about the Son is the Son's express reflection of the image of the Father, in all its brightness and glory. The Father therefore beholds in the Son all his own excellencies and perfections. In a sense, Owen is saying that the Father's love for the Son is a kind of self-love since the Son is loved because of his resemblance to the Father. Secondly, the text specifically suggests that the Father 'delights' in the fact that the Son himself 'delights' in 'the sons of men.' The Son's thoughts of kindness and redemption toward sinners who had not yet been created excites the Father's love toward the Son. *Thus, amazingly, the very love bond between the Father and the Son is contributed to by the praiseworthy design of human redemption that the Father initiates and the Son reflects.* This is a rare example in Puritan writing of a direct connection between the immanent and economic Trinity: intra-trinitarian love has a basis in the Father's and the Son's respective actions as the initiator and confirmer/reflector of the plan of redemption. This is a largely undiscovered aspect of Owen's trinitarianism, and fascinating for its connection of God's ontology to his public work. Echoes of Karl Rahner might be heard, but what we have already seen about Owen's sureness of God's 'freeness' prevents us from taking this to mean that God's identity is incomplete apart from his historic actions. More that this, Owen dropped an anchor of devotional methodology right in the middle of it all. The fact that something as eternal as intra-trinitarian self-delight is focused on the redemption of short-lived, time-bound humans shows believers that their salvation is not only eternally secure, but somehow locates their place in the universe right in the middle of the relationship of divine Father and Son. To realize such a truth instills a feeling of worth, to say the least, and 'is enough to make all that is within us, like the babe in the womb of Elisabeth, to leap for joy.'[24] Further, to recognize that we are drawn up into God's eternal intra-trinitarian love rightly provokes us to prostrate our souls 'to the lowest abasement of a humble, holy reverence, and make us rejoice before him with trembling.'[25] Owen shows that the eternality of the Father's love, when affectively discovered, produces both joy and holy fear.

We see in Owen's devotional method an oscillation between emphasis on the Calvinist concern that the objective fact of God's favor is rooted in his eternal decree and, on the other hand, the appeal that the believer subjectively apply God's love to herself as a separate act of worship for its own emotional impact. Does this meditative, subjective focus undercut Calvinist soteriology with its focus on the objective, monergistic, saving work of God in Christ? If one reads only his more devotional treatises, especially their passages that urge the believer to diligently seek after rapturous pleasure in Christ, this might be a tempting conclusion. But it cannot be forgotten that perhaps his most famous essay, *The Death of Death in the Death of Christ*, was, and in many quarters still is considered to be, the most extensive and thoroughly biblical defense of the high

---

[24] II.33
[25] II.33

Calvinist doctrine of limited atonement (and of course, if Clifford is right, even suggests that Owen is grossly more narrow and deterministic about election than Calvin was[26]). So, if Owen's subjective focus on human devotional disciplines suggests a lack of commitment to God's absolute sovereignty in accomplishing the whole of redemption himself, then it is a strange fact that he is simultaneously unsurpassed as a defender of the most unpopular formulations of sovereignty – a highly monergistic salvation where the Father sent Christ to die only for a remnant, and a remnant to whom he himself, through the Spirit, sovereignly applies that salvation.

The solution to this tension is that even Owen's strict advocacy of divine determination in salvation seems to allow that at least the present *enjoyment* of God's saving love (though not the divinely determined bestowal of it), requires the believer's own determination (a human determination that is itself enabled by the Holy Spirit, however). The vigor with which Owen demands that believers must actively and willfully take hold of the Father's love in order to fully appropriate its benefits is in part explained by the fact that Owen's Calvinist theological milieu made this emphasis less expected. Horton Davies notes that Puritan preaching and even prayers were often polemical[27] – and the target of the polemic was often the Arminian assertion that salvation was determined by a person's acceptance or rejection of the Father's offer of forgiveness through Christ, a determination of an utterly free (i.e. neutral) will. For Owen to make a claim that, without context, might have an Arminian ring would require him to state his case carefully. Any talk of 'appropriating' God's love could easily be construed to have such Arminian features. However, our surprise at hearing Owen speak so forcefully of the Christian's devotional responsibility is less warranted if we consider that even Calvinist soteriology allows (and even requires) a strong subjective aspect, though rightly placed. The devotional responsibility of the believer to 'make use' of the Father's love is no more contrary to the system of elective salvation than is the Calvinist assertion that faith, though a gift of God to the believer, is no less an active human response. Even closer to Owen's project is the orthodox Reformed understanding of sanctification – sanctification is first God's project to progressively purify the Christian, yet God's work is accomplished by renewing the human will to freely make increasingly God-honoring choices.[28] For the believer to pursue communion with the Father in love is an aspect of sanctification – God draws, but the believer is simultaneously responsible for 'eyeing' the Father. Owen shows that when genuine Calvinist

---

[26] Clifford, *Atonement*.

[27] Horton Davies, *The Worship of the English Puritans* (Ligonier, Penn.: Soli Deo Gloria) 133.

[28] *Westminster Confession of Faith*, ch. XIII.

soteriology touches ground in the world of Christian devotion, no lack of passion for seeking deeper encounter of God need result.

The goal of dwelling on the Father's love is two-fold: God's own delight and the believer's own pleasure in God. Speaking of the former, it is God's great desire that his saints subjectively recognize his loving favor toward them. Owen states the same truth conversely, 'the Lord takes nothing worse at the hands of his [own] than ... hard thoughts of him." The sin of Eden, after all, fits this pattern: the primeval couple caved in to the serpent's suggestion that God was holding them back from something wonderful lying just beyond the forbidden tree. Because of the Fall, doubting God's love remains, for Owen, perhaps the prime impetus to all other sin (that is, the sin of Christians, who ought to know their Father better), and the greatest cause of God's displeasure in his children. The reason the God of love is so grieved at 'hard thoughts of him' is not merely that his central attribute is going unadored, but that when the believer loses focus on the Father's love it is to her own great loss – and anything that damages the saints grieves the one who lovingly formed them. When a believer lacks the present awareness of divine love the Father is grieved for he knows 'full well what fruit this bitter root is like to bear, – what alienations of heart, – what drawings back, – what unbelief and tergiversations in our walking with him.'[29] To be underwhelmed at the Father's love is the beginning of spiritual decay, a sin of the affections that becomes a slippery slope toward almost all kinds of rebellion of mind and will. Once again, it is impossible to escape the reflexive, communal nature of Owen's devotional method. The pleasure of the Father and the saints are wrapped up in one another: the Father's enjoyment in the saints is piqued when they fix their affections on his love and in him find joy themselves. Such a formulation is again incredibly suggestive of the larger trinitarian theme of Owen's method, since for all practical purposes Owen encourages the believer to relate to the Father in the kind of mutual exchange of love which is blatantly reminiscent of the immanent, eternal relationship between the Father and the Son. These are elements of a devotional life that can be only lived if the doctrine of the Trinity is both true and meditated on by the believer herself.

The Pastoral Context: Confronting Apathy, Instilling Assurance

To focus on the Father's love is not what the Puritans are remembered for, and, in fact, Owen's reliance on the idea is somewhat stronger than that of his peers. In order to see the practical value of this doctrine we will examine Owen's use of it in the face of two pastoral problems of his own

---

[29] II.35

age: spiritual dryness and the lack of assurance of salvation. These are standard problems of pastoral concern in the seventeenth century, but perennial enough in the history of the church to warrant our own attention and to highlight some of the advantages of our own thesis. As it turns out, a doctrine of Fatherly love within a trinitarian context seems especially equipped to address these two spiritual problems. Owen's paradigm proves to have advantages over other Puritan techniques, which to some degree became de-centered from a doctrine of Fatherly love.

Owen assumes that even though the average Christian desires, at some level, to find delight in knowing God, she simultaneously struggles with a nagging dullness and apathy (or even antipathy) toward him. Very simply, such spiritual distemper can be diagnosed in her 'unskillfulness'[30] or 'neglect' of holding communion with the Father in love. Any other spiritual discipline will actually worsen the problem, as we will see below. Owen was not alone is his diagnosis of spiritual apathy as one of the church's leading maladies, but his prescription of Fatherly communion 'in love' as the best cure was unique.

Owen especially warned his contemporaries about overly relying on the law as an encouragement to holy living, or a cure for spiritual dryness, without first laying a strong foundation in the believer's mind of the Father's love.[31] Any focus on God's law whatever, and for that matter, any appeal to any of the Father's acts or attributes that provide benefit to the Christian, will only kill affection for God if it is not prefaced in the mind with a fixation on his eternal, immutable love: 'every other discovery of God, without this, will but make the soul fly from him.'[32] Luther had his own bitter experience in this regard as a monk. The strength of his devotion to God kept him in rigorous daily devotional exercises, yet because he simultaneously viewed the Father primarily as a holy lawgiver and himself as an incorrigible lawbreaker he began to hate

---

[30] II.36

[31] On one hand, several features of the Puritan Sunday services were expressly designed, directly or indirectly, to bring the worshipper into a more 'comfortable' walk with God, that is, to inject the same kind of vitality into Christian living that, generally speaking, Owen himself is after. What features? Davies (*The Worship of the English Puritans*, 20 and 125) has noted that many Independent congregations by Owen's day were routinely incorporating the reading of the Decalogue into their services, and Kevan (*Grace*, 195-224) makes it clear that this focus on the law was consistent with their understanding of the grace of God, which frees the believer to obey God out of a renewed spiritual nature (Calvin's 'second use' of the law was equally important – to convict the worshipper of sin and thus remind her of her need for saving grace). There is, for the Puritan, real joy to be found in obedience, though for Owen the law could still be easily misused in a way that destroys joy.

[32] II.36

the God whose righteousness always condemned him.[33] Owen's approach would lead us to say that God's legal justice is perhaps only the most obvious divine attribute which, when given primacy over his love, will inevitably provoke hostility to God. But *any* truth about God, once discovered, will cause the sinner to flee unless love is found first. We are left to imagine how else Owen might have connected various divine attributes to the 'flight from God.' Certainly, without God's loving favor, learning of his omnipotence would cause a weak soul to cower in fear, a discovery of his omniscience would lead to shame of having all one's deepest motives exposed, God's eternality would lead to despair of his own mortal insignificance. But the advantage of first 'eyeing' his love produces an equally inevitable reaction, yet now a wonderful one, for if 'the heart be once much taken up with this eminency of the Father's love, it cannot choose but be overpowered, conquered, and endeared to him.'[34] Hearts that feel his 'love shed abroad'[35] upon them are now in a posture to receive all other truth about God: believing in and returning the Father's love is the hermeneutical key to all other statements of theology proper. For, without a sense of his love, all other discoveries about God's attributes are found to be threatening and fearful, or at best, unappealing, evoking apathy and only nominal faith. Beyond this, a correct doctrine of intra-trinitarian love enforces our understanding of the Father's love of the elect. For, as we saw, the Father loves the Son in part because of the Son's own love for the elect – and all this prior to creation, prior to the Fall, prior to the Son's actual mediation. Here is a doctrine of immanent trinitarian relations that can melt the believer's heart, and which prepares her to fearlessly, and with positive desire, discover all else that is true about God. We might say that the great impetus for the sinner to love God will come when she discovers, simply, that the Father loves the Son.

What about the problem of assurance? How can one know that God is love to oneself in particular? Owen's answer is consoling, but also subtle enough to be confusing. It is worth analyzing closely:

> [God] has spoken it [God's promise to be loving to a person] as particularly to thee as to any one in the world. And for cause of love, he hath as much to fix it on thee as on any of the children of men; that is, none at all without himself. So that I shall make speedy work with this objection. Never any one from the foundation of the world, who believed such love in the Father, and made returns of love to him again, was deceived; neither shall ever any to the world's end be so, in so doing. Thou art,

---

[33] Roland Bainton, *Here I Stand: A Life of Martin Luther* (Nashville: Abingdon Press, 1978) 27-38.
[34] II.36
[35] Rom. 5:5

then, in this, upon a most sure bottom. If thou believest and receivest the Father as love, he will infallibly be so to thee, though others may fall under his severity.[36]

Such a passage absolutely confounds the hypothesis that suggests that Owen was a kind of hyper-Calvinist who portrayed God as stilted and randomly selective in his offers of love. In fact, here we are almost tempted to ask whether or not Owen the high Calvinist had changed his colors, asserting that God's love universally rests on all humanity. Was Owen's particularist soteriology becoming unhinged from his spiritual counsel? The problem cannot be evaded by assuming that Owen is speaking only of God's general promise to love all creatures through common grace. After all, the kind of love he is considering is that which is the medium for the fullest communion with God. Neither can he have meant that all will be saved, for he makes clear that some will 'fall under his severity,' which means that such persons could never have been loved with the eternal, immutable love about which Owen always speaks. If he escapes the charge of being a universalist, it may seem that Owen was at least speaking like an Arminian. Again, it may seem incredible to hear the seventeenth century's most definitive proponent of limited atonement announce so freely that God's declaration of saving love is spoken 'as particularly to thee as to any one in the world' and that simply anyone who 'believest and receivest the Father as love, he will infallibly be so to thee.' Whatever Owen meant exactly, it is impossible for him to fit the mold that Kendall casts for the English Puritans as ones who twisted Calvin's doctrine of predestination to a degree that they were prevented from freely offering the gospel to their hearers. However much William Perkin's *Golden Chaine* may have set the stage for a breed of supralapsarian Puritan preaching that could merely exhort the listener to look inward to see if God had already saved her, Owen, the thoroughly Calvinist Puritan (clearly at least in this passage), seems to have easily offered salvation to any who would truly throw themselves before the Father's love. If Owen was consistent with his Federal Theology, he was certainly applying it in a way that much contemporary assessment has not thought possible. This is a Fatherly love so free that it dare not be only narrowly offered, even granted the moral inability of sinful human wills.

A free offer of Fatherly love was not the exclusive domain of the Arminian for the following reasons. First, God's promise which is 'as particular to thee as to any' is not that God has set aside for every individual a measure of dormant saving love which is waiting to be awakened by any who will exercise faith. If this were true, then the efficient cause of salvation would be the believer himself. Owen refused this possibility, for God himself is the ultimate cause of his love to his chosen, as we have seen. The nature of the freeness of the gospel promise

---

[36] II.36-37

in Owen's understanding only requires that no one at the outset should feel disqualified from God's favor, since God's favor is bestowed on a particular person, if at all, without any reference to that person's particular inherent worthiness. This belief about unmerited favor leads to the very mystery of how the Reformed doctrine of election could be embraced by Puritans who so enthusiastically also practiced evangelistic preaching. On one hand, from the Father's own perspective, he has determined to have mercy on whom he will have mercy, and the number of the elect is therefore admittedly fixed. [37] However, since God saves those who are until that moment his enemies, humans must all consider themselves possible candidates. It becomes absurd for any sinner to complain, as Owen's objector has, 'I can believe that God is love to others...but that he will be so to me, I see no ground...no cause...no reason in the world.'[38] That there is no human ground of God's love is exactly the point. Salvation is gracious, wonder-inducing, and unexpected. Therefore, the offer of salvation must be preached to all people. Theologically speaking, this wrongheaded objection is flawless in what it observes, for it portrays an accurate self-assessment: I have done nothing and can do nothing that could merit the Father's love. However, the moment a person finishes a sentence which begins 'The reason God might save others but not me is ...' with any observation about himself, even an observation about the absence of his own faith, he has injected human contingency into God's redemptive plan. This would be to see his salvation as hinging on something in himself, rather than on God as the efficient cause and ground of it. So even while the doctrine of the decree recognized God's complete control of salvation, Puritan evangelistic preaching (except in the case of true hyper-Calvinist supralapsarians) could tell the listener that he was no better or worse a candidate for God's love than any.

While Owen shared in common with other Calvinistic Puritans the practice of freely offering of the gospel, certain differences arise with Owen when it comes to the way positive assurance one attains, differences which suggest how a robust trinitarian theology casts a larger role for human affections for God in the quest for assurance. All Puritans realized there was a difference between saying 'there is no reason God couldn't love one such as me,' and, that 'God does, in fact, love me in particular.' To arrive at this higher level of assurance, finally requires a look at the self. The standard Puritan way of providing this kind of assurance is often referred to as the 'Practical Syllogism,' which reasons:

P1: God promises to sanctify those whom he has justified.

---

[37] Rom. 9:14-18
[38] II.36

P2: I observe in myself such sanctification, that is, growth in the fruit of the Spirit, love for God, etc.

C: Therefore, God must have justified me.

Some have observed that the Practical Syllogism made the Puritans obsessively introspective regarding their level of personal holiness, but this case is often overstated.[39] As biblicists, the Puritans could not ignore that a person is not justified apart from acted faith, and secondly, a person who makes claims to faith without at least some eventual transformation of behavior and motives is likely suffering a delusion regarding his spiritual condition. God saves by his sovereign grace, but this is grace that produces observable faith and that over time causes the believer to grow in actual holiness. So admittedly, the Practical Syllogism could have the effect of centering one's attention on one's own personal holiness or decision of faith. Owen's unique way of describing the place of human response in the Syllogism might best be described by creating a sort of 'Owenian Syllogism' that features a greater role for the heart's desire for God:

P1: The Father promises that his saving love rests on any who (1) *believe that he can love such as they* (by virtue of his basic loving nature and sovereign discretion to apply that love savingly to whom he will), and who also (2) *seek to receive that love* for themselves.

P2: I *believe* the Father can savingly love such as me, and I *seek* to receive it.

C: The Father's saving love must rest on me.

Owen, like any English Calvinist who believed in some form of limited atonement, was not at first asking his objector to believe that the Bible promises that God has set aside saving love for him in particular, but only that God will be savingly loving to many. But the inquirer must believe that there is every reason that God can make him part of that many whom he justifies, for God has the character of one who will not let even the most sinful rebellion of anyone block his redemptive designs, and God can thus make a sovereign choice to savingly love anyone at all. More than this, such a sinner must desire to receive such love. The P2, which in the traditional Syllogism refers to general evidences of sanctification, refers in Owen's model to only a very narrow aspect of the Christian character: a regenerate person will believe that the Father has a family of children whom he loves eternally and immutably, and he will desire that love for himself. Therefore, P2 simply measures the presence of belief

---

[39] Leland Ryken takes aim at several similar Puritan myths in *Worldly Saints,* esp. 1-23.

and the presence of the heart's desire to be justified. If the objector looks at himself, sees such belief and such desire, then at last he can conclude that God must have savingly loved him in particular. In such a manner, the believer can comfort himself that his basic desire to be loved by the Father is evidence that he already is. Admittedly, this is close to the Practical Syllogism, yet less prone to legalism and introspection when one looks primarily to behavioral changes in order to gain feelings of peace with God. The desire for God's love, which Owen substituted for behavioral sanctification, seems more in keeping with a doctrine of God which describes the Father as, above all, affectionate toward his people. An immanent trinitarianism that has such a central place for Fatherly love (toward the divine Son and the elect whom the Son himself loves) and its power to cause a similar reflex in his beloved creatures seems to program from the start a spirituality first concerned with the heart rather than outward acts. And this is no small advantage over the traditional Syllogism.

The element of human desire for communion with God that Owen introduces into the Syllogism brings up a question about the general place of the affections in the rest of Owen's spiritual program. This point has been debated even among those who find unique value in his theology of devotion. Ferguson does not ignore the fact of his highly experiential emphasis, yet he notes that, even still, 'Owen steers a course which avoids mysticism on the one hand, and on the other, the pietism and quiescence of a later period in the Evangelical tradition, which was marred by an unhealthy subjectivism.'[40] No doubt Owen does not go as far as mystics or Quakers in his subjective focus, but David King thinks it unwise to draw too hasty a distinction between them and Owen.[41] For King, mysticism simply involves immediate knowledge of God attained through personal religious experience, and basic pietism, following Stoeffler's definition, merely requires the following four characteristics: a claim that the essence of Christianity is found in individual relationships with God made possible by a union with God, a rejection of religious nominalism (i.e. shallowness of commitment, not philosophical nominalism), a biblical emphasis, and a dissatisfaction with dominant religious patterns.[42] By these definitions, asks King, is not Owen at least somewhat of a mystic and a pietist? While King's instinct is basically right, the problem with calling Owen a mystic is that as much as he advocated a personal knowledge of God, this knowledge did not come 'immediately' but rather through the mediation of several facets of

---

[40] Ferguson, *John Owen on the Christian Life*, 224.

[41] David M. King, 'The Affective Spirituality of John Owen,' *Evangelical Quarterly* 68:3 (July 1996): 223-33.

[42] F. Ernest Stoeffler, *The Rise of Evangelical Pietism* (Leiden: E.J. Brill, 1963) 25ff, in King, 'Affective Spirituality.'

God's redemptive plan. A person only comes to experience God as knowledge of him is mediated through the Scripture, as his favor is procured through Christ's mediatorial blood-shedding, as a love of God is instilled in the believer through the Spirit's regenerative work. Mediation, not 'immediation,' is what Christian spirituality is all about, for Owen. Even the Father's intrinsic love-nature is not experienced directly. To call Owen a pietist according to Stoeffler's fairly broad definition is even somewhat defensible, but the term 'pietist' often carries with it historical baggage from the individualistic excesses of later German pietistic groups. Yet one does not need to call Owen either a mystic or a pietist to admit that he is highly oriented to religious feeling. Packer sums up Owen's balance well when he says, in speaking of Puritans in general, '[they] were not less concerned about experiential acquaintance with God than we are – rather, indeed the reverse...[but] they did not isolate this concern in their minds from their broader theological concern about the doctrine of divine grace.'[43] Indeed, Owen illustrates this holding together of the head and the heart when within one paragraph he hits on the objective, subjective, and trinitarian features of true devotion. As such, there may be no more terse and representative statement of Owen's brand of trinitarian, affective piety than this:

> The spiritual intense fixation of the mind, by contemplation on God in Christ, until the soul be as it were swallowed up in admiration and delight, and being brought unto an utter loss, through the infiniteness of those excellencies which it doth admire and adore...are things to be aimed at in prayer, and which through the riches of divine condescension, are frequently enjoyed. The soul is hereby raised and ravished, not into ecstacies or unaccountable raptures, not acted into motions above the power of its own understanding and will; but in all the faculties and affections of it, through the effectual workings of the Spirit of grace and the lively impression of divine love, 'in joy unspeakable and full of glory.'[44]

In a sense, the Father, Son, and Holy Spirit all work in distinct ways to eventually ravish the believer with the realization of the Father's love. This is a spirituality that illustrates the possibility of welding a doctrine of God to the most subjective experiences of God's love.

Communion with the Son

On one hand, Owen's treatment of the person and work of Christ is the most theologically complicated when compared to his treatment of the Father and Spirit, for here he is drawing from the deepest doctrinal rivers

---

[43] J.I. Packer, *A Quest for Godliness: The Puritan Vision of the Christian Life* (Wheaton, Illinois: Crossway, 1990) 204.
[44] IV.329-30

of Reformed scholasticism. This is a journey worth taking, however, because it illustrates the way in which even highly sophisticated theological formula that might seem arcane can be carried through quite profitably to spiritual practice. Here we will see fairly typical distinctions made by the earlier Federal Theologians, their interest to precisely define the parties and terms of various covenants they found in Scripture, and how each informs the historical unfolding of God's redemptive plan. This triune plan of redemption finds its greatest expression in Christ's mediatorial work in history – so in studying the incarnate Son's person and work we are really no further from our original interest in the Trinity's *ad extra* work and what it might mean to the worshipping Christian. This section thus deals with Owen's christology, but not as an end in itself: each facet of his christology carries through to a corresponding feature of a devotional method. Because of the rich theological trinitarianism of Covenantal Theology, we might expect that a spirituality grounded on it would also bear a trinitarian mark. And, since christology itself deals with explaining what Jesus Christ was accomplishing while in Palestine, we will see how the climax of the *historia salutis* can elicit various devotional responses. It will take some work to understand the features of Federal Theology's christology, but after doing so we will be able to see how fruitful it, and our own criteria, can be for practical spirituality.

The believer's communion with Christ is an extremely fruitful topic for Owen, and to understand its breadth, the treatment of it will be considered in two sections. Here, the meaning and effects of Christ's 'purchased grace' will be unfolded, while a separate section will deal in more detail with Owen's christological explorations as well as his more famous devotional usage of the *Song of Songs*.

As with communion with the Father, Owen wants to discover the ways in which the Son and the believer both make unique movements toward each other to complete the circuit of communion. Owen names a medium of this communion as he has with the love-medium for Fatherly communion, and in this case the believer communes with the Son through the medium of grace, both 'purchased grace' as well as what he perhaps originally coins 'personal grace.' The spheres of Christ's purchased grace and personal grace are uniquely separated by Owen in order to illuminate various aspects of communion. Functionally, this purchased grace/personal grace division serves to show the respective difference between communion as (1) a function of the forensic stages of an individual's redemption, caused by Christ's purchased grace, versus communion as (2) a function of the intimate personal relationship, which the believer is given, to Christ himself, caused by personal grace. The common theological distinction between Christ's work and Christ's person are thus preserved in Owen, yet for a different purpose than to craft scholastic theology as such. Owen, showing his recurring trait, appropriates theological categories as the foundations for categories of Christian devotional response.

Section One: Purchased Grace

The first center of communion to consider is purchased grace. By the expression, Owen means 'all that righteousness and grace which Christ has procured, or wrought out for us...by any thing that he hath done or suffered, or by anything he continueth to do as mediator.'[45] There are three sources of purchased grace: Christ's active obedience, his passive obedience (though Owen prefers the term 'suffering'), and his ongoing intercession. These three Christ-centered sources Owen also terms the 'causality' of purchased grace. The grace that Christ purchases results for the believer in three benefits: justification, sanctification, and a bundle of what Owen calls 'privileges.'[46] The relation of the three causes of purchased grace (Christ's active obedience, passive obedience, and intercession) to its three-fold manifestation (the believer's justification, sanctification, and privileges) is not to be pulled apart, rather, the first three function together to create a sort of general fund of grace which God draws on as the individual then is made to experience the three facets of redemption.

PURCHASED GRACE THROUGH CHRIST'S ACTIVE OBEDIENCE

By the term active obedience, Owen refers to Christ's actual perfect fulfillment of the entire moral law of God. Christ as the Son of God had always been subject to the Father, but this alone does no good for lost humanity. To be a successful mediator for human sinners, Christ needed to additionally submit himself to every law or ordinance that God required of fallen humanity in the Scriptures. In a sense, this was a new kind of obedience for the eternal Son, which explains what might otherwise be a confusing text from Hebrews 5:8, 'though he were a Son, yet he learned obedience.' The eternal Son, to be mediator, had to submit to the laws given to humanity in creation and other covenant contexts. A few aspects of this obedience need to be noted before we can understand how Owen finds it to impact communion with Christ.

First, the ability of Christ the man to so perfectly conform his soul to the will and mind of God flows from what Owen calls his 'habitually-inherent righteousness.'[47] Christ was of course not just a man, but a person in whom human and divine natures were united. The hypostatic

---

[45] II.154
[46] II.155, 207-22
[47] II.156

union links his human nature with God's own limitless reservoir of actual holiness, putting Christ on a plane of moral ability that is infinitely higher than even the angels. The Spirit of sanctification, which believers have only 'by measure,'[48] instead rests limitlessly on Christ, such that in him all the fullness of God dwells in bodily form.[49] Owen draws a distinction of spiritual anatomy between Christ and the believer to further highlight Christ's unique moral ability: all other creatures by virtue of their created-ness, have the limitations inherent to a dependent being; therefore, any moral ability they may have has an ultimate source outside themselves (though this is reminiscent of the Roman Catholic *donum superadditum*, it is incautious to read the doctrine into Owen; his more moderate claim seems to be that creaturliness by definition assumes dependence on the creator for moral ability, not that the creaturely state, because of some kind of inherent moral deficit, requires a supernatural added grace in order to obey God). The human nature of Christ, however, is indivisibly sealed to the person of the Son of God, and so has the 'fountain of its holiness in the strictest unity with itself.'[50] Christ obeys the law out of 'habit,' which for Owen means out of his own perfect inherent moral energy.

Had Christ not been furnished with habitual grace, he could never have fulfilled the various acts of righteousness which were required of him to obey the law in place of the many, nor could he have fulfilled the Old Testament types which required the mediator who would be sacrificed to be an absolutely unblemished lamb. In the latter regard, Owen had theological opponents who would suggest that the only function of Christ's perfect life was to establish him as a sinless sacrifice, not to merit any positive moral victory that could be imputed to others. But if such were the case, Christ's righteousness as inherent and habitual would have meant that Christ was a fit oblation immediately after his incarnation and *before* any particular acts of obedience. Why not then have Christ crucified as soon as he was born? The fact that Christ tarried on earth proves, for Owen, that his obedience served a different function than merely qualifying him to be sacrificed. As has been already suggested, Christ needed to obey God's law in real deeds in order to pass on the covenant rewards for those deeds to his chosen. We will see how this distinctive of Owen (and other Federalists) makes an impact on the spiritual life of those who believe they have received the reward for Christ's active obedience to the Father's moral law.

---

[48] Jn. 3:34
[49] Col. 1:19
[50] II.157

PURCHASED GRACE THROUGH CHRIST'S PASSIVE OBEDIENCE

The role of Christ's passive obedience has been mentioned until now more by way of contrast to active obedience, so a direct explanation is in order.[51] The passive obedience of Christ, summed up in his death and oblation, provides the second spring of communion with Christ in purchased grace. Owen proposes that Christ's passive obedience is comprised of three separate ingredients: his payment of a price, which accomplishes redemption; his offering of a sacrifice, which effects reconciliation or atonement; and his suffering a penalty to provide satisfaction to an offended party, namely, the Father.[52] It is not necessarily fruitful to delve further into these three cause-and-effects within Owen's view of the effects of passive obedience, since his understanding of the terms he uses are fairly common to Protestantism and do not seem to impact spiritual response directly. However, it is interesting that in general, Owen's view of purchased grace is that it provides something of a general trust of salvific grace from which God draws all the redemptive benefits that he gives to his elect. In other words, by Owen's general configuring, Christ's active obedience, passive obedience, and heavenly intercession together bring the sinner from the fallen state to the glorified state.[53]

---

[51] In fairness to Owen, it should be mentioned that he detested the term *passive obedience* itself, which had already established itself in Reformed circles. In one of his many passing assaults on the phrase, he says, 'it cannot be clearly evinced that there is any such thing, in propriety of speech, as *passive obedience*; *obeying is doing*, to which passion or suffering cannot belong: I know it is commonly called so, when men obey until they suffer, but properly it is not so' (II.163). As an alternative, Owen prefers the simple term 'suffering.' It seems that 'obedience' is not, for him, a word that can rightly describe an experience of suffering. Also problematic is the fact that 'passive obedience' simply appears oxymoronic. No doubt Owen's problem is more with the language of the conventional phrase than with its theological meaning. The traditional term has the advantage of reminding us of the two-sidedness of purchased grace (or three-sidedness if we follow Owen's distinction of Christ's intercession from his active and passive work), and so, with apologies to Owen, we will continue to use the term as a way to make the structure of his thought stand out more clearly.

[52] II.165; and XII.397-433

[53] Yet, at times, Owen departs from this general schema by further specifying which of Christ's acts provide exactly which benefits. For example, in a rare instance he speaks of passive obedience by saying, 'the single and most eminent part of purchased grace [which for Owen is justification] is nothing but the natural exurgency of the threefold effect of the death [i.e. passive obedience] of Christ,' (II.168). That is to say that passive obedience and justification are especially linked. Following Owen's logic, we might surmise that he would also have found a particular connection between Christ's active obedience and the believer's sanctification, since the personal holiness of Christ is parallel to the increasing personal holiness of the believer as she is made more Christ-like. Yet, as we shall soon see, Christ's passive obedience is also more fundamental for

THREE ASPECTS OF THE HUMAN RESPONSE TO CHRIST'S PURCHASED GRACE

Because Christ's purchased grace results in three benefits to the believer – justification, sanctification, and privileges – the believer holds communion with Christ in three corresponding ways. This fits well the motif seen to develop in Owen's writing: communion with God occurs when God initiates and the sinner responds with a direct 'returnal.' We might say that Christian spirituality is the sum of various human responses to specific actions of God to redeem the sinner. A restatement of the three features of purchased grace will make better sense of Owen's method. The first, justification, occurs when two things happen: the Father, through Christ, (1) removes that for which the sinner has been refused divine fellowship, and (2) bestows a more secure acceptance with God than was enjoyed even in Eden, given its probationary purpose. Thus, justification takes away the guilt and wages of sin, but further, since it is quite possible in human relations that an 'old quarrel may be laid aside, and yet no new friendship begun,'[54] justification also bestows an unlosable, alien righteousness which alone can give the 'right to the kingdom of heaven.'[55] Sanctification, the second benefit of purchased grace, proceeds from justification in that Christ now 'makes us not only *accepted*, but *acceptable*.'[56] Since justification in effect legally pronounces innocent a person who is truly and simultaneously a sinner (*simul justus et peccator*), sanctification begins the work of actually making the person inherently more holy. This occurs as the defilement of the believer's fallen nature is progressively removed, and as the actual deeds that the fallen nature produces are purified from their taint of sin so that they become pleasing to God. Both the defilement of fallen nature and the consequent defilement of deeds are removed as the 'Spirit of holiness' is made to dwell within the believer. The Spirit, once within the sinner, injects a 'new principle of life,' which effects each faculty of the

---

sanctification than is his active obedience. We should therefore not be over-eager to show exact correspondences between Christ's particular works of purchased grace and the resulting benefits. Neither does the intercession of Christ, though the third well-spring of purchased grace, obviously suggest to Owen a particular connection to the gospel 'privileges.' Owen's sometimes excruciatingly detailed schematic of the mechanics of communion with God should therefore not be seen as utterly forced. Contrary to Alan Clifford's thesis, which claims that Owen is somewhat of a slave to his system, it seems that though he is certainly systematic, he generally does not force a system where he believes the scriptures do not suggest it (Clifford, *Atonement*). This characteristic of Owen at times gives him the advantage over the systems of other Puritans (Perkins' *Golden Chaine*, for example) who may have let their desire for symmetry and order overtake exegetical simplicity.

[54] II.170
[55] II.170
[56] II.170

soul in a respective way – to the understanding it gives light; to the will, obedience; and to the affections, love.[57] Though the believer has new power to perform spiritual duties through this indwelling, he remains constantly dependent on the Spirit's enabling influences. Thus, Owen reminds us, it always remains the case that God himself must 'work in us to will and to do for his good pleasure (Phil. ii.13).'[58] The meaning of the third benefit of purchased grace, *privileges*, is almost entirely summed up by Owen in his discussions of the doctrine of adoption. Adoption and other aspects of the gospel privileges as they relate to the believer's communion with God, will be more extensively discussed below when we treat communion with the Holy Spirit. To sum up, the believer holds a sort of distinct, meditative, communion with the Christ through each of the purchased graces of justification ('acceptation' is Owen's more common word), sanctification, and privileges.

Aspect One: Responding to Christ through Justification

We turn now to consider how Owen uses such theological distinctions were taken up for the benefit of spirituality. Calvin noted that the doctrine of justification is 'the main hinge on which religion turns,' and clearly Owen sees tremendous practical value in the doctrine as well. For Owen the Reformed theologian, justification is essentially experienced passively, yet Owen the Puritan devotionalist can describe the believer's active communing with God in terms of her, in a sense, actively living out her justification. Owen's turning to a doctrine that is purely forensic as a model and impetus for a corresponding 'returnal' of spiritual exercises is one of the best illustrations of how theology can inform spirituality. Justification, in a sense, does not complete its work until the believer worshipfully responds to God's legal action: Owen goes as far as to say that after his having shown what is Christ's part in justification, 'it remains that I now show what also is required and performed on our part for the *completing* thereof.'[59] Can the believer 'complete' her justification? This is indeed surprising language. It would be impossible to suggest that Owen envisions the believer's justification as forensically incomplete, as if God's salvific determination was somehow hanging in the balance of any responsiveness in the elect. Rather, he is demonstrating his conviction that all of God's saving acts have their end, their completion, in bringing the sinner into an intimate dealing with her God. Justification makes such dealing a possibility, meaning that justification is not an end in itself.

---

[57] II.172
[58] II.172
[59] II.187, emphasis mine.

The duty of the Christian is to daily weigh all of his actions in the scales of God's justice and be reminded of the inherently damning imperfections he finds. Owen is not just talking about discovering one's active or willful sins of thought, word, or deed – the magnifying glass he offers is of a higher power than that which merely reveals disobedience. More thorough, this method of repentance involves, we might say, not only repenting of one's sins but of one's good works as well:

> Lord, what am I in my best estate? How little suitableness unto thy holiness is in my best duties! O spare me, in reference to the best thing that ever I did in my life!...When a man who lives upon convictions hath got some enlargements in duties, some conquest over a sin or temptation, he hugs himself ... But he who has communion with Christ, when he is *highest in duties of sanctification and holiness, is clearest in the apprehension of his own unprofitableness,* and rejects every thought that might arise in his heart of setting his peace in them, or upon them. He says to his soul, "Do these things seem something to thee? Alas! thou hast to do with an infinitely righteous God, who looks through and through all that vanity, which thou are but little acquainted withal; and should he deal with thee according to thy best works, thou must perish.[60]

Luther's famous expression 'all of life is repentance' is rightfully brought to mind by such passages, for to Owen, there is no imaginable good deed which does not bear entwined within it some strain of a dark motive. Even our 'good' would remove us from God. So, rather than the believer merely cataloguing what may have been displeasing to God in the course of a day, he must also repent of a taintedness in his good works, which he in his moral dullness may not even be able to specifically discern. The believer must repent even of his good deeds! There is a severity and seriousness to such daily spiritual exercises which should not be downplayed – for Owen it is right to regularly shed tears over one's sin. Even when believers enjoy assurance of their salvation, they must never graduate from the deep conviction of the sinfulness of sin, but must

> continually keep alive upon their hearts a *sense of the guilt* and evil of sin; even then when they are under some comfortable persuasions of their personal acceptance with God. Sense of pardon takes away the horror and fear, but not a due sense of the guilt of sin.[61]

However, neither would Owen have understood the criticism that such concentration on sin was spiritually morbid. In fact, his rigorous method of repentance is a necessary precursor for another of his related exercises, and, we might say, makes repentance a painful action that has an equal and opposite reaction in spiritual delight. Being first convinced of her

---

[60] II.188
[61] II.193

inherent lack of what God requires, she turns to consider Christ, whose personal holiness he has freely provided her. Owen suggests that the newly converted person who has made himself weary trying to please God, and who finally makes such a discovery of Christ's offer of this gift, will be 'surprised and amazed, and is not able to contain himself.'[62] Finding Christ's righteousness is like a starving man discovering a great dinner set before him – he may, in fact, be simply overcome with relief. Programmatically speaking, Owen does not appear to require that true Christian spirituality following conversion be regularly experienced in such ecstatic terms (though, as we will show, the raptures of the *Song of Songs* should be sought after and from time to time will be experienced). But at least, the believer's aim should be to actively consider Christ's righteousness so that his soul might 'value and rejoice' in it, to 'rest in it.'[63] The believer's savor of the feast of Christ's righteousness is not an experience of a different order than the stunned wonder of the new convert, but a more stable and matured appreciation of a now familiar gift. It would seem that Owen wants the matured believer to be so acquainted with his sin that the solution Christ offers will bring upon the soul the similar species of palpable relief that the new Christian experiences:

> This is the great mystery of faith in this business of our acceptation with God by Christ: – that whereas the soul of a believer finds enough in him and upon him to rend the very caul[64] of the heart, to fill him with fears, terror, disquietments all his days, yet through Christ he is at perfect peace with God.[65]

Again, this depths-to-heights method is Owen's program for regular spiritual exercise; it is 'our business' and not merely a description of events that are merely passively realized. It is an act, a response, a regular discipline to be worked at. The spiritual benefits are that the believer can now appear, as it were, before the face of God with 'boldness, confidence, peace, joy, assurance, – that they can call him Father, bear themselves on his love...'[66]

Now, as rich a program as this may be, one might ask how it relates to our central thesis that trinitarian theology can be helpful to spirituality. On one hand, of course, justification has reference to each member of the Trinity, even though we have been mostly describing Son's role in purchasing it. But when the believer praises the Son for justifying him,

---

[62] II.189

[63] II.188-89

[64] This is the part of the peritoneum that extends from the stomach to the large intestine.

[65] II.191

[66] II.191

even more direct trinitarian connections follow closely. It is not just the redeemed elect who praise the Son, but the Father himself. By use of Philippians 2:7-11 – where Paul describes Christ as one who made himself of no reputation, took the form of a servant, humbled himself and became obedient to death – Owen makes a scriptural connection between Christ's mediatorial acts and the diversity of praise that follows: a diversity of both the source of praise and the object of it. In this text, it is not just 'every tongue,' to speak of the human redeemed, that will confess that Jesus Christ is Lord, nor is it Jesus alone who is exalted. Rather, (1) such praise will be done 'to the glory of the Father,' and (2) for Christ's work the Father *himself* will highly exalt him by giving him the name that is above every name. Thus, the worshipping Christian joins the Father in glorifying the Son and by doing so glorifies the Father as well. We might say that the Christian, who is in union with Christ, is brought into the glorification matrix within the Trinity itself – in a sense he participates in the celebration between (and of) the Father and Son of the victory of Christ and the glorious fulfillment of the terms of the Covenant of Redemption. In this way, justification is not only the hinge of all religion, but a portal through which the believer enters into the Trinity's own glorification of itself, a glorification of its own praise-worthy attributes now most fully and publicly demonstrated. This is a way of conceiving the doctrine of justification (as well as the believer's worshipful response) that finds its wealth in a highly appropriated trinitarian theology.

What about our interest in the *historia salutis*? After 'cordially approving' of the righteousness of Christ, the second way the believer 'completes' justification is to 'make an actual commutation with the Lord Jesus'[67] as to his sins and Christ's righteousness – and this commutation is nothing if not an enacted drama which parallels Christ's own Passion. In a sense, the believer is to act out an exchange with Christ. Similar to the above step, he begins by actually tallying his sins: 'this the saints do: – they gather up their sins, lay them in the balance of the law, see and consider their weight and desert.'[68] Then he is to remind himself of the punishment and efficacious suffering that Christ underwent to satisfy God's just wrath for such sins. Christ has called him, and all people, to come with his sin burden and lay it at the foot of Christ's cross. Owen 'quotes' Christ in a sort of interpretive paraphrase of actual verses from the Gospels in order to dramatize this devotional exchange. Though it is certainly Christ's cross at Calvary that is envisioned as the location the for believer's commutation with Christ, this imagined dialogue with Jesus also appeals to the Father's involvement in the transaction. The

---

[67] II.193
[68] II.193

believer is to address himself with the words of the dying Jesus, spoken to him: 'this agreement I made with my Father, that I should come, and take thy sins, and bear them away: they were my lot. Give me thy burden, give me all thy sins... I know how to dispose of them well enough, so that God shall be glorified and thy soul delivered.'[69] Thus, as the sinner makes his transaction with Christ, he is aware that he is helping to fulfill an eternal covenant between Father and Son. The function of Christ's words in this regard is to assure the believer of the certainty that such a transaction is truly possible, for it was not only ordained from time immemorial, but also ordained by the will of a sovereign power whose saving decree through his Son would certainly be brought to reality. In addition, the believer's unloading of his sins in this quotation works ultimately so that God the Father would be glorified. Without so naming it, Owen brings in the Covenant of Redemption to serve, in this case, as an anchor of assurance to the believer in the midst of his prayers.

This 'commutation' does not function exactly like a prayer of confession of sins. Certainly, confession is an ingredient, but commutation goes beyond confession in the sense that it puts the believer in direct devotional reference to the whole breadth of features of the Reformed doctrine of justification; we might even say, if it is proper, that Owen has the believer play-acting her way through the story-line of the doctrine (perhaps 'pray-acting' expresses it better). The two movements of the believer are to lay her sins at the cross of Christ, and to take from Christ the righteousness that he has wrought for her. Such a devotional act is a near visualization (though stopping short of Julian of Norwich's elaboration) of the believer laying sins before Christ on the cross and then Christ holding out to her a gift of his procured righteousness. Strikingly, this is a devotional enactment of double-imputation, which is the legal basis for justification. In his Greater Catechism, Owen suggests such a double work, writing that justification is 'the gracious free act of God, *imputing the righteousness of Christ to a believing sinner, and* for that speaking of peace unto his conscience, *in the pardon of his sin.*'[70] Owen's catechetical formulation is therefore put into practice by the believer's exchanging her sin for Christ's righteousness. The exchange must be heartfelt, with the believer saying in the present tense, 'Here I give up my sins to him,'[71] then eagerly taking Christ's righteousness, and in so doing does he 'complete this blessed bartering and exchange of faith.'[72] Interestingly, though Owen's Reformed orthodoxy would have emphasized the completeness of Christ's active and passive obedience in history, he exhorts believers that such bartering with Christ is 'every

---

[69] II.194
[70] I.487, emphasis mine.
[71] II.194
[72] II.194

day's work; I know not how any peace can be maintained with God without it...' and regarding the propriety of this kind of devotion, it is

> ... not as though [Christ] died any more, or suffered any more; but as the faith of the saints of old made that present and done before their eyes [which had] not yet come to pass, Heb. xi.1, so faith now makes that present which was accomplished and past many generations ago. This is to know Christ crucified.[73]

As for the actual practice of the above method, Owen prescribes a combination of meditation and prayer. In meditation, the believer mentally rehearses all or part of the schema of Christ's work and his exchange with the believer. Though he suggests that the whole process be a daily exercise he also admits that the condition of the believer's heart may dictate which aspect of the program becomes the central focus at a particular time – some days the believer must seek to fill himself with the sense of his own shame and self-aborhorency; at other times, he will focus his thoughts on the righteousness of Christ and 'joy unspeakable and glorious' which it evokes. As for prayer itself, Owen gives little coaching as to how it should augment meditation, but on the above evidence we can imagine that he envisions speaking to God confessions of sin, requests for new applications of Christ's justifying blood, and perhaps direct praise and thanksgiving for the reminder of full acceptance he experiences by the Father, through the Son.

Aspect Two: Responding to Christ through Sanctification

Although sanctification is a work of the unified Trinity as is any other divine act, Christ has a unique role among the *hypostaseis* that is threefold. He first intercedes with the Father on behalf of believers, asking the Father to bestow the Spirit on them in virtue of his oblation on their behalf. Secondly, his prayer being granted, he himself sends his Spirit into the hearts of the saints to dwell there in his place. Owen defends this doctrine of dual procession with a comparison of John 14:16 to John 15:26, where Christ says first that the Father will give them the Comforter, then alternately that 'I will send the Comforter to you, from the Father.'[74] In a sense, Christ receives the Spirit from the Father, and then sends on the Comforter himself. That this mission of the Spirit is an application of Christ's purchased reserves is argued by Owen from his mediatorially-charged interpretation of John 16:14-15 (note in particular his own parenthetical exposition of the verse): 'He shall take of mine (of that which is properly and peculiarly so, – mine, as mediator, – the fruit of my life and death unto holiness), and give it unto you.'[75] Sanctification is the

---

[73] II.194
[74] II.199
[75] II.199

work of the Spirit to distribute the benefits of Christ's mediation to the elect. Thirdly, the work of Christ's sent Spirit is to bestow 'habitual grace' on the heart of the sinner, also termed by him 'habit of grace.' Comprehensively defined, such a 'habit' is

> a new, gracious, spiritual life, or principle, created, and bestowed on the soul, whereby it is changed in all its faculties and affections, fitted and enabled to go forth in the way of obedience unto every divine object that is proposed unto it, according to the mind of God.[76]

There is probably no better lens through which to observe Owen's trinitarian view of communion than his teaching on sanctification. Sanctification is God's process of effecting actual change within the believer's moral architecture. Sanctification, therefore, goes beyond the legal declaration of justification and begins to show God in progressive action, upon and throughout the psyche of the believer. In short, sanctification shows a God who is personally transforming and communing with his creatures.[77] Doctrinally speaking, God was is at work to empower believers 'to will and to do' (Phil. 2:13) so the restored human moral ability is itself a redemptive benefit already purchased by the Son from the Father. Owen does not seem willing to begin a discussion of the believer's role in sanctification without first trying to demonstrate that any of the believer's progress in personal holiness, as

---

[76] II.200. Though sanctification is usually understood in Reformed theology to be the progressive development of Christian character following conversion, Owen's definition is so encompassing that it is clear that, in a sense, he believes that a degree of sanctification must occur in order that the sinner embrace Christ in the first place, that is, as a cause of conversion itself. For example, without the Spirit's illumination of the mind, a transgressor could neither see his transgression nor believe Christ to be its solvent, nor could he determine to put his faith in Christ, nor certainly would he be able to rest in Christ with the delight and desire with which the affections, rightly operating, should embrace him. To say that this grace is a 'habit' is to say that it is constant and residing within a Christian by definition, even though it is manifested in greater or lesser degrees and in different ways. Owen adds that the Spirit will, in discrete moments, grant a particular and temporary dose of assistance or enablement so that the believer may accomplish a certain moral task – but he terms such a bestowing 'actual grace.'

[77] Not only is the immanence of God's power more greatly displayed in sanctification than justification, but Puritans who followed Augustine and Calvin in emphasizing the necessary passive role of a fallen person when she receives justification could very comfortably speak about the necessary activity, even, in a sense, cooperation of the believer with God's work, when it came to sanctification. All of this means that Puritan discussions of sanctification were unapologetically hortatory – they commanded the believer to obey God's law, resist temptation, yearn for heaven, repent of sin, forgive her enemies. One such Puritan work is Thomas Brooks' *Heaven on Earth* (Carlisle, Penn.: Banner of Truth Trust, 1996), which contains long lists of activities which will help a believer gain assurance of salvation.

well as any enabling motions of the Holy Spirit on her heart, are like withdrawals made on a limitless account of grace that Christ has been awarded by the Father on behalf of his perfect holiness and his surrender of himself to be crucified. Through various biblical passages, Owen is trying to show how the believer's federal attachment to Christ becomes the conduit by which she experiences the soul altering, Spirit-induced benefits of Christ's mediatorial purchase. [78] We might venture a new definition of communion that reflects such trinitarian and communion-centered elements: communion with God is the process by which a believer personally quickens to the direct actions of the Holy Spirit, himself sent out by Christ by virtue of the right he earned from the Father to remake his people increasingly in his own holy image. Duties and motives for holy living often make up a large part of any system of spirituality, but here we see what happens to such a system when it is born out of a doctrine of the Trinity that recognizes historically initiated and fulfilled covenantal obligations between the members of the Godhead. The great advantage is that sanctification is prevented from functionally becoming either legalistic or human-centered, since human moral energy is itself rooted in a reward to the Son from the Father. The spoils of the intra-trinitarian Covenant of Redemption accrue to the believer as her own energy for holy living. To root sanctification's power in so steady and determined an exchange between the Father and the Son is even more potent than merely saying that sanctification is somehow generally 'by grace.' Again, the connection to a doctrine of God, shaped by an intra-trinitarian covenant that was fulfilled on the stage of history, gives spirituality a concrete anchor outside the sinner that it would not otherwise have.

At this point, it may be asked what exactly the personal response of the believer amounts to. In short, she is to meditate on the purifying effects of Christ's blood, over and beyond its purely sin-atoning effects. The distinction between purification and atonement is extremely important to Owen.[79] The programmatic center, at least, of Owen's encouragement

---

[78] A few fragments of scripture show where Owen gets his exegetical support for an intra-trinitarian covenant that results in a believer's progressive spiritual growth: 'It is given unto us *for his sake* to believe on him,' (Phil. 1:29); 'We are blessed with all spiritual blessings [Owen here is thinking of sanctification as one such blessing] in heavenly places *in him*,' (Eph. 1:3); the 'pouring out of his soul unto death, and bearing the sins of many' is the foundation for not only justification ('by his knowledge he shall justify many') but also sanctification, in his 'destroying the works of the devil,' (Is. 53:10-12); 'the last Adam is made' unto believers 'a quickening Spirit' (I Cor. 15:45). II.201-2, emphases mine.

[79] On one hand, Christ's blood is the source of both atonement and purification, so even though sanctification is only directly a matter of purification rather than atonement, it still remains as grounded on the shed blood of Christ as does justification. Put more

toward mental communion with Christ through sanctification hangs upon the power of Christ's blood – shed in his act of passive obedience – as a cleanser of the mind and will.[80] How is this practiced? Owen calls the believer to 'eye' the network of truths that make up God's sanctifying

---

simply, the believer's growth in Christ-likeness is primarily grounded on what was accomplished at the cross for him, not on, say, a brute work of the Holy Spirit, and much less upon the believer's moral striving. Here also is a rare hint at how Owen relates the two causes of purchased grace (Christ's active and passive obedience) to sanctification: while Christ's active and passive obedience together create a sort of general fund of purchased grace which becomes the source of all redemptive benefits (i.e. justification, sanctification, and privileges), sanctification seems to be related more directly to Christ's passive suffering than to his active obedience.

[80] While Calvin and Owen differed on the meaning of biblical images of sprinkled blood – Calvin thought they were pictures of justification while Owen thought they illustrated sanctification – a comparison of their views helps make Owen's doctrine of sanctification more clear (cf. Calvin's *Commentary on Hebrews*, section 12). The believer's role in God's act of sprinkling (whether for the effect of justification or sanctification) is stated by both men to be 'faith': Calvin's reference above speaks of 'faith looking to an intervening blood,' and Owen likewise says that sprinkled blood becomes efficacious 'in and by a special act of faith in ourselves' (XX.360). What is significant is that Owen's most basic formulation of the believer's action in the process of sanctification is identical to what Calvin says is her involvement in justification – she exercises faith in God as the willing bestower of the gift. Since Owen everywhere agreed with Calvin's doctrine of justification through faith, he conspicuously here reveals his understanding of the practical similarity between justification and sanctification they are received by the believer. For Owen, justification and sanctification are two distinct works of God, yet in terms of the individual's devotional appropriation of such gifts, they both involve what we might call an 'actively passive' reception. Faith, after all, is a human act, but an act that involves happily consigning oneself to a strong external beneficence. Because sanctification is purchased by Christ and not attained by the believer through moral ladder-climbing, it is only consistent that the appropriation come through faith and not spiritual exercises. So, sanctification and justification identically comes through faith. This is a tremendously important and foundational piece of Owen's devotional program for two reasons. First, since Christ the mediator remains the object of both justifying and sanctifying faith, there is no divorce between the believer's experiential realization of either. Christ crucified (as well as Christ the active law-keeper) is the necessary focus not merely of the sinner seeking salvation, but also of the believer seeking spiritual growth. Christ's acts of mediation always remain in the center stage of devotion. Second, Owen's commitment to the foundational nature of sanctification as something the believer receives rather than achieves herself, allows him freedom to elaborate on what forms sanctifying faith may take without later raising questions about his fidelity to the centrality of grace over works. In other words, as we will now see, sanctifying faith is truly for Owen 'actively passive' in the sense that he prescribes an array of exercises by which the believer, in a sense, draws upon the Christ's blood to cleanse him – yet these exercises are grounded (if we read Owen properly) on passively received purchased grace, and accomplished by the believer strictly through the Spirit's enablement.

plan. So, as in justification, Owen's method is largely meditative. The believer is to think hard about his personal powerlessness to live a holy life – in his natural self he is morally bankrupt and has a fallen will that resists God at every turn. Once reminded of his ailment, he moves on to consider God's threefold promise of a remedy. God firstly has caused the Spirit of holiness to dwell in him; secondly, he has therefore been infused with a 'habit of holiness' that acts as a newfound basic instinct toward holy living; and thirdly, Christ will provide doses of actual alien assistance, through the Spirit, only by which power may he perform any moral duty. The meditative technique seems to call for a regular oscillation between thoughts of one's own inherent lack of practical holiness or moral ability and the consideration of Christ's three sanctifying gifts, which are one's only and sure hope for righteous living. Christ himself is always the object of this 'eyeing,' and doing so is 'the way, the only way, to obtain full, effectual manifestations of the Spirit's dwelling in us; to have our hearts purified, our consciences purged, our sins mortified, our graces increased, our souls made humble, holy, zealous, believing, – like to him.'[81] Even though sanctification differs from justification in that it features the active participation of the believer, it remains a grace that is passively received – sanctification comes through faith in Christ's merit just as justification does. This fact also has the effect of situating the role of the Spirit as sanctifier into a distinctively christological context. That is, sanctification comes when the believer 'eyes' Christ, and Christ in turn sends forth his Spirit as the Purifier (which, of course, carries forth the Father's loving purpose). Sanctification is therefore a project of the distinguished but unified members of the Trinity, each with its unique role to play as they condescend to respond to the sinner's prayerful meditation. Because of its roots in the Trinity's own ministrations, this is a way to practice sanctification that proves much more worship- and grace-centered than some kind of an endeavor to merely 'imitate Christ.' As with the meditative technique for justification, thoughts of the immanent love between the divine members are part of the drive to be holy, but especially central is a repeated meditation on the divine persons in their historical activities in carrying out the *historia salutis*, especially as the Son of God becomes incarnate, lives up to the Father's law, bears the law's penalty for sin, is raised, and mediates the Spirit to his people. This is a meditative spirituality to be sure, but one that has the believer glued to the divine drama for the basis of her consolation and moral energy.

---

[81] II.206-207

Section Two: Personal Grace

Communing with the Son through what he calls 'personal grace' is the other major motif in the Owenian scheme for understanding how a believer is to deal with the second person of the Trinity. One reason, I suggest, that Owen is well-suited to illustrate the often unnoticed devotional possibilities of Federal Theology can be summarized by his very coining of the phrase 'personal grace.' On one hand, nothing that he will say about the Son's personal grace to the believer is theologically or even covenantally distinct from what he has already said concerning purchased grace. But on the other hand, Owen wants to somehow emphasize that the forensic and covenantal actions of Christ are, in the end, in service of a personal, face-to-face dealing between two lovers, a groom and his bride. We might say that he is interested to show that the covenantal relationship between the Trinity and the believer is not merely legal, but also intimate and personal – this also works to undercut the common notion that Federal theologians like Owen could only speak in forensic language about divine and human relations. Here we see Owen at his most medieval. The biblical *Song of Songs* provides, according to him, a virtual manual for every detail of the believer's relationship with Jesus. Christ himself is the true bridegroom in this book, and the believer (or the church) is the bride. Accordingly, in his work on the *Song*, he pursues with abandon the allegorical method about which the Reformers were less than enthusiastic. But I suggest that once a redemptive-historical grid is in place, more use of such medieval forms is possible without the common excesses of the allegorizing of realist mysticism. Is it possible too that inheritors of early Protestant orthodoxy, like Owen, were less afraid of allegory than the first generation Reformers because their doctrine had become stable enough to provide allegorizing with some external controls? Perhaps there are advantages to pursuing the *Song* with the devotional zeal of the allegorizer who nonetheless operates with trinitarian orthodoxy and redemptive history as her guides. The result, as we shall see, accrues directly to the construction of trinitarian spirituality. What is best first considered, though, is the tradition of interpretation of the *Song* from which Owen was certainly drawing.

THE *SONG OF SONGS* IN BERNARD OF CLAIRVAUX: THE THEOLOGY OF THE KISS

No one doubts that the Reformers and post-Reformation Protestants were uniquely enthusiastic about Bernard above perhaps any other medieval writer. Calvin either quotes or names him forty-six times in the *Institutes* alone, with the number of citations growing as each new edition of his work was published. Bernard was not a left-over memory from Calvin's earlier humanist training, but was discovered by him as a great ally even as his own thinking developed. Bernard himself had sought to rescue Augustinianism from the perceived semi-Pelagianism of Peter Lombard and the Aristotelian rationalism of Peter Abelard in favor of a higher view of sin, and a consequent higher dependence on divine grace.[82] For these reasons there should be no surprise that Owen also delights in Bernard, citing him almost twenty times in his collected works. However, the really striking connection between Owen and Bernard lies in a commonality that goes beyond their shared version of Augustinianism, and, in fact, has much to do with an explicit trinitarianism.

It has been suggested by Etienne Gilson that if the philosophy of Augustine is essentially a metaphysics of conversion (because his writing is dominated by the fact of his religious experience of his own conversion), Bernard's is a theology of compunction. This monastic idea of compunction was that while man

> had lost the perfect spiritual freedom that permitted continual union with God... he can still regain that freedom. He does not despair for he knows that God became man and saved us in Jesus Christ, and that hereafter his salutary grace is at work in us. Thus, there are always two sides to the question: a deep realism that causes humility and a sure hope that gives rise to courage and optimism.[83]

This view, that authentic joy in God can only result when the believer is first experientially convinced of the depth of her lostness, is a controlling theme for Owen as well, as has been shown. Yet related to Bernard's theology of compunction is what Leclercq calls the actual 'summit of his doctrine,' a theme that finally becomes absolutely clear in Book Five of *Consideration*, Bernard's final piece of writing. The summit is his teaching about quiet contemplation of the mysteries of the Trinity and incarnation, and about the whole goal of the interior life, which is to 'instill in us the very life of the Trinity.'[84] The Augustinian and trinitarian themes in Bernard were enough to attract the Reformers and later Protestant Scholastics, yet what is perhaps less appreciated is that Bernard's vision of the spiritual life was itself thoroughly trinitarian. His vision comes close to satisfying our criteria in some ways, even if it was improved upon by those who followed his approach to the *Song*, but with added hermeneutical controls.

Bernard preached a series of sermons on the *Song of Songs* where his brand of trinitarian mysticism gets the most in-depth treatment. He followed in a long tradition beginning with Origen which held that King Solomon had written three books (Ecclesiastes, Proverbs, and the Song of Songs) of increasing difficulty by which the soul could eventually ascend

---

[82] W. Standford Reid, 'Bernard of Clairvaux in the Thought of John Calvin,' *Westminster Theological Journal* 41 (Fall 1978): 127-45.

[83] Jean Leclercq, introduction to *Bernard of Clairvaux: Selected Works* (New York: Paulist Press, 1987) 36.

[84] Leclercq, introduction to *Bernard of Clairvaux*, 26 and 45.

to the highest contemplation of God. So, Bernard was convinced that to preach the *Song* rightly meant to unlock for his listeners the key to the ultimate joy in communion with God. It would seem from these sermons that the most provocative image in the *Song* for him is that of the kiss between the lover and his beloved. In a sense, his whole devotional theology is summed up in the kiss, especially when the full allegorical meaning is drawn from it.

Everything about the kiss that is described in the *Song* contributes to a trinitarian spirituality. In the second sermon, Bernard identifies the mouth that initiates the kiss as the eternal Word who assumes human nature. The recipient of the kiss is the human flesh which the Word unites to itself in the incarnation, while the kiss itself is Jesus Christ, the person who is of both the Word and the flesh (just as a kiss is of both the giver and the receiver). This highly allegorized interpretation sees the kiss as a revelation of the christology of the God-man. But the next level of Bernard's interpretation takes the kiss in an entirely different way, this time to mean Christ's kissing the believer. At this deeper level, the kiss that is now received by the bride, the church, is derivative of the original christological kiss. When the bride contemplates the kiss of Christ and realizes that it is actually derivative of the original kiss that formed Christ's own person, the effect is to infuse her with joyous assurance. She realizes that by receiving a kiss from the one who is himself the ultimate kiss between divine and human nature, she has received a great promise of mediation between herself and the triune God:

> How, I say, shall I, who am dust and ashes, presume to think that God care about me (Sir. 10:9)? He loves his Father. He does not need me...[but] if the Mediator is to be acceptable to both sides, let God the Son of God become man; let him become the son of man, and make me sure of him with the kiss of his mouth. When I know that the Mediator who is the Son of God is mine, then I shall accept him trustingly.[85]

So, receiving a kiss from Christ confers assurance of God's favor and care, that is, that the God-man loves her, and therefore so does God the Father.

Kissing, of course, is a mutual affair, and Bernard features something close to Owen's 'returnal' of affection, now flowing from the believer toward the Son. In sermons three and four, the *Song*'s picture of the bride kissing the groom's feet is understood to mean the believer's returning of the kiss by deploring her sin and humbly responding to Christ at the initiation of the Christian life. As the believer grows in the faith, she moves upward and kisses his hands, imploring him to lift her up even higher, closer and closer to his face. At last she reaches his mouth, and by finally kissing his lips, she experiences one-ness with him. The

---

[85] Bernard of Clairvaux, *Selected Works*, 218.

kiss on the mouth is a rare experience, however, and only for advanced Christians. Bernard's ladder-climbing medieval method shows itself most strongly in this progression, and does not find much of an echo with Owen. However, Bernard's language about the mouth-kiss itself would not have been offensive to Owen – far from it: the kiss is primarily an exchange of affection between bride and groom. She does not flirt when she asks to approach his mouth, but directly tells him what she desires. Because she is drunk with love, his fearsome power does not dissuade her.[86]

The highest trinitarian ground for all of this kissing is what Bernard considers the absolute highest kiss, which is not to be experienced by creatures, but is between Father and Son. If it begins to seem difficult to sort out who is kissing whom and under what conditions, Bernard seems to not want us to obsess over finding in these sermons a clear hermeneutic or expositional rule. He is happy to move between various quite different levels of interpretation with nothing more than repeating '…but listen to another meaning…'[87] The ultimate kiss is between Father and Son, the kiss itself being the Holy Spirit who is the bond, unity, and love between Father and Son. The bride's request for her kiss then is only derivative of this kiss, a nonetheless bold request for the Spirit, 'in whom the Father and Son will reveal themselves to her. For one of them cannot be known without the other.'[88] By quoting John 17:3, 'This is everlasting life, to know that you are the true God and to know Jesus Christ whom you have sent,' he explains, 'the supreme happiness consists in the knowledge not of one but of both.'[89] Bernard is adamant that the believer even has a distinct personal knowledge of the Spirit through this:

> But someone is saying, 'Therefore it is not necessary to know the Holy Spirit, for when he said that eternal life is to have known the Father and the Son, he made no mention of the Holy Spirit.' That is so, but where the Father and Son are known fully how can their goodness, which is the Holy Spirit, not be known?…There is an implied reference to the Holy Spirit.[90]

And lastly, 'so when the Bride asks for a kiss, she begs to be flooded with the grace of this three-fold knowledge as much as mortal flesh can bear.'[91] And if any of this were to seem too sentimental, Bernard insists that the effect of this Trinity-revealing kiss on the believer is both 'light and love,' that is, both a new grasp of truth and an increased affection for

---

[86] Bernard of Clairvaux, *Works*, 231-32.
[87] Bernard of Clairvaux, *Works*, 217.
[88] Bernard of Clairvaux, *Works*, 237.
[89] Bernard of Clairvaux, *Works*, 237.
[90] Bernard of Clairvaux, *Works*, 237-38.
[91] Bernard of Clairvaux, *Works*, 238.

the Godhead, for it is the Son who offers the kiss, the kiss itself is the Holy Spirit, and the Spirit in turn reveals the Father. To say it another way, 'this kiss leaves no room for error or apathy.'[92] The trinitarian kiss received by the believer thus reveals all members of the Godhead, and leads both to love, knowledge, and even zeal for the divine husband. Here again we see the same midway course being steered between pure speculative knowledge on one hand, and unchecked mystical experience on the other, a balance we also saw Walter Hilton at pains to set forth.

The value of Bernard for trinitarian devotion cannot be overestimated, yet his method is somewhat opaque when it comes to which members of the Trinity are providing and receiving what kisses and graces. Bernard is not bothered by this because his allegorical method is happy to find overlapping and manifold meanings within the text. But would the clarity of such devotion not be increased were Bernard able to articulate the distinct contributions of grace of each hypostasis? And would the abstractness of love he speaks of not be improved with concrete ties to the historical manifestations of the love of God in the gospel events? Certainly, hints of both suggestions are found within Bernard, and overall we should see him as a great ally and pioneer in the present project. Yet to add a redemptive-historical context and reference to the properly distinguished work of the divine persons to Bernard's basic vision would make a more biblically sensitive spirituality that would be even more explicitly trinitarian.

THE *SONG* ACCORDING TO JOHN OWEN

A few brief words are justified on the matter of Owen's hermeneutic before exploring his main use of the *Song*. The words must be brief because Owen does not defend allegorizing as much as he takes it for granted, never seeming to imagine that anyone would take the opposite view that the Canticles are merely love poems. However, in 1669 Owen wrote the introduction to a commentary on the *Song* written by James Durham, a stern and renowned Scottish preacher, where he has a few direct words about method.[93] Owen says that while the *Song* is 'absolutely allegorical,' properly interpreting it still requires 'great heedfulness, skill and diligence, both in things spiritual...and in the nature of those schemes

---

[92] Bernard of Clairvaux, *Works*, 239.
[93] James Durham, *An Exposition of the Song of Solomon* (Edinburgh: Banner of Truth, 1997). Interestingly, Durham had been appointed in 1650 to Professor of Divinity in Glasgow University, but before he could take the post, the General Assembly of the church in Scotland made him chaplain to the future King Charles II. Ten years later, after Durham had died, his book on the Canticles was published and endorsed by Owen, a man who had been Cromwell's chaplain, the soldier who had, of course, approved of the execution of Charles' father.

or figures of speech.'[94] With fascination he notes that the Jewish Targums are bulkier on the Canticles than on any other book, and themselves acknowledge that in places it speaks of the Messiah.[95] For Durham himself, whose method Owen seems to endorse, two of the primary interpretive requirements when approaching the *Song* are that the student have an experiential knowledge of God's love for her own heart ('such kind of experience is one of the best commentaries upon this text') and that she be in regular 'conversing with the Bridegroom, especially by prayer,' for in these sessions of prayer, Christ may open her eyes to see him in the text.[96] Durham shares the Augustinian and Owenian conviction that the proper mental understanding is dependent on faith, especially in a book like this where one might miss Christ altogether unless the eyes of her heart were not already focused on him. More technically speaking, Durham believed that in fact all Scripture should be interpreted 'literally,' however, there are two kinds literal modes – the immediate, and the figurative (or, mediate). The Canticles is written in the latter sense – literal, though mediated by various figures and images. How does one know for sure that this literal-but-mediate method is the right way to read the *Song*? Because if the words were taken literally-*immediately*, they would have no edifying value, much less, they would even seem to contradict other moral requirements that the Bible has for human marital relationships. For example, in chapter five of the *Song*, the bridegroom advertises her lover's greatness and beauty to other women, hoping to excite their love for him as well. Surely this cannot be a Song that is really about the ideal of human marital love with such allusions to husband sharing. But beyond this insistence on a figurative literalness, as oxymoronic as that description may seem, Durham distinguishes between two types of figurative literature, the typical and the allegorical. Types refer to some truth that is grounded in objective history, they primarily deal with persons and facts, and always compare an Old Testament person or fact to a particular New Testament person or fact – such as the historical experience of Jonah in the whale's belly that typified Christ's three-day experience in the grave. Allegories, on the other hand, have no basis in history, go beyond facts to include uses of words and expressions, and are principally about doctrine or are used for other 'mystical' ends.[97] On these grounds, the *Song* is pure allegory, has no basis in any historical marriage of King Solomon, but has everything to say about how to love and be loved by Christ. It would appear that Owen endorsed Durham's hermeneutic.

---

[94] Owen, introduction to Durham, *An Exposition*, 20.
[95] Owen, introduction to Durham, *An Exposition*, 20-21.
[96] Durham, *An Exposition*, 24-25.
[97] Durham, *An Exposition*, 24-61.

Unlike Bernard, who is focused on the kiss, Owen is primarily fixed on the *Song*'s description of the husband as 'white and ruddy.' Christology is what allures him about this description, as it does Bernard in the kiss. Owen believes the 'whiteness' of the groom refers to the glory of his deity, while the 'ruddiness' suggests the preciousness of his humanity – thus, contained in these two adjectives is a miniature theology of the hypostatic union.[98] Of course, he does not point this out for mere theological interest, for he believes the union of God-ness and man-ness, together makes Christ 'comely' and 'beautiful' for the believer, and is the basis on which Christ 'provides all the wants of men.'[99] The main thing for the believer to learn about Christ in the *Song* is that, as a perfect husband to his saints, his primary goal is simply to 'convince them of his good-will to them...and upon their consent to accept of him, – which is all he requires or expects at their hands, – he engages himself in a marriage covenant to be theirs forever.'[100] Absent from his treatment of the marriage of Christ to the believer is any moralistic strain about being a good wife to Christ (as important as that may be) or a charge to not drive him off, as we saw in the *Imitatio Christi*. The purpose of the *Song* is to simply woo the believer by Christ's loveliness, for unless Christ appear desirable, there is simply no resisting the sinful desires of the flesh. The target, again for Owen, is the affections. Here his prescribed use of the *Song* is to attain what John Donne more poetically prays for in another glimpse of how the Trinity can inform an affective, even romantic, spirituality:

> Batter my heart, three person'd God; for, you
> As yet but knocke, breathe, shine, and seeke to mend;
> That I may rise, and stand, o'erthrow mee,' and bend
> Your force, to breake, blowe, burn and make me new.
> I, like an unsurpt towne, to'another due,
> Labour to'admit you, but Oh, to no end,
> Reason your viceroy in mee, mee should defend,
> But is captiv'd, and proves weake or untrue.
> Yet dearely'I love you,' and would be loved faine,
> But am betroth'd unto your enemie:
> Divorce mee,'untie, or breake that knot againe,
> Take mee to you, imprison mee, for I
> Except you'enthrall mee, never shall be free,
> Nor ever chast, except you ravish mee.[101]

---

[98] II.49
[99] II.52-53
[100] II.57
[101] John Donne, *The Complete Poetry and Select Prose of John Donne* (New York: The Modern Library, 1994) 252.

Common to both Owen and Donne is the hope that Christ will divorce the believer from her false husbands, and do it not by merely appealing to her mind, but by ravishing her. Donne's poem is remembered today, but Owen's interpretation of the *Song* is largely forgotten, probably because Owen rarely could muster glistening prose, much less poetry, and he rarely left behind the forensic language of covenant theology, which never sounds quite as romantic. But when given the chance, the practical trajectory of various facets of the redemptive covenants of Federal Theology often do translate to affective themes that are neither stilted nor sentimental, even if not quite poetic. For example, the Covenant of Redemption between Father and Son finds its way into Owen's interpretation of the Canticles when he writes:

> The thoughts of communion with the saints were the joy of [the Son's] heart from eternity. On the compact and agreement that was between his Father and him, that he should divide a portion with the strong, and save a remnant for his inheritance, his soul rejoiced in the thoughts of the pleasure and delight which he would take in them, when he should actually take them into communion with himself...So Christ did take us then into his care, and rejoiced in the thoughts of the execution of his trust.[102]

When Owen refers to 'communion with Christ through personal grace' what he means above anything else is a mutual 'delight' between Christ and his people, akin to the way an idealized marriage would work. Following delight comes 'valuation,' and then 'chastity,' but the prime place is given to delight.[103] In one section he even uses an argument from a kind of Augustinian/neo-platonic hierarchy of being to try to stir up the believer's affections: All created things that might compete for a person's love can be placed on an ascending ladder. A king is much greater than a beggar or a worm, but an angel is far greater than even a king. Even still, an angel and a worm are only separate from one another in degrees of worthiness. Jesus Christ is superior in that, and in reference to his divine nature, he transcends the ladder altogether. A created soul can only find rest in an uncreated lover. In the end, Christ can satisfy infinitely, and any creature, even the greatest, will not be substantial enough to hold up under the love that the human soul wants to pour out.[104] The requirements of the believer for covenant faithfulness and obedience to Christ, that is 'chastity,' certainly have their place, for Owen is not antinomian. He simply believes that one can only be lastingly chaste toward somebody whom one has first been deeply attracted to. And attraction comes when

---

[102] II.118-19

[103] Cf. II.118-36 for a discussion on the nature of delight, as well as II.79-117 for a lengthy digression on the topic.

[104] II.60-61

the believer humbly first sees through the imagery of the *Song* that the God-man is the kind of lover of which can be said, 'there is not the meanest, the weakest, the poorest believer on the earth, but Christ has prized more than all the world.'[105]

If it is possible that the often-derided method of allegorical interpretation becomes more exegetically reliable when it is bounded by the external controls of the biblical covenants, then a book like the *Song of Songs* may still have much use for developing devotional habits. Even someone as theologically precise as Owen could not be cured from the belief that to know the *Song* was to know how to love and be loved by Jesus, and that such love swept the believer into a whole matrix of trinitarian love. Those who become convinced of a similar covenantal matrix may find the *Song of Songs* fertile soil for deeper ways of relating to the personal love of Jesus, his Father, and the Spirit, in ways simultaneously orthodox and emotively profound.

Communion with the Holy Spirit

In this study, we have noticed that the Holy Spirit's presence in historical devotional models often tends in one of two problematic directions. He is either presented with a vague or almost modalistic identity, as if 'Spirit' were general shorthand for God's active agency, or he is emphasized in a way that is so immediate to the believer that there is no necessary or obvious connection to the biblical redemptive story driven forward by all three divine persons. The former tendency appears in the medieval realists, and the latter, in our study, among the Quakers. Both tendencies are somewhat answered by our criteria: if a properly defined and distinguished doctrine of the three persons is adhered to, the Spirit can be appreciated for his distinct personhood and work, and if the scriptural drama of unfolding redemption is seen to be the prime revealer of the triune God at work, then the ministry of the Spirit will be better connected to the accomplishment of Jesus Christ as the climax of that drama. Observing Owen's system will further illustrate the possible mechanics and added benefits of our proposal.

The foundational reason, for Owen, that believers can have direct personal access to the Holy Spirit is that, in the economy of salvation, the Spirit personally proceeds toward them from the sending of the Father and from Jesus Christ. Owen's descriptions of the dual procession emphasize both the unity and uniqueness of the Father and Son's roles in the sending of the Spirit. The Spirit is poured out, 'from the love of the Father, by the procurement of the Son; and thence is that variety of expression, of the *Father's sending* him, and the *Son's sending* him from

---

[105] II.136

the Father, he being the gift of the Father's love, and purchase of the blood of the Son.'[106] Both Father and Son send, but in reference to real hypostatic distinctions, the Father sends because of his love, and the Son sends by virtue of his mediatorial purchase. Thus, while Owen shows fidelity to the doctrine of God's unity, he does not do so at the expense of overtaxing the doctrine of appropriations when he begins to speak about God's diversity. While Owen believes the sending of the Spirit is a work of the whole Trinity, it should come as no surprise by now that, while respecting divine unity, he also makes the case for the Spirit's distinctive determination to send himself.[107] Thus, all human communion with the Holy Spirit is rooted in an undivided work of the Trinity, who makes the Spirit present to the believer, without downplaying the Spirit's distinct role in carrying the saving drama into the subjective experience of the believer.

The Spirit's Economic Procession

Owen identifies two key senses in which the Spirit may be said to proceed. Both are theologically important, but only the latter has a direct bearing on a practical theology of worship. On one hand, there is an eternal procession of the Spirit in respect to his substance or personality.[108] The reality of the procession of substance makes possible

---

[106] II.231

[107] II.226

[108] In a sense, this procession of substance is 'the first and most remote foundation of all our distinct communion with him,' (II.227), yet it is not related to communion in any obviously practical way. Because the believer can only respond to the mystery of such an eternal procession as an article of faith, not by any direct experience, the eternal procession is not a truth that Owen believes can be directly plumbed for devotional uses. Exegetically speaking, Owen does not find the procession of substance in every place that others have: even a text like John 15:26, 'But when the Comforter is come, whom I will send unto you from the Father, even the Spirit of truth, which proceedeth from the Father, he shall testify of me,' though being a classic text to prove the Spirit's eternal procession (Calvin, *Institutes*, I.13.17) does not, for Owen, directly declare the procession of substance or personality (what he terms the procession of *phusikei* or *hypostatikei*, II.226). Thomas Goodwin, whose thesis on the work of the Holy Spirit shows much affinity with Owen's general desire to unfold the doxological value of pneumatology, counters that John 15:26 is intended, at least in part, 'to shew the divine procession of the Holy Ghost, and the original and the consubstantiality of his person, to be out of the substance of the Father, proceeding from him,' (Thomas Goodwin, *The Work of the Holy Ghost in Our Salvation* in *Works*, [Carlisle, Penn.: Banner of Truth Trust, 1979 rept.] VI.5). Owen disagrees. While in the main he could give his consent to Goodwin's doctrine of the Spirit, he does not see John 15:26 as an ontological assertion as much as an economical one. Precisely because Owen and Goodwin are nearly theologically identical on so many points of doctrine, this slight difference in their

the second kind of procession, a type that has more direct implications for communion. The Spirit's economical or 'dispensatory' proceeding is a function of trinitarian grace at work, and results so that a particular saving purpose may be realized. The purpose of the Spirit's economical procession is to 'testify to men,' that is, to illumine human minds to all that Christ is and has procured on behalf of his people. The connection between the two species of procession – essential and economical – must not be missed: the eternal procession makes possible the actual dispensation, so that 'this relation *ad extra* (as they call it) of the Spirit unto the Father and the Son, in respect to operation, proves his relation *ad intra*, in respect of personal procession.'[109] Not only is Owen directly arguing for a kind of epistemological key to the Trinity's functioning – that God's outward works illuminate something of his internal being – but also he is arguing that God is most fully known when he reveals himself as a triune Savior. Here, the theological key to Owenian devotion simply reveals itself in another doctrine. The doctrine of the economic procession of the Holy Spirit carries with it an implicit trinitarianism, and therefore tells the believer that to have any communion with the eternal God, he must relate to him through his economical plan of salvation. In view of our current consideration of the Spirit, this might be phrased, 'to know God is to know his Spirit, whom the Father and the Son have sent to complete their project of redemption.'

The procession of the Spirit to undertake the role of Comforter also reveals the Father as the 'fountain' of all such 'works in the pursuit of electing love' and as well the Son's ministry of grace in sending the Spirit on the basis of his mediatorial purchase.[110] Owen conjoins the

---

exegesis of such a text makes more vivid Owen's general tendency to see scripture as the public record of a saving God in action, more than as a text describing the essence of God's spiritual anatomy. Of course, though this is his pattern, we should not be tempted to over-argue that for Owen the work of the Spirit does not illuminate something abut his eternal nature. Certainly, Owen does not avoid other ontological descriptions of the Godhead – for example, one of his arguments in *The Death of Death in the Death of Christ* regarding limited atonement is that a God who is inherently sovereign would not put into action a plan of salvation that was so open-ended as is the Arminian description. (Among other passages, X.200-208 argues that since God's primary goal in redemption is the glorification of himself, with the enjoyment of his people as an important though secondary means to this end, he would not allow the contingency of human free will to jeopardize his plan.) In that argument, ontology is actually what determines economy. To exegete a passage like John 15:26 in the way he does, however, is to show that only through the public saving work of the Trinity may one come to understand God's nature, or to put it another way, the economy of triune salvation is the primary lens through which we may grasp the nature of the immanent Trinity.

[109] II.227
[110] II.228

ontological and economical aspects of the Spirit as he describes the believer's approach to the Spirit:

> this, also, faith takes in and closeth withal, in our communion with the Comforter: — the conjunction and accord of his will with the gift of Father and Son; the one respecting the distinct operation of the Deity in the person of the Holy Ghost; the other, the economy of the whole Trinity in the work of our salvation by Jesus Christ. Here the soul rejoiceth itself in the Comforter, — that he is willing to come to him, that he is willing to be given to him.[111]

This is at once, I suggest, an affirmation of the western emphasis on divine unity while also positing the 'distinct operation' of God the Holy Spirit — and the benefit of asserting both of these aspects of trinitarian doctrine makes a fruitful impact on the way devotion is practiced. For example, there is a distinction between 'closing' with the Comforter as a member of the Godhead and closing with him as the saving agent of the Father and Son. How might such a distinction inform prayer? On one hand, for the believer to make a petition to the Father for the Spirit's presence is already put forth in the New Testament. Jesus the Son in Luke 11:13 promises that 'Your heavenly Father will give the Holy Spirit to them that ask him.' In light of this text, Owen claims that it is proper to appeal to the Father so that he will send his Spirit, thereby seeking the Spirit *indirectly* and seemingly in observance with the order of divine procession. Yet, on the other hand, Owen says that since the Holy Spirit is God, he may be invoked or called on *directly*, just as Father and Son may be.[112] How then should the believer apply for the Spirit's aid and presence — directly or through the Father as the sender? The distinction Owen makes in the above passage seems to act as a framework when he makes the case that either object of prayer is proper in its own way and for its own unique purpose:

> In our prayers that are directed *to himself*, we consider him as essentially God over all, blessed for evermore; we pray *for him* from the Father and Son, as under this mission and delegation from them. And, indeed, God having most plentifully revealed himself in the order of this dispensation to us, we are (as Christians generally do) in our communion to abound in answerable addresses; that is, not only to the person of the Holy Ghost himself, but properly to the Father and Son for him, which refers to this dispensation.[113]

Because the Holy Spirit shares in the being of God, he is, in the same sense as the other *hypostaseis*, independent, free, and omnipotent — qualities that make him able to receive and respond to prayers addressed

---

[111] II.228-29
[112] II.268, 270
[113] II.230, emphasis mine.

directly to him. It is also proper to pray to the Father and the Son to give the Spirit, for to pray in this manner respects the appropriations by which the Godhead has determined to deliver to his people the saving benefits of Christ. It is almost predictable that Owen would need to raise this question (for his audience, but it seems for himself as well) regarding which of these two routes to the Spirit is more appropriate for the worshipper – the direct or the indirect route.[114] Why so? Because two common Owenian themes seem to require both methods together: on one hand, distinct communion with any one member of the Trinity is possible and proper, and on the other, the exact nature of such communion is shaped by the role each member plays in the story of redemption. The believer can, and ought, to pray directly to the Holy Spirit because the Spirit is God – yet, the nature of such prayer, as we will see, is to thank, exult, and appeal for the Spirit's work of regeneration, conviction of sin, comfort amidst affliction, and sanctification from indwelling sin. Since these benefits have been purchased by the Son, through the design of the Father, the believer may directly appeal to the Father and Son to send these gifts through the Spirit. So, both prayer *to* the Spirit and prayer *for* the Spirit are appropriate, in their own ways. If, as we are suggesting, both a doctrine of immanent trinitarian relations and redemptive history are built into the foundations of the spiritual life, then at least something like this pattern of communion with the Spirit will result.

What exactly is the believer inviting upon herself when she prays to or for the Spirit? The answer remains oriented to the objective redemptive accomplishment of the triune God, even though the Spirit's role in salvation is often more subjectively oriented to the believer's own experience and psyche. The Spirit may be alternately described as the 'Spirit of sanctification' and the 'Spirit of consolation.'[115] The first he is to the unregenerate elect, changing them from sinful unbelievers into sinful yet forgiven believers, while the latter he is to believers as believers, bringing them an inward awareness and appreciation for what Christ has done for them. Simply put, the 'Spirit of sanctification' refers to the Spirit when his work is objective and forensic, and he is the 'Spirit of consolation' in his work within the Christian's mind to make that objective work subjectively real to the Christian. Owen's two categories though sometimes seem blurred – in one place he describes the Spirit's 'consolation' role to mean 'giving them the privileges of the death and purchase of Christ,' which might seem to include more objective acts (such as regeneration or justification).[116] However, remembering that Owen tends to use the word 'privileges' to mean something other than

---

[114] The rhetorical question is a rare literary device for Owen, yet he uses it here as he seems to frankly think his way through the believer's access to the Spirit.
[115] II.226ff, 232ff
[116] II.226

forensic benefits like justification, we are less confused when we elsewhere find him saying that sometimes the Spirit flatly refuses to provide consolation to a given believer.[117] Consolation as some kind of immediate and fully-manifested gospel privilege is not a believer's right merely on the basis of his union with Christ and Christ's purchased grace. Though the Spirit is the Spirit of consolation, he does not always act in this capacity in the same way that he is constant as sanctifier.

The benefit of this kind of thinking is that it allows the following overarching guideline for devotional expectations: The Spirit, when he consoles the believer, primarily does so with reference to the saving accomplishments of Christ. While many devotional traditions would affirm that the Spirit's work is greatly concerned with subjective benefits to the believer, a redemptive-historical model affirms and yet anchors this conviction by asserting that the Spirit's ministry to the believer was first as an actor in an historically performed salvific story. So, even the believer's subjectively experienced consolation from the Spirit is grounded in that story and not any merely subjective story of the worshipper's own making. The believer does not expect to receive only a vague sense that God generally loves her, but knows that her real consolation will come when the Spirit reminds her anew of the concrete facts of the story: of the Father's unbounded love for her evidenced at the cross; of her Lord crucified in her place and then resurrected for her as the prototype of her own future resurrection; of the descent of the Spirit at Pentecost, which reminds her that she too now is indwelled and empowered by him; even of the future event where her Lord will return and receive her as a groom receives his cherished bride. This is consolation, but not of a general or merely subjective kind. It is a consolation consciously drawn from a compelling story about a trinitarian God's acted love for her. For its rootedness in theology and history, it is also a devotion that is simultaneously deeper while less susceptible to novelty or unnecessarily complicated technique.

Indwelling

Closely linked to the sanctifying and consoling role of the Spirit is the concept of his indwelling. That the Holy Spirit is purchased for sinners by the oblation of Christ and that he is bestowed upon them through Christ's intercession with the Father is clear enough – what Owen seeks to make more clear is the exact sense in which the Spirit abides with believers. Again, Owen does not think that seeking an answer for such a metaphysical question is an exercise in theology for theology's sake, but it is crucial for the sake, as we will soon see, of the Spirit's ministry of

---

[117] II.233

consolation itself. More specifically, there is a danger that if the Christian exegete, either scholar or layman, comes to the wrong conclusion about the mode of the Spirit's indwelling, she will undercut her own sense of assurance and comfort that the Spirit offers to provide.

To put Owen's teaching succinctly, the Spirit really, literally, personally enters the believer *in interiori vestro* ('in the inmost part') in order to give her mystical union with Christ, through whom is accomplished all the purposes of the trinitarian economy toward her.[118] Owen is extremely concerned about the first aspect of this definition – that the Spirit in his actual person has come to live in the believer in the most concrete sense that such an assertion can be made of a non-physical person. The following sorts of texts must be interpreted 'literally and properly, not figuratively and metaphorically'[119]: 'I will put my Spirit within you and cause you to walk in my statutes,' (Ezek. 37:27); 'Now if any man not have the Spirit of Christ, he is none of his,' (Rom. 8:9); 'God has sent forth the Spirit of his Son into our hearts, crying "Abba, Father."' (Gal. 4:6); 'That good thing committed unto the keep by the Holy Ghost which dwelleth in us,' (2 Tim. 1:4). The reason for his vigorous arguing for a literal indwelling, and the reason he believes God gives so much scriptural revelation about it, is that 'the Lord knowing how much of our life and consolation depends on this truth, redoubles his testimony of it, that we might receive it, – even we who are dull and slow of heart to believe.'[120] There is a subtle distinction to be noticed here. Owen is not just arguing that the Spirit must personally be inside the believer in order to comfort the heart,[121] but that the believer must actually know and believe that she has the Spirit in order to be comforted. It is not just that the Spirit has 'shed abroad the love of God in our hearts'[122] in an immediate sense (though that he does, as we shall immediately see below), but also that the consolation and comfort of the gospel comes, in part, as the believer realizes that God has made himself immanent in the utmost, has come into her inmost parts, *invisceribus vestris* ('in your bowels').

As pastoral as this idea is, it is also polemic. Owen is fighting those who would say, 'It cannot be denied but that the Spirit dwells in believers, but yet this is not *personally*, but only by his grace.'[123] No opponent is named, but there are at least two (very different) strands of opposition that may have been on his mind. Ironically, his views oppose both the

---

[118] XI.331

[119] XI.332

[120] XI.333

[121] Though the larger sweep of his argument in ch. 8 of *The Perseverance of the Saints* includes this assertion, cf. XI. 329-36.

[122] Rom. 5:5, translation mine.

[123] XI.333

more conservative branch of Puritanism as well as the ideas of seventeenth-century religious rationalists. Speaking for the former group, the Presbyterian Hollinworth argues for a non-personal indwelling:

> When I speak of the Spirit's being, or dwelling in a Saint: I mean not an essential or personal in-being or in-dwelling of the Spirit, as he is God, or the third Person of the Holy Trinity:
>
> This Scriptural phrase of in-being and in-dwelling, doth import only inwardness, meer relation and close union. Hence God is said to be in Christ, as well as Christ in God, and Saints are as well said to be in, and to dwell in Christ, and to be in the Spirit, as Christ or the holy Spirit are said to be, or dwell in them; and therefore this phrase doth no more evince personal inhabitation, on the one side then on the other.
>
> The Spirit by a Metonymy, may be said to dwell in us... when we partake of his Gifts and Graces, though these be not the Spirit it self; . . . as when we say the Sun comes into a house, we mean not the body of the Sun (for that abides in its own Orb) but the Beams of it;[124]

Another Presbyterian conservative, John Howe, had said similarly, 'When we are cautioned not to "quench the Spirit", how can that be understood of the eternal uncreated Spirit himself? And the very thing produced – not merely the productive influence – in the work of regeneration is expressly called by the name (as it is no strange thing for the effect to carry the name of its cause): "That which is born of the Spirit is spirit."'[125]

---

[124] R. Hollinworth, *The Holy Ghost on the Bench* (London, 1656) 8, 10f, in Nuttall, *The Holy Spirit in Puritan Faith and Experience* (Chicago: University of Chicago Press, 1992) 49.

[125] John Howe, *Works* (Ligonier, Penn.: Soli Deo Gloria, 1990 rept.) II.80, in Nuttall, *The Holy Spirit*, 49. It also likely that Owen's argument for literal indwelling is a response to the Socianism of John Biddle, whose universalism he had already responded to in *The Death of Death*. Though Owen's main exposition on the nature of indwelling is found in *The Doctrine of the Saints' Perseverance*, and though this work, to the extent that it treats the Holy Spirit, is more in reference to the debate with Arminians (and not Socinians) regarding the irreversibility of the Spirit's work on those whom he awakens, Owen seems to broaden his attack in this book to once again include Biddle, or at least those of his ilk. And, as Trueman has shown, Owen believed that Socinianism was the logical consequence of Arminianism (in Robert Oliver, *John Owen: The Man and His Theology*, 51) The problem for Owen was that the Socinian denial of the true personality of the Holy Spirit (in favor of the Spirit as a mere appellation for the unitarian God's active agency) lends itself to the misinterpretation of Scripture's straightforward references to a real indwelling. All such texts would be demoted to mere metaphors for God's immanent involvement in a human life. Owen engages in much exegesis to show, on simple literary grounds, why he thinks a metaphorical interpretation is not defensible for many of the key texts. His main observation is that the operations or personality of the Spirit are regularly spoken of in distinct comparison with the person or work of the

And yet, does it not appear that Puritans like Hollinworth and Howe were suffering from a mistaken and unnecessary extension of the western *trinitatis ad extra sunt indivisa* doctrine? Why, otherwise, be so quick to retreat to 'Metonymy' when interpreting texts that seem to quite straightforwardly assert a personal indwelling of the Spirit in particular? Would this retreat have been necessary if Hollinworth had had no qualms about positing some kind of distinct operation of the Spirit in the project of sanctifying and indwelling sinners? We must not miss seeing the high cost to the spiritual life of such a move, for in so doing the believer must decide that the Spirit is much less personally present with her than the New Testament seems to first suggest. Certainly at least part of the believer's subjective consolation by the Spirit's ministry is owed to the fact that she believes his actual and unique presence is within her. This is a realization that is quite naturally protected when triune persons are allowed their distinct ministries in what is admittedly an overall united project.

Union with Christ and the Resulting Prospect of Trinitarian Indwelling

The primary effect of indwelling of the Spirit is to unite the believer to Christ, not to the Spirit himself. The Spirit is not united to the believer, for even the closeness of indwelling cannot unite human nature with the divine nature possessed by the Spirit. The Son of God, however, because he has taken on human nature, can be spiritually joined by the Spirit to the believer. Owen attempts to sharpen the definition of this union by saying that it is 'spiritual,' but readily admits that the exact nature of the

---

Father or the Son. That is, the Spirit cannot be just another way of saying 'Father' or 'Son' in places where both divine names, or even all three, are mentioned in the same breath. Perhaps, though, his most interesting appeal, given our focus on his practical spirituality, is a reference to the role of the Spirit as the indwelling witness to the believer of the veracity of her salvation. 'The Spirit itself beareth witness with our spirit, that we are the children of God,' (Rom. 8:16), suggests to Owen that the 'Spirit that dwells in us, bears witness in us, a distinct witness by himself, distinguished from the testimony of our own spirits here mentioned, is either an act of our natural spirits, or gracious fruit of the Spirit of God in our hearts' (XI.335). In other words, though the believer's own spirit, or psyche, may be convinced of her salvation, this is not an assurance that she has completely self-generated. Rather, her spirit has been informed by the Holy Spirit. Why would this require an actual indwelling? Because, this Spirit dwells in close enough proximity with her own spirit that such transmissions to her, though from a source outside herself, were so nearby that Paul would have needed to make the effort to separately distinguish them from her own internal thought processes. His opponents might argue a third option, that the source of assurance is a gracious fruit of the Spirit, though He does not need to personally indwell our hearts in order to provide it. It seems that for Owen, however, this degree of internal operation on the human spirit by the divine Spirit requires a kind of personal residence within the human herself.

union is beyond grasping, though not for that reason beyond enjoyment: 'The Scripture expresses it to be very eminent, near, durable, setting it out, for the most part, by similitudes and metaphorical illustrations, to lead poor weak creatures into some useful, needful acquaintance with that mystery, whose depths in this life they shall never fathom.'[126]

However hard to fathom, the basic nature of the believer's union with Christ is to be understood in reference to the Spirit himself: the substance of the union is that both Christ and the believer share the same indwelling Spirit. The Spirit, thus, not only creates the union, but is the union. Christ and the believer are united in the medium of the same Spirit they both share. Some of Owen's exegetical reasons for this conclusion will be evaluated below, but it is important to see how this definition of union is dependent on his understanding that the Spirit is literally and personally resident in the believer. For the believer to have a personal union with Christ, she must share something of what is really in and a part of her with something that is also intrinsic to Christ. If the Spirit is nothing more than the active agency of Christ (or the Father), or if the Spirit's presence is conceived in a true internal position within the believer, the personal union between Spirit-filled Christ and Spirit-filled believer becomes less substantial. But the believer who is truly indwelt with the personal Holy Spirit may savor the thought that the same Spirit is also, in some sense, present with the person of Christ whom the Spirit also indwells, and by so doing, unites her to the God-man.

Thomas Goodwin makes a somewhat similar point, though by a different means. Goodwin was also interested in making the case that the Spirit is a personal indweller, yet he was fighting the particular counter-argument that what the Spirit attaches to the believer is not the Spirit himself, but the Spirit's charismata. Goodwin's argument for personal indwelling draws into it a miniature theology of trinitarian communion – one that is less developed than Owen's perhaps, but unique in its own ways. His case is that Scripture speaks of an actual three-fold indwelling, that in addition to the Spirit, the Father and Son are also said to be resident within the regenerate soul. There is, however, an economical ordering of this indwelling. For example, scriptural texts that refer to the indwelling by either the Father or the Son seem to credit the Spirit as the ground of the others. For example, 'Ye are an inhabitation unto God by the Spirit,' (Eph. 2:22), and 'hereby we know that he abideth in us, by the Spirit which he hath given us' (1 Jn. 3:23). What does this mean? Says Goodwin, 'the other two persons are said to dwell in us, and the Godhead itself, because the Holy Ghost dwells in us, he being the person that makes entry, and takes possession first, in the name and for the use of

---

[126] XI.336

the other two, and so bringeth them in.'[127] Goodwin's aim is to show that if the Spirit is the pioneer for the indwelling of the other two persons, then his indwelling can be no less personal than theirs is clearly said to be. In fact, the Spirit as the primary indweller means that his coming in is uniquely *immediationi suppositi*, in a special and immediate class by itself. Practically speaking, the Spirit gives the believer the assurance of the presence of the other two because him we can 'feel dwelling and working in our hearts.'[128]

For Goodwin, the mechanics of the Godhead's indwelling the believer is somewhat illuminated by the way Jesus himself experienced a divine indwelling.[129] The substance of the divine Son of God dwells in the human nature of Christ, allowing for the expression: 'in him dwelleth all of the fulness of the Godhead bodily' (Col. 2:9). Thus, the person of the Son, and therefore the substance of the Godhead himself, dwells personally in the human nature of Christ. To this extent, the hypostatic union can be understood as a model of the Spirit's divine and personal indwelling in the human nature of any believer. Goodwin acknowledges that the degree of one-ness is not as great between the believer and the Spirit as it is between Christ's human nature and the divine Son, since nowhere is the Spirit's mode of indwelling a believer anywhere described as being 'made flesh' (Jn. 1:14). There is a *unio personarum* between the believer's human nature and the Spirit – an immediate union of persons that preserves the individuality of each – but not a *unio personalis*, the becoming of one person, as in the two natures of Christ.[130]

But Goodwin observes something else in the incarnation that is more directly instructive for the believer. The actual distinction between the *unio personarum* and the *unio personalis* is itself demonstrated in Jesus. The Spirit and the Father both dwell in Christ in a real way, though not by way of personal union. To say so would be to go beyond the correct assertion that Christ's human nature is one person with the Son of God (which he is, by way of the *unio personalis*), and also to erroneously make his human nature one person with both the Spirit and the Father (which would be to destroy any personal distinctions within the Godhead). Christ's human nature then is *unio personalis* with the divine Son, while being *unio personarum* with the Holy Spirit and the Father. Again, for Goodwin, the believer and Christ enjoy a basically identical

---

[127] Thomas Goodwin, *Works*, VI.64
[128] Thomas Goodwin, *Works*, VI.64
[129] Thomas Goodwin, *Works*, VI.66-67
[130] This concession might seem to limit the extent of the usefulness of Christ as a rubric for understanding something true of the believer, and frankly, it does seem like a bit of a false start for Goodwin to cite the hypostatic union as somehow telling of the believer's relationship with the Spirit and then to have to so substantially qualify himself.

unio personarum with the Spirit. In the case of the believer, the Spirit's unique *immediationi suppositi* draws in the Father and the Son for a kind of secondary indwelling.

Somewhat comparable material in Owen is found in his exposition of Jesus' prayer in John 17:21, 'that they all may be one, as the Father is in him, and he in the Father, that they may be one in the Father and the Son,' and verse 22, 'Let them be one, even as we are one.' Like Goodwin, Owen believes that, somehow, the relationship of the Son to the Father helps us to unlock the nature of the believer's own union with Christ. The difficulty is determining whether it is the Son's eternal intra-trinitarian relationship to the Father that is the most fruitful paradigm for the believer's experience, or whether it is something else that is true of the Son only after the incarnation. The following passage is somewhat tangled, but is our best source for unraveling Owen's own struggles with this question. In commenting on Jesus' petition in John 17:23, 'I in them, and thou in me,' he writes:

> This union, then, with him, our Saviour declares by, or at least illustrates by, resemblance unto his union with the Father. Whether this be understood of the union of the divine persons of Father and Son in the blessed Trinity (the union, I mean, that they have with themselves in their distinct personality, and not their unity of essence), or the union which was between Father and Son as incarnate, it comes all to one as to the declaration of that union we have with him. The Spirit is *Vinculum Trinitatis*, 'The bond of the Trinity,' as is commonly, and not inaptly spoken. Proceeding from both the other persons, being the love and power of them both, he gives that union to the trinity of persons, whose substratum and ground is the inestimable unity of essence wherein they are one. Or if you take it from the union of the Father with the Son incarnate, it is evident and beyond inquiry or dispute, that as the personal union of the Divine Word and the human nature was by the assumption of that nature into one personal substance with itself; so the person of the Father hath no other union with the human nature of Christ, immediately and not by the union of his own nature thereunto in the person of his Son, but what consists in that indwelling of his Spirit in all fulness in the man Christ Jesus. Now, saith our Saviour, 'This union I desire that they may have with me, by the dwelling of the same Spirit in me and them, whereby I am in them, and they in me, as I am one with thee, O Father.'[131]

So, the problem for Owen is whether Jesus was explaining the believer's union with him as being similar to his own eternal immanent bond as the Son to the Father, or to the incarnate Son's union with the Father in history. Owen seems to be saying that the question is moot because the personal cause of both unions are identical – the Holy Spirit. On one hand, the substance of the immanent union between eternal Father and Son is the eternal Spirit, the very bond of the Trinity. In this

---

[131] XI.338-39

sense (echoing in part the Augustinian language), the Spirit is the love passed between Father and Son, as well as the 'power' which they both share. On the other hand, the personal union between the Father and the human nature of Christ in history can be described in no other way than as a function of the indwelling of the same Spirit, which occurred after the incarnation and as a part of the drama of redemption.

Whichever proposal is the best interpretation of John 17:23 ('I in them and thou in me'), what makes the Son's (incarnate or pre-incarnate) union with the Father similar to the believer's union with the Son is the presence and work of the Holy Spirit. This allows the Christian to think about her Spirit-indwelled identity in terms of Jesus Christ's own identity with respect to the Spirit and the Father. To be indwelled by the Spirit means, somehow, that she and her Lord share a common experience of the Spirit's presence and of his ministry to convey communion with the Father. There is a richness to this kind of thinking about indwelling that is difficult to enjoy without a fully functioning trinitarian doctrine and an appreciation for how the Spirit was active in the life of Christ and his mission in behalf of believers.

The Meaning of the Believer's 'Participation in the Divine Nature'

But Owen wanted to push further into the nature of the union with Christ that Goodwin had said the Spirit pioneers. If the primary effect of the Spirit's indwelling is to bring the believer into union with the God-man, then what further can be said about the nature of that union? Scripturally speaking, through the Spirit, believers come to an actual 'participation in the divine nature' (2 Pet. 1:4). Owen is certain that this text is an implicit commentary on the nature of the believer's union with Christ, but he is cautious to avoid two extreme positions on the meaning of *phusis theia*. Typically, he counters what he would have considered a reductionist rationalism which interprets the divine nature within the believer as simply referring to a divine-like way of living and acting. In this mode of thinking, to have God's Spirit inside merely means to be made to act and live in a Christ-like spiritual way. This interpretation might seem to be the domain of Socinians alone, but might we not say that Howe and Hollinworth's otherwise orthodox doctrine also tips toward such reductionist conclusions? No doubt the Spirit influences the believer towards Christ-likeness, and certainly a regenerate Christian has a new God-born nature. Beyond these realities, Owen is convinced that a believer has union with something else in God that is not exhausted by merely referencing her own regenerate essence or behavioral renewal. Owen sought to recover a true supernaturalism when it came to the presence of the Spirit within the soul. His boldness about trinitarian distinctions likely prepared him to make such a move, and the benefits to the spiritual life (to say nothing of exegetical elegance) should be clear in what follows. On the other hand, we also find Owen at pains to avoid the opposite extreme as regards the human-divine union – as he puts it, the 'pretended high and spiritual, but indeed gross and carnal, conceits of some from hence, destructive to the nature of God and man,' by which he was probably referring to the enthusiast tendencies of Quakerism.[132]

Towards the end of his life, in 1677, Owen found a slightly broader meaning of 2 Pet.1:4 – or at least a broader application of the text. In his earlier *The Perseverance of the Saints* (the work cited above), his guess is that Peter was referring to the ontology of God by his use of the phrase 'divine nature.' However, by the time he wrote of *The Gospel Grounds and Evidences of the Faith of God's Elect*, his understanding has changed. He here seems to suggest that the believer's participation with the divine nature is actually describing the renewed human nature, which is being made over to increasingly reflect the *imago dei*. Like Luther, Owen believed that fallen humanity had completely lost the *imago*, that 'man in his fallen condition doth no more represent God; there is nothing in him that hath any thing of the likeness or image of God in it.'[133] The Christian's regenerate nature, on the other hand, is created by God to restore her ability to represent the righteousness of God, and doing so, to that extent, makes her a partaker in the divine nature.[134]

For our purposes, Owen's 'participation in image' is worth examining because of the motivational value he finds in it for the Christian's pursuit of holy living. Without here delving too deeply into Owen's understanding of the mechanics of sanctification, it might be said that he identifies two competing systems that may serve to motivate a person toward obedience to God. The first is the fear of eternal and temporal consequences and even lower forms of the experience of a 'prick' of conscience.[135] Such motives may keep a person from some gross sins, but they are motives of such low order that they may even be found in the unregenerate – there is nothing gospel-centered about them. On the other hand, a higher motivation comes from recognizing and becoming attracted to the 'the beauty and glory of the new creation in some measure, as that which bears the image of God,' by which Owen suggests

---

[132] XI.337

[133] V.430

[134] This is not to say that the Christian's union with Christ and her participation in God's nature is proportional to the degree of God-likeness that she individually manifests. Owen's shift in emphasis from what we might call 'participation in essence' to 'participation in image' does not negate the unchanging fact that a Christian, by definition and without subject to degrees, has a Spirit-given new nature. The *imago dei* has been truly restored to the believer, though it will continue to mature in its actual reflection of God's holiness.

[135] V.431-32

that the Christian's renewed nature enables her to appreciate the beauty of God's holiness, and therefore to savor the glimpses of that same holiness when it is reflected in herself.[136] To love God is also to love seeing the qualities God in oneself, the very possibility of which is implied by the *imago*.

A comparison of both systems highlights the shallowness of the former and the way in which the greatness of the latter is rooted in the sanctified affections of the Christian:

> the consequents of sin, with an apprehension of some advantages which are to be obtained by a sober life and the profession of religion, do steer and regulate the minds of unbelievers... but the minds of believers are influenced by a view of the glory of the image and likeness of God... this gives them love unto it, delight and complacency in it, enabling them to look upon it as its own reward.[137]

As the affections operate in this capacity, they find their ultimate purpose finally restored. The Spirit who has regenerated the affections by uniting the believer to Christ's purchased grace, now delights them with a participation in Christ:

> Hereby are the faculties of our souls exalted, elevated, and enabled to act primigenial powers, with respect to God and our enjoyment of him; which is our utmost end and blessedness. Hereby are our affections placed on their proper objects (such as they were created meet for, and in closing wherewith their satisfaction, order, and rest do consist), — namely, God and his goodness, or God as revealed in Jesus Christ by the gospel.[138]

The last line is a tremendously helpful glance at a definition of human affections that holds together what Owen says in many places, but is rarely stated so succinctly in one passage: God has designed human emotions to rest most happily on himself, and especially on the presentation of himself found in his Son in his saving capacity. From the point of view of the affections, the New Covenant is crucial because only with its inauguration does God reveal himself in the way that can fully satisfy human desire. From a trinitarian perspective, believers cannot experience this enjoyment apart from the Spirit showing them the glory of the Father by first joining them to the Son. Again, the progressive re-forming of the *imago dei* in the believer delivers some of this joy as the believer sees the object of her affections, Christ, reflected in her own thinking and living. This is, for Owen, virtually the highest human pleasure,

---

[136] V.430
[137] V.432
[138] V.433

> There is a secret joy and spiritual refreshment rising in the soul from a sense of its renovation into the image of God; and all the actings and increases of the life of God in it augment this joy. Herein consists its gradual return unto its primitive order and rectitude, with a blessed addition of supernatural light and grace by Christ Jesus; it finds itself herein coming home to God from its old apostasy, in the way of approaching to eternal rest and blessedness: and there is not satisfaction like unto that which it receives therein.[139]

We might say that for Owen, the history of redemption occurs not only in cosmic dimensions, but also within the microcosm of an individual soul. Such a redemptive history-in-miniature occurs as the mind and affections of a soul are progressively re-tuned to their creational design, with the trinitarian God as not only the active agency of this transformation, but also the very object of the renewed soul's delights – a delight in the Father who has renewed it through the Son, by the ministry of the Spirit. There is a similarity here with Walter Hilton's descriptions of the soul being re-tuned to the trinitarian image in which it was created, yet the large difference is that, with Owen's whole system in mind, there is more than a (vaguely defined) trinitarian *imago*, but a communion with, and delight in, three distinct divine persons through the distinct media of their own saving overtures. These observations about Owen's system help us to see that our own two criteria are, in a sense, always linked. If we begin to ask about the relationship of the triune persons, a full answer eventually requires a reference to what redemptive history has revealed about them. The drama itself, when examined, is shot through with the distinct actions of the Father, Son, and Holy Spirit. But lastly, both of these considerations cry out to be the constituent parts not only of Christian thinking, but of the spiritual life before God. As it turns out, what this triune God is up to in the grand drama of redemption is to reveal himself to and in his redeemed in order to maximize in them a delight and satisfaction. Unitarian spirituality is not only doctrinally unrealized and historically blind, but is, for these very reasons, ill-equipped to deliver this kind of joy in God.

---

[139] V.435-36

CHAPTER 6

Conclusions, and the Significance of Owenian Devotion

The Slipperiness of Evangelical Spirituality

Christian spirituality as a contemporary discipline suffers from several factors that have slowed its progress toward a common language and set of goals. As D.A. Carson notes, the wide-spread techniques of various spiritualities cover-up the fact that 'mutually contradictory theologies may undergird these person-variable definitions of spirituality, the degree of real commonality among those working on the topic may be minimal.'[1] Often, spirituality operates without a theological core. Even in the case of a recent work entitled *Reformed Spirituality: An Introduction for Believers*, the content and techniques suggested inside would not be recognizable to many as drawing from historic Protestant theology.[2] In other cases, works of spirituality produced by those with known Evangelical theological convictions have much to say about technique, but little to say about the content or end of such practices. Richard J. Foster's *Celebration of Discipline*, for example, reintroduces various monastic techniques to Evangelicals, who may stand in need of lessons about quietness and fasting in a world that is increasingly loud and gluttonous. However, Foster freely admits that the book dwells more on technique than on theological affirmations about the nature of the believer's union with God or on what basis it is first realized. The weakness of such an approach is not in the techniques themselves, but the fact that anyone with any doctrine of God could find it equally useful without being confronted with the particular God of Christianity. The problem with defining spirituality primarily in terms of technique is that the source and end of Christian salvation – the trinitarian theological substance of the gospel itself – can be left unstated, or worse, unpracticed.

How does one practice the gospel? To seek a definition of spirituality in this way is to require the input of theology. J.I. Packer's inaugural address as a chair of theology at Regent College showcased such a concern, asserting that the tasks of both spirituality and theology are mutually dependant. For Packer, twin errors of theology's scope must

---

[1] D.A. Carson, 'When is Spirituality Spiritual?' *Journal of the Evangelical Theological Society* 37 (1994): 381-394.

[2] H.L. Rice, *Reformed Spirituality: An Introduction for Believers* (Louisville: Westminster/John Knox, 1991).

themselves be avoided: theology is not merely Christian ideas and feelings about God (the error of subjectivists), nor merely the biblically exegeted and synthetically formulated truth about God (he somewhat pessimistically identifies this error with Scholastic objectivists), but the scripturally revealed God who shows us how to relate to him in trust and love.[3] As we have learned to expect, when theology remarries spirituality, the shape of the union is trinitarian:

> Sound spirituality needs to be thoroughly trinitarian. In our fellowship with God we must learn to do full justice to all three Persons and the part that each plays in the team job (please allow me that bold phrase) of saving us from sin, restoring our ruined humanness, and bringing us finally to glory. Neglect the Son, lose your focus on this mediation and blood atonement and heavenly intercession, and you slip back into the legalism that is fallen man's natural religion, the treadmill religion of works...neglect the Spirit, lose your focus on the fellowship with Christ that he creates, the renewing of nature that he effects, the assurance and joy that he evokes...and you slip back into orthodoxy and formalism, the religion of low expectations, deep ruts, and grooves that become graves....neglect the Father, lose your focus on the tasks he prescribes and the discipline he inflicts, and you become a mushy, soft-centred, self-indulgent, unsteady, lazy spoiled child in the divine family.[4]

If spirituality is to be distinctively Christian, it must describe the life of the believer before the distinctively Christian God, the triune Father, Son, and Holy Spirit. When spirituality becomes trinitarian in this way, it does better than to merely 'submit to exegetical controls'[5] in the narrow sense of avoiding subjectivity, but becomes grounded at every point on the particular God who reveals himself in scripture, and the particular mode of that God's pattern of relating to his people.

But in order to be more specific about what should be meant by a trinitarian spirituality, two criteria were originally proposed. The first was the test of the Great Tradition of classical theology: does the spirituality in question rely in any obvious way on the depth of trinitarian doctrine as the church has derived it? To put this more strictly, would the very heart of the spirituality come undone if the received doctrine of the Trinity were proved untrue, or could it go on functioning with certain modifications? The second criterion was that of redemptive history: given that the triune God has revealed his nature in a story-line of historical events which unfolded his saving purposes, does the spiritual model draw from this history, the triune God's own mode of self-disclosure? Stated

---

[3] J.I. Packer, 'An Introduction to Systematic Spirituality,' *Crux* 26.1 (March 1990): 2-8.

[4] Packer, 'Systematic Spirituality,' 7.

[5] Carson, 'When is Spirituality Spiritual,' 381.

another way, is the spirituality dependent on the economic Trinity, God-in-action, rather than merely the triune God as he is in himself?

John Owen's writing has been of particular interest for our thesis, since the content and mode of his devotional theology has shown a rare coupling of a heavy reliance on the classical doctrine of God with an interest in the *historia salutis* as the mental touchstone for a believer's acts of worship. The degree to which Owen satisfies our criteria merit some concluding remarks, for his observations not only resolve some long-standing difficulties in Western theology, but open up new avenues between theology and history and their combined value to the worshipping Christian.

The First Test: A One *Substantia*, Three *Persona* Spirituality

Owen and Alignment with the Western Theological/Spiritual Tradition

Again, the reason we are concerned about Owen's orthodoxy is that a vote for or against his adherence to Western doctrine is in some sense a determination of the very possibilities for a trinitarian spirituality within Western theological boundaries. Certainly, less orthodox ways of reconnecting spirituality with a doctrine of God are easy to come by, from the Pelagianism of Gabriel Biel, who invites the worshipper to make the soul habitable to the Trinity before receiving from God the grace of divine friendship, to the Eckhartian strains of Nicholas of Cusa, which eventually blur the distinction between creator and creature. Owen seems different, both in regards to basic orthodoxy and in his sustained efforts to appropriate such nuances of the historic doctrine of God for devotional purposes. But much of what this book has found helpful in his practical works may be moot if his presuppositions about distinctions in trinitarian action prove illegitimate. Certainly also, we have seen orthodox understandings of the Trinity produce devotional models still quite different from Owen's. Put another way, though we have discovered other spiritualities that mention the Trinity as a high point for religious meditation, we have not found apart from Owen a version which is so dependant on the distinct activity of each divine person. Julian of Norwich saw in the crucifixion of Christ a portrait of the love shown her by the whole Trinity, but her consequent meditation on the Trinity tended to indiscriminately credit each divine person with various works of creation and redemption. Relatively speaking, Julian's 'showings' are quite trinitarian, and certainly do not stray beyond the boundaries of trinitarian orthodoxy. However, neither do they take full advantage of the depth of trinitarian description found in even the early creedal definitions.

Certainly the previous two chapters have shown in John Owen a devotional model that is at pains to draw out the distinct operations of each divine person as they induce particular responses from the believer. Yet this tendency in Owen raises the question of whether or not his devotional system actually goes beyond or even against the traditional doctrine's emphasis on God's unity. Is Owen's highly differentiated way of dealing with the saving activity/worshipful response consistent with what our criterion asks, or is he being innovative by positing too much in the way of differentiated hypostatic activity? While Owen himself clearly endorsed the principle of *opera trinitatis ad extra sunt indivisa*, he also made an exception to the rule: in the divine activity of saving the elect, some unique operations are rightly attributed to one divine person to the exclusion of the others. The Son in his saving mission is one example, for only the Son actually incarnated and joined with human nature; a second example is the saving office of the Spirit, who alone can be said to anoint and indwell the Christ. Owen was aware that he might be charged with novelty on this point and so mentioned the precedent of John of Damascus, who believed that some of the works of the individual *hypostaseis* take place 'wherein others have no concurrence but by approbation and consent.'[6]

Perhaps the fairest way to finally judge Owen on this point is to say that he qualified the classic indivisibility doctrine in bold ways without undoing its primary intent. The doctrine of appropriations had already made some allowance for the distinction of divine activity, even if in its nervousness about tritheism it cast those divisions merely in terms of how, from the human vantage point, one may *ascribe* primary authorship to an individual divine person in contrast to the others. Even the scholastic doctrine of the *modus agendi* provides additional room for development in the ways that Owen would eventually much more fully pursue. For the *modus agendi* doctrine, in any trinitarian action the Father is conceived as the *fons actionis*, the Son as the *medium actionis*, and the Spirit as the *terminus actionis* – that is, each hypostasis has a distinct kind of activity in what may be, albeit, a unified final result. Certainly Owen goes further than these somewhat nebulous categories of hypostatic agency when he says that the Son incarnates with nothing but the approbation and consent of the Father and Spirit – but is his saying so a contradiction of allowing, as the *modus agendi* doctrine does, that the Father would be differently active in the work of the Son, for example, as the *fons actionis* of the Son's incarnation? It seems that the *modus agendi* doctrine already allows that the Father could be credited with the fountain-head role as initiator of the whole plan of salvation, including the Incarnation of the Son, without necessarily ruling out the unique position of the Son as the

---

[6] III.94

only divine person who actively incarnates. While the dominate strain in the Western tradition was certainly in the direction of the unified action of the Trinity, Owen exploits a halting allowance that the tradition always featured, its own built-in, latent exception to its overarching rule about divine unity.

The value of Owen for Christian devotion is that he presses beyond the narrow allowances of the doctrine of appropriations and the *modus agendi* to freely attribute certain redemptive actions to the Son and Spirit, respectively. This helps to answer Rahner's just outcry that if 'our future happiness will consist precisely in face-to-face vision of this triune God' then how can each of the divine persons have 'no real ontological relation [to us], something more than appropriation?'[7] Owen's system assumes that, in fact, the old appropriation doctrine as it is often applied is too confining, and that the Son has loved us particularly as the Son by condescending to incarnate as a human, and the Spirit has loved us uniquely by indwelling and empowering Christ for his mediatorial task. However, Owen's model also avoids Rahner's other tendency, which is to over-identify the divine missions with the Godhead's immanent processions. Owen, while emphasizing that the *ad extra* actions of the Trinity in the plan of salvation are unique to each divine person, also believes that they are not what actually constitute the immanent relations among the persons. The triune work of salvation is not the way God becomes himself, but the free act of a God who chooses to most clearly reveal his eternal triune identity through highly distinguished works of redeeming sinners through Christ. Owen then transcends the historical hesitance to speak about differentiated saving work of the divine persons without overindulging the sometimes modern tendency in economic trinitarianism to make such actions constitutive of the immanent relations. The Rahnerian tradition suggests that the only way to secure the value of the acts of God is to make them constitutive of the being of God, but Owen's commitment to the freedom of God shows it is possible to identify distinct hypostatic actions without going to that unnecessary extreme. The result is that the Christian worshipper may approach a God who is irreducibly triune even apart from and before any of his *ad extra* actions, yet whose triunity is never more clearly *revealed* than in those works.

Owen's Spirit-Christology as a Key Ingredient for a Trinitarian Spirituality

Very closely related to the above discussion is the place of Owen's christology in his overall spiritual method. Spence rightly argues that

---

[7] Rahner, *The Trinity*, 15.

because Owen was able to posit such distinct activity of the Son and the Spirit, he overcame an impasse in traditional 'one-sided' christologies. The historic pattern since the ancient controversies between the Alexandrian 'incarnational' christology and the Antiochene 'inspirational' view has been to think about the identity of Christ as either primarily a function of the Son's work (in incarnation) or the Spirit's indwelling (inspiration). The purely incarnational view has led toward docetism, since it eclipses the real human nature of Christ by its emphasis on the Son's direct determination of Christ's human nature. Solely inspirational christology has its problems as well, since it breaks down the real mystical union of Christ's human nature with the Son's divine nature in favor of Spirit-induced unity merely of purpose and action. The Definition of Chalcedon tried to affirm both the substantial unity of Christ's person (to shore up the weakness of the potentially Nestorian, Antiochene model) as well as the fullness of Christ's human nature (against the inherent weakness of the Alexandrian incarnational model); however, no single christology in that era was able to explain clearly how both these emphases might cohere. Owen closed the gap by first drawing in a third stream of tradition, the Latin emphasis on Christ as mediator, but more significantly, 'it was his pneumatology, his understanding of the Spirit's work as the dynamic unifying principle of Christ's personal activity, which enabled him to integrate successfully an Alexandrian and Antiochene Christology.'[8] In this understanding, Christ the man has a real union with the divine Son, but is not *acted* on by the divine Son in a direct way, but instead, through the motions of the Spirit. Jesus Christ is God-in-the-flesh, but relies on the ongoing empowerment and anointing of the Spirit to accomplish his saving mission in the world. When the Latin emphasis on Christ as mediator is also kept in view, the resulting christology is strikingly trinitarian: Jesus Christ cannot be fully understood apart from (1) his God-ness, by virtue of the Son's incarnation; (2) his need, according to his human nature, for the regular empowerment of the Spirit; and (3) his task, assigned particularly by the Father, to mediate for sinners he was sent to save.

How does such a christology impact devotion? Few of the earlier devotional traditions examined in this work had much difficulty with the incarnational aspect of Christ's identity. The neo-platonic strain that has long been present in Western mysticism is comfortable enough with the divine nature of Jesus Christ. More necessary for inheritors of the Augustinian tradition is to recover the inspirational identity of Christ as a man-in-the-Spirit. Spence says, 'an adequate understanding of Christ must conceive of him as both the giver and the receiver of the Spirit; as

---

[8] Spence, 'Incarnation and Inspiration: John Owen and the Coherence of Christology' (unpublished dissertation, Kings College, University of London, 1990) 138.

God among us and as a prototype man of faith totally dependent on God.'⁹ In contemporary Reformed/Evangelical spirituality, the idea of Christ as giver and receiver of the Spirit is the most necessary of the two sides of Christ's identity to reassert in spiritual practice (that is, an inspirational christology rather than just an incarnational christology). On one hand, the value of this reassertion is to make Christ more of an active model of how to depend on the Holy Spirit for moral strength and for making kingdom-centered priorities, and, forensically speaking, to provide a great assurance to the believer that Christ has, in his active obedience to the Spirit (to put a slight twist on the Reformed scholastic notion) already performed as the perfect dependant in the believer's place. This two-sided view of Christ is rich in devotional balance because Christ becomes a perfect and clear role model of how to follow God's law (i.e. through reliance on he Holy Spirit), yet the believer is not led toward the slippery slope of legalism because she realizes the same Christ is the one-and-only perfect obedient whose law-keeping was itself a ministry to her as the Father imputed his obedience to her account.

Another particularly fruitful direction for practical spirituality implied by what I term Owen's Spirit-christology is in the Christian's practice of mortification of the flesh. To say that the divine nature of the Son acts on the Christ-the-man primarily indirectly, through the Holy Spirit, has implications for any spirituality that deals with the ongoing problem of the Christian's sin nature. Mortification becomes a discipline to be practiced in direct reference to Christ's own anointing by the Spirit as the power by which he himself resisted sin. Haller notes that fighting temptation indeed was 'the central experience of Puritan morality,'[10] but, it should also be realized, this fight was generally first conceived as the Spirit's own fight against the believer's sin-nature, not a moralistic self-propelled fight of the believer on her own. The way a Spirit-christology informs such a fight is that the same Holy Spirit who strengthened Christ in the face of temptation can be appealed to in order work for the same ends in the believer who is herself in union with that Christ. Those united to Christ have the same divine agent he was anointed with, the Spirit of holiness. When Christ's own life is seen to be fundamentally guided by the Spirit in this sense, and, to put it more strongly, when we realize that our very christology is inadequate without seeing Christ's human nature as reliant on the Spirit for his every act of active and passive obedience, we are able then to undercut the pervasive human tendency to think of the process of sanctification as a merely humanly powered response to God's law, or even a response to his previous grace. The quite literally

---

[9] Spence, 'Incarnation,' 126.

[10] William Haller, *Rise of Puritanism* (New York: Harper Torchbooks, 1957 rept.) 153.

'Christian' way to avoid sin, that is, the way Christ first did it, is to appeal to the Spirit's own preserving power at work within us. Protestant spiritualities that are often so clear about the free gift of justification by virtue of Christ's work frequently neglect the idea that sanctification is also tied to Christ's person in any practical sense. Owen's christology helps maintain the idea that daily mortification is by grace as much as is regeneration; mortification is a grace of the Spirit of Christ who will afford the same helps to Christians as he did to their Lord with whom they are in union.

The other pitfall in spirituality that is remedied by such a christology is the mistake of overly abstracting the helping work of the Spirit as a kind of naked power, without particular reference to Christ. This weakness is not the same as the legalistic modes of sanctification mentioned above, but occurs when one is genuinely seeking to rely on the Spirit's grace but still ignoring the Christ-centered means of the Spirit's help. This problem more predictably appears in some popular Charismatic settings where the emphasis on Spirit can eclipse the work of Christ, but many spiritualities that fail to have a clear theological connection between Christ and the Spirit tend, when the Spirit's help is sought, to do so in a way that would be unaffected had Christ not been crucified. Yet, if Owen is right, the way the Spirit accomplishes moral transformation is not merely through 'a real physical efficiency on the root and habit of sin'[11] (though it is at least that), for to say so would be to state the Spirit's ministry in terms of his direct moral empowerment of the believer, but without reference to Christ's person nor his mediatorial work in history.

How then does the Spirit transform a human psyche? He 'brings the cross of Christ into the heart of the sinner by faith.'[12] And here is the key: the same Spirit who directly assisted Jesus Christ to avoid sin is now active to the same ends in Christians by only a slightly different means – Jesus Christ who committed no sin was helped directly by the Spirit to avoid sin, while Christian sinners are now helped by the Spirit *indirectly*, by his making real in their minds the virtues of Christ's mediatorial work for their persuasive power on the morally weak mind. The forensic basis of sanctification in Christ's active obedience is not at issue here – I suggest that the contribution of a Spirit-christology in sanctification is rather a reference to the agency (not the grounds) for such ongoing transformation. *The Spirit's support of the believer is through the specific agency of making a sensible impression on the mind and affections, an impression of how Christ has loved her through his mediatorial work.* In this way, the cross of Christ in particular is not only looked back on as the source of the sinner's justification, but also as the ongoing source of her

---

[11] VI.19
[12] VI.19

sanctification, her flesh's mortification, for the Spirit 'alone brings the cross of Christ into our hearts with its sin-killing power; for by the Spirit we are baptized into the death of Christ.'[13] Again, this strategy assumes the forensic benefit of Christ's death as a presupposition, but goes on the say that the Spirit's ongoing ministry is to make that forensic work emotively compelling to the believer as a way to build up an aversion to sin. The Spirit may be appealed to directly for this influence, but because in the economy of salvation the Spirit was so closely tied to the empowerment and success of Jesus' original earthly mission, his present help is to mediate an existential savor of Christ's accomplishments that the Spirit himself first enabled, not just to be a naked force of spiritual strengthening. From the human perspective, the way to be sanctified is to invoke the Spirit's power to make Christ's own Spirit-empowered saving deeds, especially his willing death, vivid and compelling. Calvin said that 'bearing the cross of Christ' was central to Christian experience,[14] but Owen made this idea more concrete. The Spirit helps the believer

> store the heart with the sense of the love of God in Christ, with the eternal design of his grace, with the taste of the blood of Christ, and his love in the shedding of it; get a relish of the privileges we have thereby...and thou wilt, in an ordinary course of walking with God, have great peace and security as to the disturbance of temptations.[15]

Owen's Spirit-christology rounds out the fully trinitarian nature of Christ's ministry, for Christ does his work as part of a saving plan that is originated by the Father, accepted by the Son, and lastly, empowered by the Spirit. It also helps make a believer's own appeals to the Spirit oriented to the Spirit's first work as guarantor of Christ's earthly obedience (passive and active), and not any other less Christ-centered conception of power. Spiritual power for the believer is not even categorically different than what it was for Christ – for him the Spirit aided his obedience to the Father, which purchased salvation for Christians, and for Christians it makes the benefits of Christ's obedience real to them as motivation to respond to such saving grace with their own trust and obedience. If mortification is a central aspect of Christian spirituality, here is a model of mortification that would have neither means nor end without reference to trinitarian agency. More broadly stated, Owen's model for the Christian life relies so heavily on various aspects of classic trinitarian doctrine that we see in it a marriage between theology and spirituality that illustrates how both disciplines quite effortlessly reinforce one another.

---

[13] VI.86
[14] Calvin, *Institutes*, III.viii
[15] VI.134

The Second Test: The Devotional Use of Divine Drama

The other reason that Owen's spirituality proved to be so highly trinitarian is because of his heavy reliance on the drama of redemption, both in its overarching narrative and its various sub-plots. Why should we conclude that the *historia salutis* is so helpful for constituting a trinitarian spirituality? One way to answer this question is to remind ourselves that Protestant scholastic theology, even when articulating a doctrine of God, is always drawing upon the grand story-line of God's historical actions. Owen should be seen as a late contributor to the tradition of Federal Theology, which was interested to draw out the various divine-human covenants in scripture, and their successive role in increasing the content of God's self-revelation over time. Federal Theology and its covenantal structure is often used by Owen to justify the distinctions he makes between the gracious motions of each divine person, as well as to tie together the unfolding plot of the entire scripture. All to say, when redemptive history is the focus, a particularly triune God comes into view as the Lord of that history. For this Federalist tradition, the story of the Bible (which is, in a sense, the story that interprets all history) involves the cutting of diverse covenants between God and his people, all of which reveal special things about God's nature, his law, his grace, his kingdom purposes, etc. But for all of the diversity, each covenant plays a role in shaping the believer's holistic devotional response to what turns out to be a triune God bent on making worshippers of those he has determined to love.

As we have seen, the heart of Federal Theology is really a plot-structure, and a particularly trinitarian one at that. We have focused on Owen in particular because he is the most successful of the Federal theologians in taking this linear redemptive structure into the realm of devotion. He encourages the Christian to meditate not on God's attributes in any abstract sense, but on the particular actions of each of the divine *hypostaseis* as they occur in time, in the unfolding public history of their dealings with the world. The ironic criticism of Reformed scholasticism and Federal Theology has been (among other things) that it replaced the warm-hearted religion of the first-generation Reformers with an overly elaborate system of covenants. But in the case of Owen, a high-scholastic by any count, the covenantal structure of Federal Theology provides an important framework for a method of devotion. The structuring is somewhat elaborate, yes, but wondrously elaborate in the same sense that an epic play slowly draws the audience into another vast world of characters, conflicts, sub-plots, and even cathartic resolution. While it is certainly possible to linger in the extremely precise details of some of the

Protestant scholastic writings (Owen's included) and be spiritually distracted from the doxological goal of all theology, the meta-themes of the three great covenants (of Redemption, of Works, of Grace) are uniquely helpful in actualizing a robust trinitarian devotion that few other ages were able to produce. The narrative/covenant arrangement has the advantage of introducing to the believer (and reintroducing, through her own ongoing acts of meditation on it) the Father, Son, and Spirit in a way that induces worship more obviously that any other non-covenantal, non-historical way: One may imagine the final scene of another great romance where Romeo finds the body of Juliet in the crypt, realizing that she had killed herself because she thought he was dead – he moans, and then turns the same dagger on himself. But what if instead of enacting this scene, a stage company tried to achieve catharsis in an audience by simply bringing Romeo onstage while an invisible narrator says, 'This is Romeo. He loves Juliet so much he'd rather die than not be with her'? Needless to say, the audience would be informed, but not moved. Emplotment captures us in a way that static explanations do not, so it should be no surprise that a God who intends us to worship him has revealed himself in moving history. The redemptive-historical model of Christian devotion stages a love-narrative in front of the believer with resulting advantages that are hard to otherwise realize.

Even from a merely sociological level we would expect redemptive-historical devotion to achieve certain unique results. Martha Nussbaum has argued that societies imbue their children with their accepted repertoire of emotions primarily by telling them certain stories.[16] If the emotional life is to be reformed, she says, success will not come first by argumentation, but by the 'unwriting of stories,' and, I might add, by the telling of a new one, a better story than any we compose autonomously, a story that is accompanied by divine power to affect its audience. The Christian in his devotional life is, among other things, seeking to have his emotional life retrained so that it approximates Christ's emotional make-up – to rejoice in the good, to be saddened and outraged at what compromises God's glory, etc. Might we not expect that this goal would best be achieved, if Nussbaum is correct, by immersing ourselves in the covenantal narrative that virtually declares from the start that it aims to grip us with the work of Christ as not only the high-point of history, but also as it tells us about our own Spirit-wrought union with this historical Christ, that is, the decisive turning point of our own personal story?

Today, few methods of devotion lean heavily on the triune God's historical accomplishments to inaugurate his redemptive kingdom. What

---

[16] Martha Nussbaum, 'Narrative Emotions: Beckett's Genealogy of Love,' in *Why Narrative: Readings in Narrative Theology*, eds. Stanley Hauerwas and L. Gregory Jones, (Grand Rapids: Eerdmans, 1989) 216-48.

we find instead are devotional methods closer to Hodge's kind of pre-critical prolegomena that we described in the second chapter. If Hodge begins the study of theology by first deciding that the Bible is a mine of theological facts without particular historical emplotment, then a Hodgean devotionalist (for lack of a better term) imports a similar pre-critical expectation for how to nurture his spiritual life before considering the biblical drama's own diagnosis and prescription of the needs of his soul. At best, while such a devotionalist still enters the Scriptures to find guidance, his presuppositions may threaten his ability to read the Bible in its covenantal context. Worse, in our particularly subjective age, pre-critical, pre-biblical methods of spirituality often look first to the self to ascertain its spiritual need, then turn the believer to various cultivated spiritual experiences to meet that need. Increasingly, spirituality is furthered with reference to expertly derived technique in a variety of disciplines. Evangelical spirituality, to say nothing of Liberal Protestant models, makes increasing use of, for example, secular psychological observations and personality inventories (as helpful as both these may be, in their place) as the way to diagnose human weaknesses and prescribe paths to healing. In America, Evangelicals are increasingly convinced about their spiritual need for large-group experiences (stadium revivals, multi-church song festivals, etc.) as a primary means for re-kindling one's love for God and one-another again.[17] High-quality worship music is often believed to make-or-break a particular church's viability, for without good music one is thought to be almost fundamentally hindered in the ability to emotionally respond to God.

None of this is to say that cultivated group experiences, common grace psychological observations, or good worship music has no place in a model for spiritual growth – the real concern is how they have been allocated a relative weight in forming the methodology (and sometimes ends) of Christian spirituality, with less conviction about the primacy or spiritual usefulness of the biblical drama that heralds God's call to spiritual living in the first place. By contrast, the thing that made 'our hearts burn within us' for the disciples on the road to Emmaus was something as simple yet profound as Jesus' narrated tour through the whole Scriptures (not just the Prophets, but the historical books as well) as they revealed Christ the future Savior. Jesus' own method of affecting hearts in Luke 24 was to reveal himself to his people through the biblical drama that climaxed in his death and resurrection. Evangelicalism is

---

[17] The Promise-Keepers phenomena is one example, though as that particular movement has declined, other para-church rallies have not slowed. Cf. Campus Crusade for Christ's regional Christmas Conferences and InterVarsity Christian Fellowship's Urbana Missions Conference. The latter has gradually changed its focus toward corporate worship and a rally atmosphere from an earlier emphasis on biblical exposition of missions themes.

fairly stable in its emphasis that the Bible should determine our doctrine (once doctrine can be abstracted from the story, that is), but less sure that the Bible tells us much about spirituality (apart from, again, spiritual exemplars who can become models to us only after we abstract them from their role in the overarching narrative and covenantal context). For example, one will find many sermons preached about David's defeat of Goliath that holds him up as a general model for how we can trust in God in the face of any great trial. Yet reading the story that way abstracts a universal spiritual lesson that has no real connection to the grand trajectory of the main biblical plot. A better spiritual application of David's story would encourage us to take comfort in the Greater David who has been our representative champion to defeat what really threatens us, the enemies of sin and death. This kind of devotional use of Old Testament typology has a long but often forgotten tradition.[18] In the first model, David's defeat of Goliath is a spiritual lesson that only happens to be embedded in a more detailed plot. In the latter, the incredible narrative detail of the story can all be put to use to rouse the believer's affections for Christ, her humble champion who trusted in his Father to bring about his seemingly unlikely victory, and to save the lives of the people he stands for. The David story is a miniature retelling of the Great Story, which is the only story that can really touch the heart at its deepest need.

As the alternative to eschatologically insensitive spirituality, we must first turn to the covenantal storyline to discover what the agenda for spirituality should be at the outset. The story is deep enough to tell us not only who God is, but who we are, what is wrong with us, what the cure is, and even where the Lord of the story is surely taking us in the final act. This is a story that has doctrinal content, yes, but it also has an epic power to strike at the heart. Says Dorothy Sayers,

> it is the dogma that is the drama – not beautiful phrases, nor comforting sentiments, nor vague aspirations to loving-kindness and uplift, nor the promise of something nice after death – but the terrifying assertion that the same God who made the world lived in the world and passed through the grave and gate of death... the Christian faith is the most staggering drama that ever staggered the imagination of man – and the dogma is the drama.[19]

Such a drama sets the agenda for a whole method of spirituality. If a methodology can be framed in terms of questions it poses, the devotion that grows out of biblical drama confronts the believer with something like the following: Are you in awe of the Glory you were created to reflect? Do you sense the depth of the personal catastrophe that Adam's

---

[18] A classic nineteenth-century example is Patrick Fairbairn, *The Typology of Scripture* (Grand Rapids: Kregel, 1989).

[19] Dorothy Sayers, *Creed or Chaos*, 36.

and your sin brought to your personal standing with God? Does it melt you to see how much the Father loves you by what he gave to cover your dismissal of him? Are you humbled and encouraged by what the Son condescended to do when he united himself with human nature? How is it affecting you to know that he lived the life you should have lived, died the death you deserved to die, all so you might share his right before the Father as a son yourself, with all the attendant glory once enjoyed by the divine Son before his Father? Does the Spirit's presence in you now give you a sense of God's love shed abroad in your heart? Do you desire him to re-make you into the image of the Son? Does the love of the triune God so demonstrated motivate you to obey his laws and to desire his renown, which he says will soon fill the earth?

What can be said about these questions? First, they are inescapably oriented to the human affections. According to Jonathan Edwards, exalted affections for Christ are what glorifies him the most, and are therefore what are, in subjective terms, the greatest goal in the practice of spirituality. 'Being in awe,' 'melted,' 'encouraged,' 'humbled,' – this is the language of the Puritan devotionalists, and, I think, language that is most unforced when such phenomena are seen to arise from observing the divine drama. That is, while drama itself may be suited to touch the affections, it is only the redemptive-historical drama that touches them in a distinctively Christian way. When a devotional practice seeks to evoke these emotions through other devices, apart from reference to God's triune performance in history, one of two affective failures often takes place. On one hand, a kind of platonic, hyper-spirituality results when a model of spirituality suggests that meditating on God's attributes by themselves will affect a person to the core. This spirituality becomes esoteric, because most people will not be gripped at the affective level even by the claim 'God is love' without a situatedness to such an attribute. On the other end of the spectrum, revivalistic spiritualities that are rightly pessimistic about the emotional payoff of platonized meditation may still seek to manufacture emotion through other means (sentimental music, forceful oratory), then somehow attach that emotional response to God. In a different way, the biblical drama is still ignored. Any effects of such revivalistic spirituality are maudlin and short-lived because the emotional response is really tied to a transitory object. The proper desire for Christian affective response to God can avoid being esoteric by grounding itself to a particular showcase of God's attributes, and can avoid being maudlin by letting God's own dramatic actions do the work of wooing the affections. Redemptive-historical spirituality is certainly emotional when practiced, but since the emotions are always triggered by public and objectively real events, they are neither arbitrary nor self-authenticated.

Finally, in the extent to which these questions dwell on the eschatological progression of scripture, they are unavoidably trinitarian. Only, then, by staying within the story do we find ourselves face-to-face with the richness of God's character as a three-in-one creator/redeemer. Non-dramatic spiritualities, it seems, will always be playing catch-up when they try to articulate which God in fact we are trying to live before. And, since the covenantal drama is one in which the believer is an actor in the same play as this trinitarian God, such a spirituality is clear from the start about what the worshipper's own roles are before God. She is not blown to-and-fro with each passing wind of contemporary spiritual technique – she knows to get herself into his script in order that she may respond to his past actions (for her redemption was accomplished by Christ when she was still off-stage herself, so to speak). She lives her life as not as an extempore actor, but as if the triune God is the star and her role is to react to him. She thanks the Father for his fore-ordaining love before she took the stage herself, she makes continual exchanges with the Son – her sin for his righteousness – and she continually invites the Spirit to work within her to make her more like Christ, in expectation of his immanent return in the final scene.

Selected Bibliography

Alleine, Joseph. (1995 rept.) *A Sure Guide to Heaven* (Edinburgh: Banner of Truth Trust).
Ames, William. (1997 rept.) *The Marrow of Theology* (Grand Rapids: Baker).
Andrewes, Lancelot. (1648) *A Manual of the Private Devotions and Meditations of Lancelot Andrewes* (London: Humphrey Moseley).
Anonymous. (1996 rept.) *The Cloud of Unknowing and The Book of Privy Counseling* (New York: Doubleday Publishing).
Armstrong, Brian G. (1969) *Calvinism and the Amyraut Heresy: Protestant Scholasticism and Humanism in Seventeenth-Century France* (Madison: University of Wisconsin Press).
Augustine. (1961) *Confessions*, trans. R.S. Pine-Coffin (London: Penguin).
———. (1991) *On the Trinity*, trans. Edmund Hill (New York: New City).
———. (1994) *On Christian Doctrine*, trans. R.P.H. Green (Oxford: Oxford University Press).
Barth, Karl. (1969) *Church Dogmatics,* ed. Geoffrey W. Bromily and T.F. Torrance, 13 volumes (Edinburgh: T. & T. Clark).
Battles, Ford Lewis. (1996) *Interpreting John Calvin,* ed. Robert Bendetto (Grand Rapids: Baker).
Baxter, Richard. (1675) *Catholick Theologie: Plain, Pure, Peaceable: For Pacification of the Dogmatic Word-Warriors* (London: Robert White).
———. (1846) *A Christian Directory* (London: George Virtue).
———. (1976) *A Call to the Unconverted* (Welwyn: Evangelical Press).
———. (1989) *The Reformed Pastor* (Edinburgh: Banner of Truth Trust).
———. (1962) *The Saints Everlasting Rest* (New York: Revell).
Bayly, Lewis. (1995 rept.) *The Practice of Piety: A Puritan Devotional Manual* (Morgan, Penn.: Soli Deo Gloria).
Becon, Thomas. (1560) *The Flower of Godly Prayers* in *The Second Part of the Bokes, which Thomas Beacon hath made* (London: John Day).
———. (1564) *The Pathway unto Prayer* in *The Bokes, which Thomas Beacn hath made*, Part I. (London: John Day).
———. (1560) *The Pomaunder of Prayer* (London: John Day).
Beeke, Joel R. (1991) *Assurance of Faith: Calvin, English Puritanism, and the Dutch Second Reformation* (New York: Peter Lang).

_____. (1994) 'Does Assurance Belong to the Essence of Faith? Calvin and the Calvinists,' *The Master's Seminary Journal* 5.1: 43-71.

_____. (1993) 'Personal Assurance of Faith: The Puritans and Chapter 18.2 of the Westminster Confession,' *Westminster Theological Journal* 55: 1-30.

_____. (1999) *Puritan Evangelism: A Biblical Approach* (Grand Rapids: Reformation Heritage).

Beeke, Joel R. and Sinclair B. Ferguson. (1999) *Reformed Confessions Harmonized: With an Annotated Bibliography of Reformed Doctrinal Works* (Grand Rapids: Baker).

Belarmine, Robert. (1989) *Robert Bellarmine: Spiritual Writings* (*The Mind's Ascent to God* and *The Art of Dying Well*) (Mahwah, New Jersey: Paulist).

Bennett, Arthur, ed. (1975) *The Valley of Vision: A Collection of Puritan Prayers and Devotions* (Edinburgh: Banner of Truth Trust).

Bernard of Clairvaux. (1987) *Bernard of Clairvaux: Selected Works* (New York: Paulist).

Beza, Theodore. (1992) *The Christian Faith*, trans. James Clark (East Sussex: Christian Focus).

Bierma, Lyle D. (1999) 'Law and Grace in Ursinus' Doctrine of the Natural Covenant,' in *Protestant Scholasticism: Essays in Reassessment*, ed. Carl. R. Trueman and R.S. Clark (Carlisle: Paternoster).

Bolton, Samuel. (1996 rept.) 'Sin: The Greatest Evil,' in *The Puritans on Conversion*, ed. D. Kistler (Morgan, Penn.: Soli Deo Gloria).

Bradford, John. (1848) *Godly Meditations on the Lord's Prayer, Belief, and Ten Commandments, with other Exercises*, in *The Writings of John Bradford*, ed. Aubrey Townsend (Cambridge: Parker Society).

_____. (1567) *Godly Meditations Upon the Ten Commandments, the Articles of the Fayth, and the Lord's Prayer* (London: William Seres).

_____. (1848) *Private Prayers and Meditations, with Other Exercises*, *The Writings of John Bradford*, ed. Aubrey Townsend (Cambridge: Parker Society).

Brauer, Jerald C. (1987) 'Types of Puritan Piety,' *Church History* 56: 39-58.

Brook, Benjamin. (1997 rept.) *The Lives of the Puritans* (Morgan, Penn.: Soli Deo Gloria).

Brooks, Thomas. (1996 rept.) *Heaven on Earth: A Treatise on Christian Assurance* (Edinburgh: Banner of Truth Trust).

_____. (1993 rept.) *Precious Remedies Against Satan's Devices* (Edinburgh: Banner of Truth Trust).

Bucer, Martin. (1969) *De Regno Christi*, ed. Wihelm Pauck, Library of Christian Classics (Philadelphia: Westminster).

Bunyan, John. (1901) *Holy War Made by Shaddai Upon Diabolus* (London: J.M. Dent).

_____. (1990) *The Pilgrim's Progress* (London: Penguin).
_____. (1955) *Grace Abounding to the Chief of Sinners* (London: SCM).
Burgess, Anthony. (1647) *Vindiciae Legis: or, A Vindication of the Morall Law and The Covenants, From the Errours of the Papists, Arminians, Socinians, and More Especially, Antinomians* (London: Thomas Underhill).
Burleigh, J.H.S., ed. (1953) *Augustine: Earlier Writings* (Philadelphia: Westminster).
Burnaby, John. (1955) *Augustine: Later Works* (Philadelphia: Westminster).
Burroughs, Jeremiah. (1998 rept.) *The Rare Jewel of Christian Contentment* (Edinburgh: Banner of Truth Trust).
Butin, Philip Walker. (1994) *Revelation, Redemption and Response: Calvin's Trinitarian Understanding of the Divine-Human Relationship* (Oxford: Oxford University Press).
Calvin, John. (1960) *The Institutes of the Christian Religion*, trans. Ford Lewis Battles (Philadelphia: Westminster).
_____. (1979) *Calvin's* New Testament Commentaries (Grand Rapids: Baker).
Carson, D.A.(1994) 'When is Spirituality Spiritual? Reflections and Problems of Definition,' *Journal of the Evangelical Theological Society* 37: 381-394.
Chadwick, Owen. (1964) *The Reformation, Vol. 3*, The Penguin History of the Church (London: Penguin).
Chan, Simon. (1998) *Spiritual Theology: A Systematic Study of the Christian Life* (Downer's Grove, Ill.: InterVarsity).
Chapman, Collin. (1990) *Shadows of the Supernatural: A Guide to Popular Religion* (Oxford: Lion).
Charnock, Steven. (1996 rept.) *The Existence and Attributes of God* (Grand Rapids: Baker).
Clark, Mary T. (1989) 'The Trinity in Latin Christianity,' in *Christian Spirituality, Vol. 1*, ed. Louis Dupre and Don E. Saliers (New York: Crossroad) 276-290.
Clifford, Alan. (1990) *Atonement and Justification: English Evangelical Theology 1640-1790* (Oxford: Oxford University Press).
Cohen, Charles Lloyd. (1986) *God's Caress: The Psychology of Puritan Religious Experience* (New York: Oxford University Press).
Collinson, Patrick. (1967) *The Elizabethan Puritan Movement* (Berkeley: University of California Press).
Cunningham, David S. (1998) *These Three Are One: The Practice of Trinitarian Theology* (London: Blackwell).
Davies, Horton. (1997 rept.) *The Worship of the English Puritans* (Morgan, Penn.: Soli Deo Gloria).

_____. (1996 rept.) *Worship and Theology in England: From Cranmer to Baxter and Fox 1534-1690* (Grand Rapids: Eerdman).
Davies, Oliver, ed. (1999) *Celtic Spirituality* (Mahwah, New Jersey: Paulist).
Dent, Arthur. (1994 reprint) *The Plain Man's Pathway to Heaven* (Pittsburgh: Soli Deo Gloria).
Donne, John. (1994 rept.) *The Complete Poetry and Selected Prose of John Donne* (New York: Random House).
_____. (1923) *Devotions Upon Emergent Occassions*, ed. John Sparrow (Cambridge: Cambridge University Press).
Dupre, Louis and Don E. Saliers. (1989) *Christian Spirituality Vol. 3: Post Reformation and Modern* (New York: Crossroad).
Durham, James. (1997) *An Exposition of the Song of Solomon* (Edinburgh: Banner of Truth Trust).
Ebeling, Gerhard. (1967) 'The Hermeneutical Locus of the Doctrine of God in Peter Lombard and Thomas Aquinas,' in *Distinctive Protestant and Catholic Themes Reconsidered*, ed. Ernest Kasemann, *et al.* (New York: Harper and Row) 70-100.
Ecumenical Creeds and Reformed Confessions. (1988 rept.) (Grand Rapids: CRC).
Edwards, David L. (1980) *Christian England: Its Story to the Reformation* (New York: Oxford University Press).
Edwards, Jonathan. (1773, 2003 rept.) *A History of Redemption* (Whitefish, Montana: Kessinger).
_____. (1984 rept.) *Religious Affections* (Minneapolis: Bethany House).
Fairweather, Eugene R., ed. (1956) *A Scholastic Miscellany: Anselm to Ockham* (Philadelphia: Westminster).
Ferguson, Sinclair. (1988) 'Christian Spirituality: The Reformed View,' in *Christian Spirituality: Five Views of Sanctification*, ed. Donald L. Alexander (Downer's Grove, Ill.: InterVarsity) 47-76.
_____. (1987) *John Owen on the Christian Life* (Edinburgh: Banner of Truth Trust).
The First and Second Prayer Books of King Edward VI. (1968 rept.) (London: Everyman).
Forde, Gerhard O. (1988) 'Christian Spirituality: The Lutheran View,' in *Christian Spirituality: Five Views of Sanctification*, ed. Donald L. Alexander (Downer's Grove, Ill.: InterVarsity) 13-32.
Fortman, Edmund J. (1982) *The Triune God: A Historical Study of the Doctrine of the Trinity* (Grand Rapids: Baker).
Frances de Sales. (1632) *An Introduction to a Devout Life* (Rouen: Cardin Hamillon).

Gleason, Randall C. (1995) *John Calvin and John Owen on Mortification: A Comparative Study in Reformed Spirituality* (New York: Peter Lang).
Goodwin, John. (1651) *Redemption Redeemed* (London).
Goodwin, Thomas. (1855) *The Works of Thomas Goodwin*, eleven volumes (Edinburgh: James Nichol)
Green, Brad. (1999) 'Did Augustine's Trinitarian Theology Lead the West Astray?: A Look at a Contemporary Trend in Theology,' unpubl. paper delivered at 51st meeting of the Evangelical Theological Society, 17-19 Nov., Danvers, Massachusetts.
Greenslade, S.L. (1956) *Early Latin Theology* (Philadelphia: Westminster).
Gunton, Colin. (1997) *The Promise of Trinitarian Theology* (Edinburgh: T. & T. Clark).
Hall, Basil. (1966) 'Calvin Against the Calvinists,' in *John Calvin*, ed. G.E. Duffield (Grand Rapids: Eerdmans).
_____. (1965) 'Puritanism and the Problem of Definition,' in *Studies in Church History*, ed. G.J.Crummey (London: T. & T. Clark).
Hall, David D. (1990) *The Antinomian Controversy, 1636-1638: A Documentary History*, second ed. (Chapel Hill, North Carolina: Duke University Press).
Haller, William. (1957 rept.) *The Rise of Puritanism* (New York: Harper Torchbooks).
Hambrick-Stowe, Charles. (1982) *The Practice of Piety: Puritan Devotional Disciplines in Seventeenth-Century New England* (Chapel Hill: University of North Carolina Press).
Hardin, Michael. (1992) 'The Trinity as Hermeneutic: A Pietistic Perspective,' *The Covenant Quarterly* 50: 20-33.
Hardy, Edward R., ed. (1954) *Christology of the Later Fathers* (Philadelphia: Westminster).
Harman, Allan M. (1994) 'The Psalms and Reformed Spirituality,' *The Reformed Theological Review* 53: 53-62.
Helm, Paul. (1982) *Calvin and the Calvinists* (Edinburgh: Banner of Truth Trust).
Henry, Matthew. (1991 rept.) *Matthew Henry's Commentary on the Whole Bible Complete and Unabridged* (Peabody, Mass.: Hendrickson).
_____. (1994 rept.) *A Method for Prayer with Scripture Expressions proper to be used under each head* (Fearn, Scotland: Christian Focus).
_____. (1991 rept.) *The Secret of Communion with God* (Grand Rapids: Kregel).
Hetherington, William. (1856 rept.) *History of the Westminster Assembly of Divines* (Edmonton, Alberta: Still Waters Revival).

Hill, Christopher. (1970) *God's Englishman: Oliver Cromwell and the English Revolution* (New York: Harper and Row).
Hilton, Walter. (1991) *Walter Hilton: The Scale of Perfection* (Mahwah, New Jersey: Paulist).
Hinson, Glenn. (1988) 'Christian Spirituality: The Contemplative View,' in *Christian Spirituality: Five Views of Sanctification*, ed. Donald L. Alexander (Downer's Grove, Ill.: InterVarsity) 171-189.
Hoekema, Anthony. (1967) 'The Covenant of Grace in Calvin's Teaching,' *Calvin Theological Journal* 2: 130-166.
Holmes, Rolston, III. (1970) 'Responsible Man in Reformed Theology: Calvin vs. The Westminster Confession,' *Scottish Journal of Theology* 23.2: 129-56.
_____. (1982) *Calvin versus the Westminster Confession* (Philadelphia: Westminster).
Hopko, Thomas. (1989) 'The Trinity in the Cappadocians,' in *Christian Spirituality, Vol. 1*, ed. Louis Dupre and Don E. Saliers (New York: Crossroad) 260-275.
Horton, Michael S. (1997) 'Thomas Goodwin and the Puritan Doctrine of Assurance: Continuity and Discontinuity in the Reformed Tradition, 1600-1680,' Ph.D. dissertation, Wycliffe Hall and the University of Coventry.
_____. (2002) *Covenant and Eschatology* (Philadelphia: Westminster/John Knox).
Ignatius of Loyola. (2000) *The Spiritual Exercises of St. Ignatius*, trans. Louis J. Puhl (New York: Random House).
Kelly, J.N.D. (1978) *Early Christian Doctrines* (San Francisco: Harper Collins).
Kempis, Thomas à. (1999) *Imitation of Christ*, tr. Aloysius Croft and Harold Bolton (Nashville: Thomas Nelson).
Kendall, R.T. (1981) *Calvin and English Calvinism to 1649* (Oxford: Oxford University Press).
Kevan, Ernest F. (1993 reprint) *The Grace of Law: A Study in Puritan Theology* (Ligonier, Penn.: Soli Deo Gloria).
King, David M. (1996) 'The Affective Spirituality of John Owen,' *Evangelical Quarterly* 68.3: 223-233.
Kistler, Donald. ed. (1990) *The Puritans on Conversion* (Morgan, Penn.: Soli Deo Gloria).
_____. (1995) *The Puritans on Prayer* (Morgan, Penn.: Soli Deo Gloria).
Knappen, M.M. (1939) *Tudor Puritanism* (Chicago: University of Chicago Press).
LaCugna, Catherine Mowry. (1993) *God for Us: The Trinity and Christian Life* (San Francisco: HarperSan Francisco).

Lee, Samuel. (1995 rept.) 'Secret Prayer,' in *The Puritans on Prayer*, ed. D. Kistler (Morgan, Penn.: Soli Deo Gloria).
Letham, Robert. (1986) 'Theodore Beza: A Reassesment,' *Scottish Journal of Theology* 40: 25-40.
Lewis, Peter. (1977) *The Genius of Puritanism* (London: Carey).
Lovelace, Richard. (1979) *Dynamics of Spiritual Life: An Evangelical Theology of Renewal* (Downer's Grove, Ill.: InterVarsity).
Lundgaard, Kris. (1998) *The Enemy Within* (Phillipsburg, New Jersey: Presbyterian and Reformed Publishing).
Luther, Martin. (1957) *The Bondage of the Will*, trans. J.I. Packer and O.R. Johnson (Grand Rapids: Revell).
_____. (1979) *Commentary on Galatians* (Grand Rapids: Baker).
Mackey, James. (1983) *The Christian Experience of God as Trinity* (London: SCM).
McGowan, Andrew T.B. (1984) 'Federal Theology as a Theology of Grace,' *Scottish Bulletin of Evangelical Theology* 2: 41-50.
McGrath, Alister E. (1986) *Iustitia Dei: A History of the Christian Doctrine of Justification* (Cambidge: Cambridge University Press).
McGrath, Gavin J. (1994) *But We Preach Christ Crucified: The Cross of Christ in the Pastoral Theology of John Owen (1616-1683)* (St. Antholin's Lectureship Charity Lecture).
Melanchthon, Philip. (1969) *Melanchthon on Christian Doctrine (Loci Communes, 1521)*, trans. Lowell Satre and ed. Wilhelm Pauck, Library of Christian Classics (Philadelphia: Westminster).
_____. (1556) *A Godlye Treatyse of Prayer*, trans. John Bradforde (London: John Wight).
Miller, Gordon. (1996) *The Way of the English Mystics: An Anthology and Guide for Pilgrims* (Harrisburg, Penn.: Morehouse).
Miller, Perry. (1939) *The New England Mind: The Seventeenth Century* (Cambridge: Harvard University Press).
Milton, John. (1975) *Paradise Lost*, ed. Scott Elledge (New York: Norton).
Moller, J.G. (1963) 'The Beginnings of Puritan Covenant Theology,' *Journal of Ecclesiastical History* 14: 46-67.
Muller, Richard A. (1986) *Christ and the Decree: Christology and Predestination in Reformed Theology from Calvin to Perkins* (Durham, North Carolina: Labyrinth).
_____. (1995) 'Calvin and the "Calvinists": Assessing Continuities and Discontinuities Between The Reformation and Orthodoxy,' *Calvin Theological Journal* 30: 345-75.
_____. (1985) *Dictionary of Latin and Greek Theological Terms* (Grand Rapids: Baker).
_____. (1978) 'Perkins' *A Golden Chaine*: Predestinarian System or Schematized *Ordo Salutis*?' *Sixteenth Century Journal* 9.1: 69-81.

———. (2001) 'The Problem of Protestant Scholasticism: A Review and Definition,' in *Reformation and Scholasticism: An Ecumenical Enterprise*, ed. W.J. van Asselt and E. Dekker (Grand Rapids: Baker Academic) 45-64.

———. (1999) 'The Use and Abuse of a Document: Beza's *Tabula praedestinationis*, the Bolsec Controversy, and the Origins of Reformed Orthodoxy,' in *Protestant Scholasticism: Essays in Reassessment*, ed. Carl. R. Trueman and R.S. Clark (Carlisle: Paternoster).

Nuttall, Geoffrey, F. (1975) 'Puritan and Quaker Mysticism' *Theology* 78 :518-31.

———. (1992) *The Holy Spirit in Puritan Faith and Experience* (Chicago: University of Chicago Press).

Oberman, Heiko A. (2000) *The Harvest of Medieval Theology* (Grand Rapids: Baker).

———. (1966) *Forerunners of the Reformation* (Philadelphia: Fortress).

———. (1994) *The Reformation: Roots and Ramifications* (Edinburgh: T. & T. Clark).

Olevianus, Caspar. (1995) *A Firm Foundation: An Aid to Interpreting the Heidelberg Catechism*, trans. and ed. Lyle D. Bierma (Grand Rapids: Baker).

Oliver, Robert. (1999) 'Is John Owen Still Reliable?,' *Banner of Truth* 428: 15-17.

Owen, John. (1996 rept.) *Biblical Theology or Theologumena Pantadapa*, trans. Stephen P. Westcott (Morgan, Penn.: Soli Deo Gloria).

———. (1970) *The Correspondance of John Owen (1616-1683) with and Account of His Life and Work*, ed. Peter Toon (Cambridge: James Clarke and Company).

———.(1854 rept) *Works*, 23 vols., ed. W.H. Goold (London: Johnstone and Hunter).

———. (1971) *The Oxford Orations of John Owen*, ed. Peter Toon (Cornwall, Linkinhorne House).

Packer, J.I. (1990) 'An Introduction to Systematic Spirituality,' *Crux* 26.1: 2-8.

———. (1990) *A Quest for Godliness: The Puritan Vision of the Christian Life* (Wheaton: Crossway).

———. (1954) 'The Redemption and Restoration of Man in the Thought of Richard Baxter,' D.Phil. dissertation, Oxford University.

Parsons, William. (1530) *The Pomander of Prayer* (London: Robert Coplande).

Perkins, William. (1608) *The Foundation of Christian Religion* (Cambridge: Cambridge University Press).

Petry, Ray C., ed. (1967) *Late Medieval Mysticism* (Philadelphia: Westminster).
Pink, Arthur W., (rept., no date) *Spiritual Union and Communion* (Pensacola, Florida: Mt. Zion).
Preston, John. (1995 rept.) 'The Saint's Daily Exercise,' in *The Puritans on Prayer*, ed. D. Kistler (Morgan, Penn.: Soli Deo Gloria).
Rachovian Catechism. (1818) trans. T. Rees (London: Longman).
Rehnman, Sebastian. (2002) *Divine Discourse: John Owen's Theology of Revelation* (Grand Rapids: Baker Academic).
_____. (2001) 'John Owen: A Reformed Scholastic at Oxford,' in *Reformation and Scholasticism: An Ecumenical Enterprise*, ed. W.J. van Asselt and E. Dekker (Grand Rapids: Baker Academic) 181-203.
Rice, Howard L. (1991) *Reformed Spirituality* (Louisville: Westminster/John Knox).
Rogers, Richard. (1632) *A Garden of Spirituall Flowers. Planted by* Ri. Ro[gers], Will. Per[kins], R. Green[ham], M. M[ead], and Geo. Web[be] (London: R. B[adger] for Robert Bird).
Rolle, Richard. (1988) *Richard Rolle: The English Writings* (Mahwah, New Jersey: Paulist).
Rupp, E. Gordon and Philip Watson. (1969) *Luther and Erasmus: Free Will and Salvation* (Philadelphia: Westminster).
Ryken, Leland. (1986) *Wordly Saints: The Puritans as They Really Were* (Grand Rapids: Zondervan Academie).
Ryken, P.G. (1999) 'Scottish Reformed Scholasticism,' in *Protestant Scholasticism: Essays in Reassessment*, ed. Carl. R. Trueman and R.S. Clark (Carlisle: Paternoster).
Saltmarsh, J.(1646) *Free Grace* (London).
Schaefer, Paul R. 'Protestant Scholasticism at Elizabethan Cambridge: William Perkins and a Reformed Theology of the Heart,' in *Protestant Scholasticism: Essays in Reassessment*, ed. Carl. R. Trueman and R.S. Clark (Carlisle: Paternoster).
Schaff, Philip, ed. (1931, 1983 rept.) *The Creeds of Christendom* (Grand Rapids: Baker).
Sibbes, Richard. (1998 rept.) *The Bruised Reed* (Edinburgh: Banner of Truth Trust).
Spence, Alan. (1989) 'Inspiration and Incarnation: John Owen and the Coherence of Christology,' *King's Theological Review* 12.2: 52-55.
_____. (1990) 'John Owen and Trinitarian Agency,' *Scottish Journal of Theology* 43.2: 157-73.
Spitz, Lewis. (1971) *The Renaissance and Reformation Movements*, two vols. (Chicago: Rand McNally).
Steinmetz, David C. (1999) 'The Scholastic Calvin,' in *Protestant Scholasticism: Essays in Reassessment*, ed. Carl. R. Trueman and R.S. Clark (Carlisle: Paternoster).

Taylor, Jeremy. (1901) *The Rule and Exercises of Holy Living*, ed. A.R. Waller (London, orig. pub. date 1650).
_____. (1901) *The Rule and Exercises of Holy Dying*, ed. A.R. Waller (London, orig. pub. date 1657).
Thomas, I.D.E., ed. (1997) *A Puritan Golden Treasury* (Edinburgh: Banner of Truth Trust).
Thompson, John. (1994) *Modern Trinitarian Perspectives* (New York: Oxford University Press).
Toon, Peter. (1971) *God's Statesman: The Life and Work of John Owen* (Exeter: Paternoster).
Torrance, Alan J. (1996) *Persons in Communion: Trinitarian Description and Human Participation* (Edinburgh: T. & T. Clark).
Torrance, James B. (1984) 'The Incarnation and "Limited Atonement",' *Scottish Bulletin of Evangelical Theology* 2: 32-40.
_____. (1996) *Worship, Community, and the Triune God of Grace* (Downer's Grove, Ill.: InterVarsity).
Trinterud, Leonard J. 'The Origins of Puritanism,' *Church History* 20: 37-58.
Trueman, Carl R. and R.S. Clark, eds. *Protestant Scholasticism: Essays in Reassessment* (Carlisle: Paternoster).
Trueman, Carl R. (2001) 'Puritan Theology as Historical Event: A Linguistic Approach to the Ecumenical Context,' in *Reformation and Scholasticism: An Ecumenical Enterprise* (ed. W.J. van Asselt and E. Dekker; Grand Rapids: Baker Academic) 253-275.
_____. (1998) *The Claims of Truth: John Owen's Trinitarian Theology* (Carlisle: Paternoster).
_____. (1999) 'A Small Step Towards Rationalism: The Impact of the Metaphysics of Tommaso Campanella on the Theology of Richard Baxter,' in *Protestant Scholasticism: Essays in Reassessment*, ed. Carl. R. Trueman and R.S. Clark (Carlisle: Paternoster).
Tudor Jones, R. (1990) 'Union with Christ: The Existential Nerve of Puritan Piety' *Tyndale Bulletin* 41: 186-208.
Turretin, Francis. (1992) *Institutes of Elenctic Theology*, two volumes, trans. George Musgrave Giger, ed. Jams T. Dennison, Jr. (Philipsburg, New Jersey: Presbyterian and Reformed Press).
Tyacke, Nicholas. (1987) *Anti-Calvinists: The Rise of English Arminianism* (Oxford: Oxford University Press).
Ursinus, Zacharias. (1852 reproduction) *Commentary on the Heidelberg Catechism* (New Jersey: Presbyterian and Reformed).
van Asselt, William J. and Eef Dekker. (2001) *The Reformation and Scholasticism: An Ecumenical Enterprise* (Grand Rapids: Baker Academic).
Van Engen, John. ed. (1988) *Devotio Moderna: Basic Writings* (New York: Paulist).

Vincent, Nathaniel. (1997 rept.) *A Discourse Concerning Love* (Morgan, Penn.: Soli Deo Gloria).
_____. (1996 rept.) 'The Conversion of a Sinner,' in *The Puritans on Conversion*, ed. D. Kistler (Morgan, Penn.: Soli Deo Gloria).
_____. (1995 rept.) 'The Spirit of Prayer,' in *The Puritans on Prayer*, ed. D. Kistler (Morgan, Penn.: Soli Deo Gloria).
Wainwright, Arthur. (1962) *The Trinity in the New Testament* (London: S.P.C.K.).
Wakefield, Gordon S. (1957) *Puritan Devotion: Its Place in the Development of Christian Piety* (London: Epworth).
_____, ed. (1983) *The Westminster Dictionary of Christian Spirituality* (Philadelphia: Westminster).
Wallace, Dewey D. (1987) *The Spirituality of the Later English Puritans* (Macon, Georgia: Mercer University Press).
Watson, Thomas. (1986 rept.) *A Body of Divinity* (Edinburgh: Banner of Truth Trust).
_____. (1994 rept.) *All Things for Good*, orig. *A Divine Cordial* (Edinburgh: Banner of Truth Trust).
_____. (1996 rept.) 'The One Thing Necessary,' in *The Puritans on Conversion*, ed. D. Kistler (Morgan, Penn.: Soli Deo Gloria).
Weir, David A. (1990) *The Origins of the Federal Theology in Sixteenth-Century Reformation Thought* (Oxford: Oxford University Press).
Wendell, Francois. (1963) *Calvin: Origins and Development of His Religious Thought* (New York: Harper and Row).
White, Helen C. (1966) *English Devotional Literature [Prose] 1600-1640* (New York: Haskell House).
_____. (1951) *The Tudor Books of Private Devotion* (Madison: University of Wisconsin Press).
Wilson, Jonathan R. (1993) 'Toward a Trinitarian Rule of Worship,' *Crux* 39: 35-40.
Won, Jonathan Jong-Chun. (1989) *Communion with Christ: An Exposition and Comparison of the Doctrine of Union and Communion with Christ in Calvin and the English Puritans*, PhD dissertation, Westminster Theological Seminary, Philadelphia.
Wood, Lawrence. (1988) 'Christian Spirituality: The Wesleyan View,' in *Christian Spirituality: Five Views of Sanctification*, ed. Donald L. Alexander (Downer's Grove, Ill.: InterVarsity).
Wood, T. (1952) *English Causistical Divinity* (London: S.P.C.K.).
Woodhouse, A.S.P., ed. (1992 rept.) *Puritanism and Liberty: Being the Army Debates (1647-49) from the Clarke Manuscripts* (London: J.M. Dent and Sons).

General Index

Abelard, Peter, 13, 162
Active Obedience, 147-48, 149, 159, 191, 192
Alexandrian, 190
antinomian, 168
appropriation, 4, 20, 28, 54, 106, 159, 189; appropriations, 20, 36, 104, 108, 109, 113, 170, 173, 188, 189
Aquinas, Thomas, 14, 16, 20, 57, 59, 63, 95
Arians, 33
Aristotle, 50, 57, 95, 100, 111, 114-15; Aristotelian, 2, 13, 61, 99, 100, 125, 162
Arius, 33
Athanasius, 34, 107
atonement, 24, 43, 137, 141, 143, 149, 158, 171, 186
Augustine, 1, 12, 57, 65, 66, 72, 73, 84, 89, 94, 106, 108-11, 157, 162; Augustinian, 6, 41, 61, 68, 79, 88, 89, 93, 94, 96, 97, 162, 166, 168, 181, 190; augustinian/neo-platonic, 168

Barth, Karl, 3, 9, 17-19, 23, 29, 109; Barthian, 18-19, 20
Basil Caesarea, 34, 107
Baxter, 65
Bayly, Lewis, 55-56
Berkhof, Louis, 91
Bernard of Clairvaux, 12, 60, 66, 72, 73, 81, 84, 161-65, 167
Beza, 5, 52, 57, 113
'Biblical Theology', 39, 43
Biel, Gabriel, 92, 93, 94, 95, 187

Bonaventure, 16, 119
Book of Privy Counseling, The, 62
Bradwardine, Thomas, 94, 95, 96, 97
Brinckerink, John, 80
Bullinger, Heinrich, 52
Bultmann, Rudolf, 23; Bultmannian, 24
Bunny, Edmund, 65
Bunyan, John, 48-49, 54

Calvin, John, 2, 4, 5, 41, 51, 57, 58, 64, 94, 95, 105, 137, 19, 141, 151, 157, 159, 161, 162, 170, 193
Calvinist, 42, 66, 134, 136, 137, 141, 143
Cappadocian Fathers, 34, 106, 108, 110, 111
Catholic, 8, 14, 20, 58, 64, 65, 66, 87, 96, 148
Catholicism, 48, 75
Chalmers, Thomas, 71
Chrysostom, John, 57
circumincessio, 34
Clifford, Alan C., 2, 5, 51, 137, 150
Cloud of Unknowing, The, 61, 62-64, 66, 72
contemplatio, 13, 133
Covenant Theology, 28, 42, 52, 57, 109, 127
covenants, 6, 39, 41, 43, 52, 93, 102, 117, 130, 146, 168, 194
Cunningham, David, 9

deism, 44
Dent, Arthur, 54, 56
devotio moderna, 5, 16, 59, 75, 76, 79-80, 81, 84, 85, 86
docetism, 190
Donne, John, 167-68
Durham, James, 51, 65, 165, 166

Eckhart, Meister, 5, 16, 60, 61, 63, 72, 74, 76, 92, 130; eckhartian, 60, 76, 187
Edwards, Jonathan, 6, 132, 198
English Methodists, 86
English Mystics, 5, 62, 66, 67

facienti quod in se est Deus non denegat gratiam, 92
Federalism, 25, 124, 130; Federal Theologians, 146; Federal Theology, 5, 6, 7, 52, 124, 141, 146, 161, 168, 194
Ferguson, Sinclair B., 2, 118, 144
fons actionis, 35, 188
Fox, George, 5, 46, 47, 48, 50

Gerson, Jean, 16, 92
Gilson, Etienne, 162
Gomarus, Franciscus, 58
Goodwin, John, 56, 95
Goodwin, Thomas, 170, 178-80, 181
gratia gratum faciens, 93
Green, Brad, 110, 111
Gregory of Nazianzus, 34, 107
Gregory of Nyssa, 34, 62, 107, 108, 118-19
Grote, Geert, 75-78, 79, 84, 103
Grotius, Hugo, 57
Guido (or Guigo), 13
Gunton, Colin, 9, 106, 110-11

Hammond, Henry, 95, 96
Harnack, Adolf, 23

Heidelberg Catechism, 50, 54, 91
Hick, John, 23
Hill, Edmund, 111
Hilton, Walter, 5, 65, 66, 71-74, 84, 165, 184
historia salutis, 4, 7, 15, 23, 30, 37, 46, 54, 62, 67, 81, 101, 146, 154, 160, 187, 194
Hodge, Charles, 42-44, 196; Hodgean, 44, 196
Hollinworth, Richard, 176-77, 181
homoousios, 33, 106
Horton, Michael S., 37, 38, 39, 40, 41, 137
Howe, John, 176-77, 181
hypostaseis, 6, 14, 17, 21, 28, 34, 41, 45, 48, 52, 56, 69, 96, 98, 106, 123, 156, 172, 188, 194
hypostasis, 3, 34, 35, 110, 120, 123, 165, 188
hypostatic, 35, 71, 104, 105, 111, 147, 167, 170, 179, 188, 189

immediationi suppositi, 179-80
incarnation, 18, 21, 24, 25, 53, 56, 69, 70, 102, 110, 112, 114, 116, 127, 148, 162, 163, 179, 180, 181, 188, 190
indwelling, 15, 34, 89, 112, 151, 173, 174, 175, 176, 177, 178, 179, 180, 181, 189, 190
intra-trinitarian, 6, 51, 128, 136, 140, 158, 180

Jensen, Robert, 9, 10
Julian of Norwich, 5, 66-68, 70, 72, 155, 187
justification, 90, 91, 93, 128, 131, 147, 149, 150-55, 157-60, 173, 192

Kempe, Margery, 66
Kendall, R.T., 2, 5, 51, 100, 141

LaCugna, Catherine Mowry, 9, 126
Leclercq, Jean, 13, 162
lectio divina, 13, 133
Lombard, Peter, 14, 161
Lucian of Samosata, 33
Luther, Martin, 40, 57, 75, 80, 89, 94, 131, 139, 140, 152, 182

Mackey, James, 106
Marshal, Walter, 119
Martyr, Justin, 57
meditating, 7, 70, 71, 77, 79, 135, 198
Moltmann, Jurgen, 3, 9, 25-26, 29, 40
monarchianism, 33; monarchian, 33
mortification, 10, 37, 61, 85, 89, 90, 191, 193
mysticism, 5, 12, 16, 39, 44, 45, 59, 60, 61, 65, 81, 92, 118, 133, 144, 161, 162

New Covenant, 53, 77, 117, 120, 183
Nicholas of Cusa, 16, 187
Nietzsche, Frederick, 39
nominalism, 59, 76, 94-96, 144; nominalist, 16, 59, 76, 92, 97; nominalistic, 59, 92; nominalists, 60, 97
Nussbaum, Martha, 195

Oberman, Heiko, 57, 60, 75, 93, 94
Ockham, William of, 92, 95
Oden, Thomas, 30
Old Covenant, 21, 120, 126
opera Dei essentiala, 35-36
opera Dei personalia, 35
opera trinitatis ad extra sunt indivisia, 35, 177, 188
opus Dei essentialis, 35
ordo salutis, 54, 117, 135
Origen, 57, 162
origin, 47, 118
'Owenian Syllogism', 143
Oxford, 55, 56, 94, 96

Packer, J.I., 145, 185-86
Pannenberg, Wolfhart, 14
pantheism, 45, 48
Paris, 16, 66, 76, 92, 94
Penn, William, 47, 48, 50
perichoresis, 34, 69
perichoretic, 15, 22
Perkins, Willliam, 5, 51, 150
platonism, 60
Plotinus, 61, 99
postliberalism, 37
potentia absoluta, 92
potentia ordinata, 92
Practical Syllogism, 142-44
Princeton, 42, 43
probationary, 52, 150
prolegomena, 5, 43, 44, 196
Protestant Scholastics, 11, 14, 28, 30, 162

Rahner, Karl, 3, 8, 9, 14-15, 18, 20-23, 26, 29, 136, 189
Ramus, Peter, 50
redemptive-historical, 38, 40, 42, 44, 58, 78, 124, 161, 165, 174, 195, 198
redemptive-history, 43, 44
reformation, 74
regeneration, 54, 95, 113, 119, 173, 176, 192
Rolle, Richard, 5, 66, 73

Sayers, Dorothy, 39, 197
Scale of Perfection, The, 65, 72-75

Schneiders, Sandra, 11
scholasticism, 2, 5, 29, 32, 42, 45, 50, 51, 53, 58, 59, 61, 80, 91, 92, 95, 112, 124, 128, 133, 135, 146, 194; scholastics, 4, 5, 22, 34, 35, 43, 51, 52, 54, 56, 57, 91, 95
sentimentalism, 133
Sheldrake, Philip, 11, 14, 16
simul justus et peccator, 150
Socinus, 57
Spence, Alan, 99, 100, 101, 104, 106, 107, 108, 109, 111, 112, 189, 190-91
substantia, 33, 34
supralapsarians, 141, 142

Tertullian, 33, 34, 57
Thomas à Kempis, 84-89
Torrance, Alan, 9
trinitatis ad extra sunt indivisa, 35, 177, 188

unio personalis, 36, 179
unio personarum, 179
Ursinus, Zacharius, 5, 52, 58, 91, 113

Vermigli, Peter Martyr, 5, 52, 58, 113
via moderna, 59, 92, 93, 94
via negationis, 99
via negativa, 99
viator, 93
Victorines, The, 16
Vos, Geerhardus, 43-44

Warfield, B.B., 31-32, 42, 43
Westminster Confession, 5, 90, 118, 132, 137

Zanchius, Jerome, 5, 52, 113, 128
Zizioulas, John, 9, 106, 110

Studies in Christian History and Thought
(All titles uniform with this volume)
Dates in bold are of projected publication

David Bebbington
Holiness in Nineteenth-Century England
David Bebbington stresses the relationship of movements of spirituality to changes in their cultural setting, especially the legacies of the Enlightenment and Romanticism. He shows that these broad shifts in ideological mood had a profound effect on the ways in which piety was conceptualized and practised. Holiness was intimately bound up with the spirit of the age.
2000 / 0-85364-981-2 / viii + 98pp

J. William Black
Reformation Pastors
Richard Baxter and the Ideal of the Reformed Pastor
This work examines Richard Baxter's *Gildas Salvianus, The Reformed Pastor* (1656) and explores each aspect of his pastoral strategy in light of his own concern for 'reformation' and in the broader context of Edwardian, Elizabethan and early Stuart pastoral ideals and practice.
2003 / 1-84227-190-3 / xxii + 308pp

James Bruce
Prophecy, Miracles, Angels, *and* Heavenly Light?
The Eschatology, Pneumatology and Missiology of Adomnán's Life of Columba
This book surveys approaches to the marvellous in hagiography, providing the first critique of Plummer's hypothesis of Irish saga origin. It then analyses the uniquely systematized phenomena in the *Life of Columba* from Adomnán's seventh-century theological perspective, identifying the coming of the eschatological Kingdom as the key to understanding.
2004 / 1-84227-227-6 / xviii + 286pp

Colin J. Bulley
The Priesthood of Some Believers
Developments from the General to the Special Priesthood in the Christian Literature of the First Three Centuries
The first in-depth treatment of early Christian texts on the priesthood of all believers shows that the developing priesthood of the ordained related closely to the division between laity and clergy and had deleterious effects on the practice of the general priesthood.
2000 / 1-84227-034-6 / xii + 336pp

Anthony R. Cross (ed.)
Ecumenism and History
Studies in Honour of John H.Y. Briggs
This collection of essays examines the inter-relationships between the two fields in which Professor Briggs has contributed so much: history—particularly Baptist and Nonconformist—and the ecumenical movement. With contributions from colleagues and former research students from Britain, Europe and North America, *Ecumenism and History* provides wide-ranging studies in important aspects of Christian history, theology and ecumenical studies.

2002 / 1-84227-135-0 / xx + 362pp

Maggi Dawn
Confessions of an Inquiring Spirit
Form as Constitutive of Meaning in S.T. Coleridge's Theological Writing
This study of Coleridge's *Confessions* focuses on its confessional, epistolary and fragmentary form, suggesting that attention to these features significantly affects its interpretation. Bringing a close study of these three literary forms, the author suggests ways in which they nuance the text with particular understandings of the Trinity, and of a kenotic christology. Some parallels are drawn between Romantic and postmodern dilemmas concerning the authority of the biblical text.

2006 / 1-84227-255-1 / approx. 224 pp

Ruth Gouldbourne
The Flesh and the Feminine
Gender and Theology in the Writings of Caspar Schwenckfeld
Caspar Schwenckfeld and his movement exemplify one of the radical communities of the sixteenth century. Challenging theological and liturgical norms, they also found themselves challenging social and particularly gender assumptions. In this book, the issues of the relationship between radical theology and the understanding of gender are considered.

2005 / 1-84227-048-6 / approx. 304pp

Crawford Gribben
Puritan Millennialism
Literature and Theology, 1550–1682
Puritan Millennialism surveys the growth, impact and eventual decline of puritan millennialism throughout England, Scotland and Ireland, arguing that it was much more diverse than has frequently been suggested. This Paternoster edition is revised and extended from the original 2000 text.

2007 / 1-84227-372-8 / approx. 320pp

Galen K. Johnson
Prisoner of Conscience
John Bunyan on Self, Community and Christian Faith
This is an interdisciplinary study of John Bunyan's understanding of conscience across his autobiographical, theological and fictional writings, investigating whether conscience always deserves fidelity, and how Bunyan's view of conscience affects his relationship both to modern Western individualism and historic Christianity.
2003 / 1-84227-223-3 / xvi + 236pp

R.T. Kendall
Calvin and English Calvinism to 1649
The author's thesis is that those who formed the Westminster Confession of Faith, which is regarded as Calvinism, in fact departed from John Calvin on two points: (1) the extent of the atonement and (2) the ground of assurance of salvation.
1997 / 0-85364-827-1 / xii + 264pp

Timothy Larsen
Friends of Religious Equality
Nonconformist Politics in Mid-Victorian England
During the middle decades of the nineteenth century the English Nonconformist community developed a coherent political philosophy of its own, of which a central tenet was the principle of religious equality (in contrast to the stereotype of Evangelical Dissenters). The Dissenting community fought for the civil rights of Roman Catholics, non-Christians and even atheists on an issue of principle which had its flowering in the enthusiastic and undivided support which Nonconformity gave to the campaign for Jewish emancipation. This reissued study examines the political efforts and ideas of English Nonconformists during the period, covering the whole range of national issues raised, from state education to the Crimean War. It offers a case study of a theologically conservative group defending religious pluralism in the civic sphere, showing that the concept of religious equality was a grand vision at the centre of the political philosophy of the Dissenters.
2007 / 1-84227-402-3 / x + 300pp

July 2005

Byung-Ho Moon
Christ the Mediator of the Law
Calvin's Christological Understanding of the Law as the Rule of Living and Life-Giving

This book explores the coherence between Christology and soteriology in Calvin's theology of the law, examining its intellectual origins and his position on the concept and extent of Christ's mediation of the law. A comparative study between Calvin and contemporary Reformers—Luther, Bucer, Melancthon and Bullinger—and his opponent Michael Servetus is made for the purpose of pointing out the unique feature of Calvin's Christological understanding of the law.

2005 / 1-84227-318-3 / approx. 370pp

John Eifion Morgan-Wynne
Holy Spirit and Religious Experience in Christian Writings, c.AD 90–200

This study examines how far Christians in the third to fifth generations (c.AD 90–200) attributed their sense of encounter with the divine presence, their sense of illumination in the truth or guidance in decision-making, and their sense of ethical empowerment to the activity of the Holy Spirit in their lives.

2005 / 1-84227-319-1 / approx. 350pp

James I. Packer
The Redemption and Restoration of Man in the Thought of Richard Baxter

James I. Packer provides a full and sympathetic exposition of Richard Baxter's doctrine of humanity, created and fallen; its redemption by Christ Jesus; and its restoration in the image of God through the obedience of faith by the power of the Holy Spirit.

2002 / 1-84227-147-4 / 432pp

Andrew Partington,
Church and State
The Contribution of the Church of England Bishops to the House of Lords during the Thatcher Years

In *Church and State*, Andrew Partington argues that the contribution of the Church of England bishops to the House of Lords during the Thatcher years was overwhelmingly critical of the government; failed to have a significant influence in the public realm; was inefficient, being undertaken by a minority of those eligible to sit on the Bench of Bishops; and was insufficiently moral and spiritual in its content to be distinctive. On the basis of this, and the likely reduction of the number of places available for Church of England bishops in a fully reformed Second Chamber, the author argues for an evolution in the Church of England's approach to the service of its bishops in the House of Lords. He proposes the Church of England works to overcome the genuine obstacles which hinder busy diocesan bishops from contributing to the debates of the House of Lords and to its life more informally.

2005 / 1-84227-334-5 / approx. 324pp

Michael Pasquarello III
God's Ploughman
Hugh Latimer: A 'Preaching Life' (1490–1555)

This construction of a 'preaching life' situates Hugh Latimer within the larger religious, political and intellectual world of late medieval England. Neither biography, intellectual history, nor analysis of discrete sermon texts, this book is a work of homiletic history which draws from the details of Latimer's milieu to construct an interpretive framework for the preaching performances that formed the core of his identity as a religious reformer. Its goal is to illumine the practical wisdom embodied in the content, form and style of Latimer's preaching, and to recapture a sense of its overarching purpose, movement, and transforming force during the reform of sixteenth-century England.

2006 / 1-84227-336-1 / approx. 250pp

Alan P.F. Sell
Enlightenment, Ecumenism, Evangel
Theological Themes and Thinkers 1550–2000

This book consists of papers in which such interlocking topics as the Enlightenment, the problem of authority, the development of doctrine, spirituality, ecumenism, theological method and the heart of the gospel are discussed. Issues of significance to the church at large are explored with special reference to writers from the Reformed and Dissenting traditions.

2005 / 1-84227-330-2 / xviii + 422pp

Alan P.F. Sell
Hinterland Theology
Some Reformed and Dissenting Adjustments

Many books have been written on theology's 'giants' and significant trends, but what of those lesser-known writers who adjusted to them? In this book some hinterland theologians of the British Reformed and Dissenting traditions, who followed in the wake of toleration, the Evangelical Revival, the rise of modern biblical criticism and Karl Barth, are allowed to have their say. They include Thomas Ridgley, Ralph Wardlaw, T.V. Tymms and N.H.G. Robinson.

2006 / 1-84227-331-0 / approx. 350pp

Alan P.F. Sell and Anthony R. Cross (eds)
Protestant Nonconformity in the Twentieth Century

In this collection of essays scholars representative of a number of Nonconformist traditions reflect thematically on Nonconformists' life and witness during the twentieth century. Among the subjects reviewed are biblical studies, theology, worship, evangelism and spirituality, and ecumenism. Over and above its immediate interest, this collection provides a marker to future scholars and others wishing to know how some of their forebears assessed Nonconformity's contribution to a variety of fields during the century leading up to Christianity's third millennium.

2003 / 1-84227-221-7 / x + 398pp

Mark Smith
Religion in Industrial Society
Oldham and Saddleworth 1740–1865

This book analyses the way British churches sought to meet the challenge of industrialization and urbanization during the period 1740–1865. Working from a case-study of Oldham and Saddleworth, Mark Smith challenges the received view that the Anglican Church in the eighteenth century was characterized by complacency and inertia, and reveals Anglicanism's vigorous and creative response to the new conditions. He reassesses the significance of the centrally directed church reforms of the mid-nineteenth century, and emphasizes the importance of local energy and enthusiasm. Charting the growth of denominational pluralism in Oldham and Saddleworth, Dr Smith compares the strengths and weaknesses of the various Anglican and Nonconformist approaches to promoting church growth. He also demonstrates the extent to which all the churches participated in a common culture shaped by the influence of evangelicalism, and shows that active co-operation between the churches rather than denominational conflict dominated. This revised and updated edition of Dr Smith's challenging and original study makes an important contribution both to the social history of religion and to urban studies.

2006 / 1-84227-335-3 / approx. 300pp

Martin Sutherland
Peace, Toleration and Decay
The Ecclesiology of Later Stuart Dissent
This fresh analysis brings to light the complexity and fragility of the later Stuart Nonconformist consensus. Recent findings on wider seventeenth-century thought are incorporated into a new picture of the dynamics of Dissent and the roots of evangelicalism.
2003 / 1-84227-152-0 / xxii + 216pp

G. Michael Thomas
The Extent of the Atonement
A Dilemma for Reformed Theology from Calvin to the Consensus
A study of the way Reformed theology addressed the question, 'Did Christ die for all, or for the elect only?', commencing with John Calvin, and including debates with Lutheranism, the Synod of Dort and the teaching of Moïse Amyraut.
1997 / 0-85364-828-X / x + 278pp

David M. Thompson
Baptism, Church and Society in Britain from the Evangelical Revival to *Baptism, Eucharist and Ministry*
The theology and practice of baptism have not received the attention they deserve. How important is faith? What does baptismal regeneration mean? Is baptism a bond of unity between Christians? This book discusses the theology of baptism and popular belief and practice in England and Wales from the Evangelical Revival to the publication of the World Council of Churches' consensus statement on *Baptism, Eucharist and Ministry* (1982).
2005 / 1-84227-393-0 / approx. 224pp

Mark D. Thompson
A Sure Ground on Which to Stand
The Relation of Authority and Interpretive Method of Luther's Approach to Scripture
The best interpreter of Luther is Luther himself. Unfortunately many modern studies have superimposed contemporary agendas upon this sixteenth-century Reformer's writings. This fresh study examines Luther's own words to find an explanation for his robust confidence in the Scriptures, a confidence that generated the famous 'stand' at Worms in 1521.
2004 / 1-84227-145-8 / xvi + 322pp

Carl R. Trueman and R.S. Clark (eds)
Protestant Scholasticism
Essays in Reassessment

Traditionally Protestant theology, between Luther's early reforming career and the dawn of the Enlightenment, has been seen in terms of decline and fall into the wastelands of rationalism and scholastic speculation. In this volume a number of scholars question such an interpretation. The editors argue that the development of post-Reformation Protestantism can only be understood when a proper historical model of doctrinal change is adopted. This historical concern underlies the subsequent studies of theologians such as Calvin, Beza, Olevian, Baxter, and the two Turrentini. The result is a significantly different reading of the development of Protestant Orthodoxy, one which both challenges the older scholarly interpretations and clichés about the relationship of Protestantism to, among other things, scholasticism and rationalism, and which demonstrates the fruitfulness of the new, historical approach.

1999 / 0-85364-853-0 / xx + 344pp

Shawn D. Wright
Our Sovereign Refuge
The Pastoral Theology of Theodore Beza

Our Sovereign Refuge is a study of the pastoral theology of the Protestant reformer who inherited the mantle of leadership in the Reformed church from John Calvin. Countering a common view of Beza as supremely a 'scholastic' theologian who deviated from Calvin's biblical focus, Wright uncovers a new portrait. He was not a cold and rigid academic theologian obsessed with probing the eternal decrees of God. Rather, by placing him in his pastoral context and by noting his concerns in his pastoral and biblical treatises, Wright shows that Beza was fundamentally a committed Christian who was troubled by the vicissitudes of life in the second half of the sixteenth century. He believed that the biblical truth of the supreme sovereignty of God alone could support Christians on their earthly pilgrimage to heaven. This pastoral and personal portrait forms the heart of Wright's argument.

2004 / 1-84227-252-7 / xviii + 308pp

Paternoster
9 Holdom Avenue,
Bletchley,
Milton Keynes MK1 1QR,
United Kingdom
Web: www.authenticmedia.co.uk/paternoster